GREAT MOUNTAIN DAYS
IN
SNOWDONIA

ABOUT THE AUTHOR

Born into a Lancashire mining family, I was destined for employment with the National Coal Board, but 'escaped' by securing a job in the Town Clerk's office in St Helens. Rising to become Deputy Town Clerk in Bangor, North Wales, and then Leigh in Lancashire, I spent thirty years in the cloisters of local government. Much of it, looking back, was professionally enjoyable, but compared with what I do now, it was like a very long prison sentence for a crime I hadn't committed.

My interest in Snowdonia began in 1970 when I moved to live and work in Bangor. With the Carneddau in view from my living room window, and far too much of a temptation to resist, I soon became a voluntary warden in the Snowdonia National Park. It was here in Snowdonia that I learned and then honed the crafts and skills of hillwalking, building a foundation of experience on which my career (and survival) has rested. My first book was *The Summits of Snowdonia*, published in 1984, which was followed a year later by *The Mountains of Wales*, which took me a little further afield.

These days, based back in Lancashire, I am a full-time writer and photographer specialising in the outdoors and travel in the UK, Australia, Ireland, France, Madeira and the Azores, which is quite enough to be going on with. I like to get into the culture of the countries I visit, and when I'm walking and writing new guidebooks, the history of the place and its people are important facets, helping me to understand how landscapes were shaped by man, as well as geologically. Never having had the chance to go to university – in the early 1960s, that wasn't for miners' sons – I am also proud to have obtained a Masters Degree with Distinction in Lake District Studies from the University of Lancaster.

Now, almost 40 years since those first faltering steps on Welsh rock, I have been fortunate to be able to return to walk the mountains and valleys of North Wales anew, seeing them with more experienced eyes, and understanding, as much as any Englishman can, the role they have played in the lives and culture of the Welsh people.

Terry Marsh, 2010

GREAT MOUNTAIN DAYS
IN
SNOWDONIA

by
Terry Marsh

2 POLICE SQUARE, MILNTHORPE, CUMBRIA LA7 7PY
www.cicerone.co.uk

First edition 2010
ISBN-13: 978 1 85284 581 0
Reprinted 2013 (with updates)
Printed by KHL Printing, Singapore
A catalogue record for this book is available from the British Library.
Photographs by the author. Line drawings by Mark Richards.

 Maps are reproduced with permission from HARVEY Maps, www.harveymaps.co.uk.

ACKNOWLEDGEMENTS

Thanks are due to Dr Barbara Jones, Upland Ecologist (Ecolegydd yr Ucheldir) with the Countryside Council for Wales (Cyngor Cefn Gwlad Cymru) for permission to reproduce an article on 'Recreation and the mountain environment', and for general help and advice about the mountains of Snowdonia.

WARNING

Mountain walking can be a dangerous activity carrying a risk of personal injury or death. It should be undertaken only by those with a full understanding of the risks and with the training and/or experience to evaluate them. While every care and effort has been taken in the preparation of this guide, the user should be aware that conditions can be highly variable and can change quickly, thus materially affecting the seriousness of a mountain walk.

Therefore, except for any liability which cannot be excluded by law, neither Cicerone nor the author accept liability for damage of any nature (including damage to property, personal injury or death) arising directly or indirectly from the information in this book.

To call out the Mountain Rescue, phone 999 or the international emergency number 112: this will connect you via any available network. Once connected to the emergency operator, ask for the police.

INTERNATIONAL DISTRESS SIGNAL

The recognised distress signal is six whistle blasts (or torch flashes in the dark) spread over one minute, followed by a minute's pause. Repeat until an answer is received (which will be three signals per minute followed by a minute's pause).

ADVICE TO READERS

While every effort is made by our authors to ensure the accuracy of guidebooks as they go to print, changes can occur during the lifetime of an edition. If we know of any, there will be an Updates tab on this book's page on the Cicerone website (www.cicerone.co.uk), so please check before planning your trip. We also advise that you check information about such things as transport, accommodation and shops locally. Even rights of way can be altered over time. We are always grateful for information about any discrepancies between a guidebook and the facts on the ground, sent by email to info@cicerone.co.uk or by post to Cicerone, 2 Police Square, Milnthorpe LA7 7PY, United Kingdom.

Front cover: Y Garn and Llyn Idwal

CONTENTS

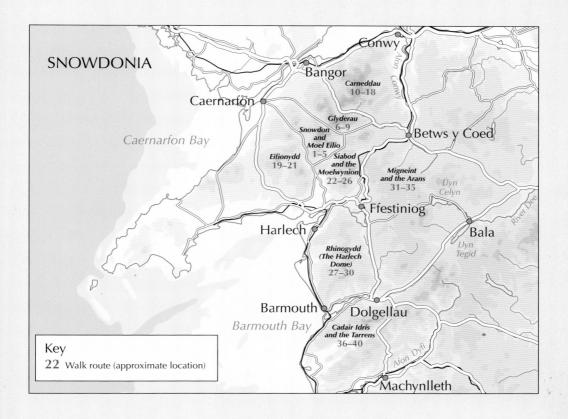

SNOWDONIA

Caernarfon Bay

Conwy

Bangor

Caernarfon

Carneddau
10–18

Glyderau
6–9

Snowdon
and
Moel Eilio
1–5

Betws y Coed

Afon Conwy

Eifionydd
19–21

Siabod
and the
Moelwynion
22–26

Migneint
and the Arans
31–35

Llyn
Celyn

River Dee

Ffestiniog

Harlech

Bala

Llyn
Tegid

Rhinogydd
(The Harlech
Dome)
27–30

Barmouth

Dolgellau

Barmouth Bay

Cadair Idris
and the Tarrens
36–40

Afon Dyfi

Machynlleth

Key

22 Walk route (approximate location)

HARVEY MAP KEY

	Llyn, pond
	River, footbridge
	Wide stream
	Narrow stream
	Peat hags
	Marshy ground

	Contour (15m interval)
	Index contour (75m interval)
	Auxiliary contour
	Scree, spoil heap
	Boulder field
	Scattered rock and boulders
	Predominantly rocky ground
	Major crag, large boulder
	O.S. trig pillar, large cairn
805	Spot height (from air survey)

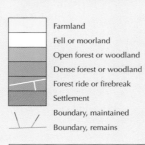

	Farmland
	Fell or moorland
	Open forest or woodland
	Dense forest or woodland
	Forest ride or firebreak
	Settlement
	Boundary, maintained
	Boundary, remains

On moorland, walls, ruined walls and
fences are shown. For farmland, only the
outer boundary wall or fence is shown.

Contours change from brown to grey where
the ground is predominantly rocky outcrops,
small crags and other bare rock.

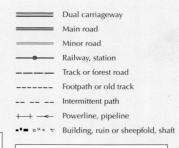

	Dual carriageway
	Main road
	Minor road
	Railway, station
	Track or forest road
	Footpath or old track
	Intermittent path
	Powerline, pipeline
	Building, ruin or sheepfold, shaft

The representation of a road, track or footpath
is no evidence of the existence of a right of way.

SCALE 1 : 40,000

0 Kilometres   1

0 Miles   1

PREFACE

In 1984, my first book *The Summits of Snowdonia* was published. Ironically, having lived, rock climbed and walked in North Wales in the early 1970s, by the time of publication I was living back in my native county of Lancashire, and spending my time walking and climbing in a much wider arena. But those first impressions, and a wealth of exquisite literature, principal among which were Amory Lovin's *Eryri, The Mountains of Longing*, Showell Styles' *The Mountains of North Wales*, and Carr and Lister's *The Mountains of Snowdonia*, remained with me over the years. 1985 saw the publication of my book *The Mountains of Wales*, which embraced all the mountains of the principality. The present work is a modern interpretation of these two books, combining the exploration of those early writing years with countless return visits over the intervening period, as well as, one would hope, a surer and more accomplished hand on the literary tiller, and a mind on the wiser side of 60.

It was in Snowdonia that I first found my feet; here I worked as a voluntary warden in the National Park, and learned the skills and hazards of rock climbing. But most of all, it was here that I acquired a love of mountains, of recreational walking and days at ease among the hills. Everything I've achieved as a writer, photographer and lover of wild landscapes is built on foundations laid here in Snowdonia.

The 40 walks offered here will take you through landscapes of peerless beauty, along ways that are easy and ways that are tough, frequently remote, wild, rugged, demanding, occasionally pastoral, but, above all, imbued with everything that brings unending joy to those of us who walk the hills.

Terry Marsh, 2010

INTRODUCTION

In the minds of many visitors, only the mountain ranges that dominate the north-west of Wales are known by the name 'Snowdonia' – 'Eryri' in the old Welsh. In fact, Snowdonia covers a much wider area, over 2,000km² (840 square miles), a domain extending far south to Bala, Cadair Idris and beyond, from the northern edge of Cardigan Bay to Anglesey.

Throughout history the mountains of Snowdonia have performed two roles. For hundreds of years, since the Romans sought to colonise the area, they have been a secure and strong defensive barrier, but over the last 200 years they have become an adventure playground. These two opposing views of the mountains might be said to represent those of the Welsh, who live among them, and those of the English, who come to explore. For centuries, the mountains not only provided the local people with pasture for their flocks and the raw building materials for their homesteads, but also hampered the penetration of the pagan attitudes sweeping across England and threatening the flame of Christianity that burned so brightly within Wales.

Today, for better or worse, the mountains of Snowdonia are everyone's playground. Nevertheless, in these Great Mountain Days you will discover the companionship of solitude, the sound of silence and the tang of wild places, for all are still here, waiting.

About this guide

The 40 walks in this book are grouped into areas defined by valleys, starting from the Snowdon massif, and then rippling away southwards to the Tarrens north of Machynlleth – more a matter of convenience than geographical or geological significance.

Each route description starts with a box containing all the key information about your walk: the distance, height gain, time and grade, and details of suitable parking places. (Some of the parking suggestions are Pay and Display car parks; others are roadside or off-road parking areas where the key thing is to park without causing inconvenience to local people and businesses.) Also provided here are details of places for refreshment after the walk, where they conveniently exist.

Appendix 1 summarises all this route information at a glance.

Walk grades

The grading of walks anywhere is a very subjective issue; what is 'easy' for one walker can be a scary experience for someone less experienced. In reality, nothing in Snowdonia can safely be regarded as easy; the terrain is often bouldery and complex, marshy and trackless, or, more usually, a mix of all of these conditions. But, in order to convey some notion of the effort and walking skill involved in each route, four grades have been employed.

← *Tryfan from the slopes of Pen yr Helgi Du (Walk 6)*   ↑ *On Crib Goch (Walk 1)*

THE LAND OF EAGLES

Welsh scholars tell us that from time immemorial this untamed, rugged region has been known as Eryri, the land of eagles, 'eryri' coming from 'eryr', meaning eagle. But it might equally be derived from 'eira', making it the land of snow. Some latter-day scholars prefer yet another, rather more prosaic, translation – simply 'High Land' or the 'Land of Mountains' – a derivation from the Medieval Welsh for high place. The truth is, no one knows, so you can choose whichever suits you.

I take the view that the lands of Snowdonia are named after eagles, especially as eagles were once here all year round, while snow most certainly wasn't. These majestic birds have soared above the crags and cwms across the ages, and provided substance for bards, singers and story-tellers. Gerald of Wales (Giraldus Cambrensis), one of the most colourful, extrovert and dynamic of churchmen in the 12th century, writes of

a remarkable eagle which lives in the mountains of Snowdonia. Every fifth

feast-day it perches on a particular stone, hoping to satiate its hunger with the bodies of dead men, for on that day it thinks that war will break out.

The stone on which the eagle is said to stand is known as the 'Stone of Destiny', thought by some to be Carreg yr Eryr, near Llyn Dinas in Nant Gwynant, and close to Dinas Emrys, the hill fort believed to be the spot that King Gwrtheyrn, better known as Vortigern, chose for his retreat from the unwanted attentions of Anglo-Saxon invaders.

In the 16th century, Thomas Price of Plas Iolyn sends an eagle on an errand to other poets, writing later of the 'king of mountain fowl' that dwelt on the 'clear-cut heights above the rock-bound tarn' in such a way that it is evident that he was writing about something he had actually seen. But by the early 19th century, Snowdonia's eagles were reduced to a wandering bird, 'skulking on the precipices'.

Castell y Gwynt (The Castle of the Winds), Glyders (Walk 6)

Pen yr Ole Wen from Cwm Idwal (Walk 6)

- **Moderate**: the easiest routes, involving walks of any length over any type of terrain; map and compass skills may be necessary.
- **Energetic**: devoid of serious hazard in good conditions, but requiring map-reading and compass skills, generally but not always on clear paths.
- **Strenuous**: involving a fair commitment in terms of time and energy; these may well be rugged walks involving many hours' walking.
- **Arduous**: covering rough ground, sometimes in remote locations; there may be mild to moderate scrambling. These walks are not necessarily long or time consuming, but they are demanding both of a level of fitness and mountain competency.

Timings

As with grades, timings are also subjective; those given are the times taken by the author (40 years' experience, and a pensioner, but no slouch – for the present), plus a little extra. It is far better to learn by experience what your own pace is, and then use the distance and height gain information to get an idea of how long it will take you given your personal level of fitness. But be sure to allow for the difficulty of the terrain: for example, the ascent of Tryfan by the North Ridge has a horizontal distance of 1km (just over half a mile), and height gain of 615m (2020ft). This would suggest you could be jumping from Adam to Eve in less than 90 minutes, and indeed some can (I did it myself in 45 minutes, but that was a long, long time ago), but for many walkers, two hours would be nearer the mark because of the nature of the terrain.

Mapping

To aid visualisation, routes are depicted both as line diagrams and as customised HARVEY maps. The former, drawn by author and artist Mark Richards, give an aerial perspective of the walks, while the latter pinpoint the key detail covered in the route description. Harvey maps owe their origins to orienteering, and their bold symbols and distinctive colours make them well suited to outdoor use. Note that key landmarks that feature on the maps and/or diagrams appear in **bold** in the text to help you plot the route.

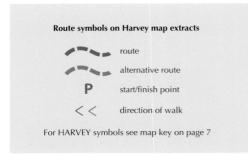

Route symbols on Harvey map extracts

route

alternative route

P   start/finish point

< <   direction of walk

For HARVEY symbols see map key on page 7

Although the guide contains map extracts and diagrams, you are strongly advised always to take with you the relevant sheet map for the route, not only for safety reasons, but also to give a wider picture of the landscapes you are walking through.

At present, **HARVEY** publish three 1:25,000 **Superwalker** maps of Snowdonia: *Snowdon and the Moelwynion*, *The Glyderau and the Carneddau* and *Snowdonia South*, covering the Rhinogs, as well as a 1:40,000 British Mountain Map *Snowdonia*.

Alternatively, the following 1:25,000 Ordnance Survey **Explorer** maps cover the areas described: OL17 Snowdon/Yr Wyddfa, OL18 Harlech, Porthmadog and Bala and OL23 Cadair Iris and Lyn Tegid.

Welsh place names

The Welsh language (*Cymraeg*) is an ancient one, emerging in the sixth century from the Brythonic languages, the common ancestor of Welsh, Cumbric, Breton and Cornish. It is a phonetic language, and once the pronunciation of the alphabet has been acquired, a fair stab can be made at the actual words of the language. However, over the years inconsistencies have arisen, most of no great consequence, but sufficient to cause confusion if not explained. Spellings of many Welsh place names have changed over the past 50 years, as use of the proper Welsh language and spelling has gained ground.

For this book, the spelling shown on maps has generally been retained, but not always, especially where it is known to be wrong. (One notable such exception is the spelling of Carnedd Llywelyn.

The Lord of Snowdonia was Prince **Llywelyn** ap Gruffudd, not **Llewelyn**, as some maps suggest. So Carnedd Llywelyn is used here.) In general correct Welsh has been followed: Cwm y Llan, south of Snowdon, is rendered on maps as Cwm Llan but Cwm y Llan is used in the text. (There is a subtle linguistic difference, but that need not trouble us here.) But this example highlights another issue that crops up throughout the maps of Snowdonia, and varying between OS and Harvey versions. Should it be Cwm y Llan or Cwm-y-llan? Guidance has been taken on these thorny issues from a Welsh-speaker and this accounts for some further variance from the maps for the sake of linguistic accuracy without compromising the clarity of the route descriptions.

In addition, many names have become Anglicised over the years. In most instances, this book uses what is believed to be the correct Welsh version, departing only rarely in the most widely-accepted cases of Anglicisation, for example the use of Snowdon instead of Yr Wyddfa and Conwy Mountain instead of Mynydd y Dref. Moreover, the author's local knowledge has led him to name features sometimes not named on the maps at all. Appendix 3 also contains a glossary of Welsh words that you are likely to encounter on your great mountain days in Snowdonia.

↑ *Y Garn and Llyn Idwal (Walk 7)*

Weather to walk?

Mountains everywhere tend to generate their own climate, while remaining subject to whatever is going on nationally. Proximity to the Irish Sea can and does make a difference at times, making conditions change in an instance. So, while out on the hills, you need always to be aware of what is happening to the weather: is the wind changing direction? – are clouds gathering? – is it getting hotter, or colder? Make allowance for the fact that conditions on the tops are generally more severe than in the valleys.

You can get some indication of what *might* happen by checking the weather forecast both the day before you go and again on the morning you intend to walk. The internet is the best way of checking this, as the websites are regularly updated:

- www.metoffice.gov.uk/loutdoor/ mountainsafety/snowdonia/ snowdonia_latest_pressure.html
- www.news.bbc.co.uk/weather
- www.mwis.org.uk/sd.php

IN CASE OF EMERGENCY

There are four key mountain rescue services operating in Snowdonia:

- Llanberis Mountain Rescue Team (www.llanberismountainrescue.co.uk)
- Aberglaslyn Mountain Rescue Team (www.aberglaslyn-mrt.org)
- South Snowdonia Search and Rescue Team (www.southsnowdoniamountain rescueteam.co.uk)
- Ogwen Valley Mountain Rescue Team (www.ogwen-rescue.org.uk)

The following information is provided by Llanberis Mountain Rescue Team, who, as do other teams, produce excellent information on safety in the hills; theirs is available for download from www.llanberismountainrescue.co.uk. This is what to do if you need a mountain rescue team:

- Call 999 or 112 and ask for Mountain Rescue.

- Tell them where the 'incident' has occurred by giving an accurate grid reference, and the nature of the incident. Give them a contact phone number.

- The messengers may be required to wait by the phone for further instructions, and may be used to guide the Team to the exact location of the incident, so they should be the fittest group members if possible.

- Be prepared for a long wait – comprised of the time it takes for your messengers to reach a phone, the team callout and assembly time, and the time required for the team to walk to your location with heavy equipment. You may decide that if there is a danger of hypothermia it is best to evacuate most of the party and leave a small group remaining with the casualty. You may also decide that it is necessary to move the casualty to a more sheltered or safer location (if so, ensure that someone will be on hand to guide the Team to your new location). →

- Consider how group members or passers by can best be deployed, and how the equipment carried by the group can best be redistributed and utilised.

- Consider 'alternative' uses for the equipment you are carrying, for example camera flashes can be used to attract attention in the dark, a rope laid out along the ground will maximise your chances of being located in poor visibility, and a survival bag can be used for attracting attention.

- The standard distress signal is six sharp whistle blasts (or torch flashes) followed by a one minute silence, repeated.

- Don't lose touch with common sense when coming to any decisions!

Before you start

What to wear

Someone once said: 'There's no such thing as bad weather, just inadequate clothing.' Well, as everyone knows, there *is* such a thing as bad weather, sometimes so bad that no amount of clothing will prove adequate. But the anonymous optimist makes a fair point, and, unless you aspire to being no more than a fair weather walker, then going adequately and suitably clothed facilitates walking regardless of all but the most severe weather conditions. Regular walkers will talk at length (usually in a bar), about days spent in the hills battling wind and rain; it's a circumstance that breeds its own delightful perversity, a dash of self-esteem at having coped safely with a bad weather day, an exhilaration that is often breathtaking in more ways than one. Let's face it, if you have to wait for the sun to shine before venturing out, you may never begin.

Being adequately clothed makes all the difference, and well-equipped walkers, enveloped in wind- and waterproof garments, have little to fear from a moderately inclement day.

So, what to wear?

This question can be answered only in general terms for the simple reason that each of us is physically different, we have different metabolisms, our bodies function in different ways when exercising, and the way, and amount, we perspire varies, too. All these factors generate bodily conditions that are specific to each of us and which require individual solutions.

To complicate things even further, there are numerous clothing and equipment manufacturers clamouring to sell you their own brand, but without the certainty that one brand is any more suitable for *you* than another. It is purely a process of trial and error, often over a period of time, sometimes years. But eventually, you find a combination that works best for you. When you do, stick with it. Just as important, when you settle on the type of clothing that suits you and decide to kit yourself out, go for the best you can afford. Quality really does count when it comes to outdoor clothing.

What to carry

So, what is considered essential? It is not intended that this list should be slavishly followed in every detail by every person in a group, but is suggested as a guide or checklist. Small groups may manage without some items, but if the group is such that it may become fragmented, then it pays to have the key items throughout the group.

- **Map** – everyone should carry a map for the area of the walk, and know how to read it.
- **Compass** – much the same; map and compass are essential.
- **Whistle** – every individual should carry a whistle; it is vital as a means of communication in the event of an emergency. There are numerous, inexpensive mountain and survival whistles available, but any whistle will do.
- **Torch** – you may not intend to be out after dark, but a torch will prove useful if you are. Make sure that every individual carries their own torch, even if there are only two of you. There are many suitable pocket torches on the market, and be sure to carry spare batteries, too. A torch is also useful for signalling in an emergency.
- **First aid kit** – there is nothing worse than a developing blister, or a bad scratch from a bramble. Even the smallest of first aid kits contain plasters or skin compounds like Dr Scholl's® Moleskin, or Compeed® Blister Packs that can ease the

irritation. The kit does not need to be huge, but should include a good cross-section of contemporary first aid products, including ointments and creams suitable for easing insect stings and bites. Today's outdoor market offers plastic first aid 'bottle' kits containing everything you are likely to need for minor emergencies.

- **Food** – it is important to carry day rations sufficient both for the walk you are planning to follow *and* for emergencies. Every rucksack should contain some emergency foods, like Kendal Mint Cake, chocolate bars or glucose tablets, that remain forever in your pack – although it is a good idea to replenish them at regular intervals.

- **Drink –** liquids are vital, especially in hot conditions, and in winter a stainless steel Thermos of hot drink goes down a treat. Cold liquids can be carried in water bottles or a pliable water container with a plastic suction tube that can be led from your rucksack over your shoulder.

- **Spare clothing** – there is no need to duplicate everything you wear or would normally carry, but some extras kept permanently in your rucksack will prove beneficial – T-shirt, sweater, scarf, spare socks (to double as gloves, if necessary), spare laces

- **Other bits and pieces** – strong string (can double as emergency laces), small towel (for drying post-paddling feet during summer months), notebook, pencil, pocket knife and a thermal blanket or survival bag for emergencies. With luck you will never use it, but half a roll of toilet tissue in a sealable plastic bag can ease many an embarrassing moment.

Cwm Eigiau from Craig yr Ysfa (Walk 15)

RECREATION AND THE MOUNTAIN ENVIRONMENT

[Reproduced with the consent of the Countryside Council for Wales. More information about the need to protect the mountains of Snowdonia, and how that can be achieved, is available from the Council.]

Carnedd Ugain (Crib y Ddysgl) in winter (Walk 1)

Mountains have withstood the rigours of millions of years of geological processes – including mountain building, erosion and glaciation, but, paradoxically, their environments are fragile and very special. Their fragility comes from the harsh climate and landforms which affect the way in which plants and animals can survive there. And they are special because mountains are one of the least human impacted environments. The mountains of Britain support a number of rare species of plants and animals. The effects of ice during the last glacial advance are responsible somewhat for the botanical wealth, producing steep, north facing rocks which provide a suitable habitat for relict arctic–alpine plants which need the cool conditions and freedom from competition from more aggressive grassland species. They also provide a refuge from the attentions of sheep, which manage to graze vegetation

Heather

in most places in the British uplands, except steep rock faces and fenced enclosures. It is no accident that the best sites to botanise in the uplands are often on rock faces and very steep ground which are effectively mountain 'islands', with little surviving woodland or scrub and surrounded by agricultural and urbanised lowlands.

Tenacious hawthorn

Although the effects of recreation in the uplands may appear insignificant compared to those of other, more substantial and widespread pressures on the countryside, the potential impact is magnified because of the very nature of the sports which we undertake in some of the hitherto least affected areas. These cliffs and summit areas are precisely those last remaining refuges which are so valuable and which conservation organisations are trying to protect. Whether is it ground nesting birds, arctic–alpine flora, blanket bog or the fragile montane heath on the very highest summits, there is a need to be aware of and to protect the special features of the environment we use. There is also the added burden of possible climate change and the results this may have for our upland species.

Generally, most walkers and climbers are sensitive to these concerns and co-operate fully to avoid damage to the special vegetation found in Snowdonia. Examples of damage are rare, but an awareness of the issues is important, particularly as not everyone knows of the special sites or the potential for damage.

Rock lichen

Wild pony, Eastern Carneddau (Walk 12)

SNOWDON
AND MOEL EILIO

Llyn Llydaw from Bwlch y Ciliau (Walk 1)

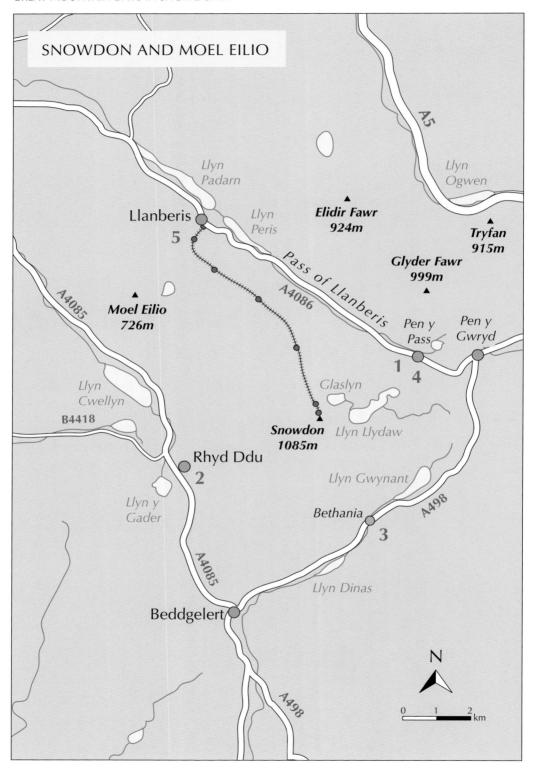

SNOWDON AND MOEL EILIO

Llyn
Padarn

Llyn
Peris

Elidir Fawr
924m

Llyn
Ogwen

A5

Llanberis

5

▲ **Moel Eilio**
726m

A4085

A4086

Pass of Llanberis

Tryfan
915m

Glyder Fawr
999m
▲

Pen y
Pass

Pen y
Gwryd

1

4

Glaslyn

Snowdon
1085m
Llyn Llydaw

Llyn
Cwellyn

B4418

Rhyd Ddu

2

Llyn y
Gader

Llyn Gwynant

Bethania

3

A498

A4085

Llyn Dinas

Beddgelert

A498

N

0   1   2
km

SNOWDON AND MOEL EILIO

The popularity of Snowdon, Yr Wyddfa in Welsh, has scarcely diminished since the first recorded ascent by the botanist Thomas Johnson in 1639. However, the 18th-century Welsh historian Thomas Pennant mentions a 'triumphal fair upon this our chief of mountains' following Edward I's conquest of Wales in 1284, which, if true, indicates the likelihood of significantly earlier ascents. And although all the early ascents were by scientists of one breed or another, by the time Norfolk-born author George Borrow appeared on the scene to quote Welsh poetry from Snowdon's summit in the middle of the 19th century, he and his companion were 'far from being the only visitors to the hill...groups of people, or single individuals, might be seen going up or descending the path as far as the eye could reach.'

Yr Wyddfa is known to everyone as 'Snowdon', the highest and arguably the most popular summit in England and Wales. The name Yr Wyddfa, like that of Pen y Gadair to the south, is a name with origins in legend. It is said, although there is no archaeological evidence to support it, that the summit of Yr Wyddfa is the tomb of Rhita Gawr, a fierce, king-killing giant who dressed himself in a cloak made from the beards of those he had killed. Rhita was eventually slain by King Arthur, who had a great cairn thrown over the giant on top of the highest mountain in Eryri.

In 1857, an anonymous writer commented on the number of walkers, saying: 'Snowdon is ascended by everyone because it is the highest top; no one seems to ascend the other mountains but the shepherds of the country. Snowdon is the Righi of Wales, with a trifle worse inn at the top.' Snowdon is certainly the highest mountain in England and Wales but it has so much more to offer than its bare altitude. It has something for everyone, easy ways and hard ways. In the words of the English judge and sometime Member of Parliament for his home town of Reading, Sir Thomas Noon Talfourd, who, comparing it with Cadair Idris, Helvellyn and Ben Nevis, wrote: Snowdon 'forms... the noblest aggregate, because, except on the side opposite Caernarvon, its upper portion is all mighty frame-work, a top uplifted on vast buttresses, disdaining the round lumpish earth, spreading out skeleton arms towards heaven, and embracing on each side huge hollows, made more awful by the red tints of the copper ore which deepens among its shadows, and gleams through the scanty herbage of its loveliest pathways' – which really says it all.

There is a history of refreshments being served on the summit dating back to 1838, a licence to sell intoxicating liquor being granted in 1845. When the Snowdon Mountain Railway was opened in 1896, a hotel was built a short distance below the summit.

In the 1930s, this was replaced by a restaurant to a design by Sir Clough Williams-Ellis. By the end of the 20th century, this was operating as a café and shop complex. However, it was becoming increasingly dilapidated and its state led to a campaign to replace the old building. In April 2006, Snowdonia National Park Authority agreed to start work on a new café and visitor centre complex. By mid-October 2006, the old building had been largely demolished. The shell of the new visitor centre was erected during 2007 and finally opened on 12 June 2009, and named Hafod Eryri – 'Eryri' in English is 'Snowdonia', but there is no adequate translation for 'Hafod', an old Welsh term for a residence on high land.

The steep cliffs in the Snowdon group hold an important place in the history of British rock climbing. The first recorded climb was the 1798 ascent of the Eastern Terrace of Clogwyn Du'r Arddu (Cloggy, as it is affectionately now known among the climbing fraternity) by the Reverends Peter Williams and William Bingley, botanists looking for alpine plants. What prompted them to complete the climb was summed up by Bingley, who wrote: 'I believe it was the prospect downwards that determined us to brave every difficulty.' Nothing has changed on Cloggy.

The north face of Y Lliwedd was explored in the late 19th century, and in 1909 became the subject of one of the first British climbing guides, *The Climbs on Lliwedd* by J M A Thompson and A W Andrews. The testing nature of Snowdon's wall is testified to by the fact that Edmund Hillary trained here in preparation for his successful ascent of Everest in 1953.

Amazingly, for all its trampled ways, Snowdon remains an impressive mountain, with a menu of ascents to suit all abilities and dispositions, and although, as Pennant observed 'It is very rare that the traveller gets a proper day to ascend the hill', when perfect days do come, the extent of view is remarkable, reaching as far as the hills of southern Scotland.

Overshadowed somewhat by the mountains that radiate from Snowdon, those of the Moel Eilio range to the north-west have the advantage of solitude, which has merit, especially on a fine summer's day, that should not be undervalued. Lying near to Llanberis, the four grassy summits comprising this group present splendid views of Mynydd Mawr across Llyn Cwellyn, the Nantlle ridge and of the sombre precipices of Clogwyn Du'r Arddu. The complete round of the four summits is no mean undertaking, and a perfect antidote to the much-trammelled hills close by.

Y Lliwedd from the summit of Snowdon (Walk 1)

Snowdon Horseshoe

*T*his route is **the** classic walk in North Wales, arguably in the whole of Wales, and is a must for all strong walkers. 'Strong' is the operative word here, because the circuit is very tiring and can leave even experienced walkers jaded towards the end. Sadly, its appeal draws walkers who are not prepared for the exposed narrowness of the Crib Goch ridge, nor the descent of Snowdon followed by a weary climb onto Y Lliwedd. But it is quite spectacular and deservedly popular.

The Route

The early part of the circuit is shared with the so-called **Pyg Track** (see Walk Four), which leaves the Pen y Pass car park in a westerly direction, heading for the pointed cone of Crib Goch seen in the distance. The track rises in a series of rocky steps beneath the long ridge leading to an unnamed minor summit just to the east of Bwlch y Moch. This ridge, which can be gained quite easily after the initial steepness of the Pyg Track, is by far a more rewarding way to begin the ascent not least because the unnamed summit is technically the first nail in the Snowdon horseshoe – one for the purists, then.

At **Bwlch y Moch** (*Pass of the Pigs*), the path forks, left (and actually descending for a short while) to continue following the Pyg Track, and right, to tackle the steep rocky slopes of Crib Goch.

The ascent and traverse of **Crib Goch** is one of the finest ridge walks in Britain, although 'walk' is hardly the right word. This is hands-on, and the ridge wants only for more length to make it a hugely different undertaking. From Bwlch y Moch the way up Crib Goch is so popular and therefore well-defined that there is little need to attempt to describe the route in detail. In any case, the physical configuration of the many rock outcrops is such that a description would

↑ The Snowdon Horseshoe from above Capel Curig

ROUTE INFORMATION

Distance	11km/6¾ miles
Height gain	1110m/3640ft
Time	5–6 hours
Grade	arduous
Start point	Pen y Pass SH647555

Getting there
Pen y Pass car park; fills quite quickly, so consider taking the hourly Snowdon Sherpa shuttle bus from Llanberis or Nant Peris

Maps
(Harvey Superwalker) Snowdonia and the Moelwynion; (Ordnance Survey) OL17 Snowdon/Yr Wyddfa

After-walk refreshment
Pen y Pass; Pen y Gwryd; Nant Peris; Llanberis

be difficult to follow. The way, however, is not confusing; at half height there is a brief rock wall which may seem intimidating (more so in descent), but there are ample hand holds to facilitate a scrambly passage to easier ground above, and then by a final pull to the eastern end of the summit ridge. Take time, frequently, to pause

and study the way you are going before you move. Do not blindly follow the person in front.

Contrary to popular belief, the actual **summit** of Crib Goch is not at this eastern end, but nearer to the middle of the ridge, marked by a tiny cairn placed on the very edge of the steep drop into Cwm Glas to the north; most people never even notice it.

The crossing of the ridge requires a good head for heights and will be made considerably more difficult in strong winds (from any direction). Keeping to the crest all the way is nigh on impossible, and the best way, when the ridge narrows dramatically, is to keep to the left (southern) side, which allows hands to be used more readily. In winter conditions, Crib Goch is a place for only the most experienced and properly equipped walkers.

At the far end of the ridge lie the Pinnacles, which can be either crossed with care, or bypassed on the southern side to gain respite on a brief col before pressing on up **Crib y Ddysgl** and on to **Carnedd Ugain**. A short descent from the Pinnacles leads to a narrow ridge with a minor bump in the middle, and then a more grassy section before it finally comes

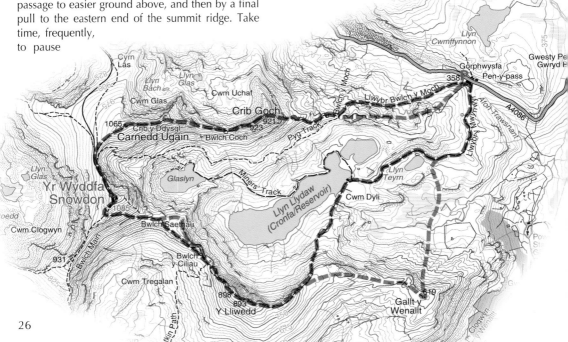

up against a shattered rock wall. Most walkers at this point tend to go left a little, to scramble through the rocks. But there is a satisfactory alternative directly ahead, up a short and narrow rock gully from the top of which it is possible to keep nearer to the crest of the ridge with correspondingly better views to the left and right. A short distance further on, the ridge narrows abruptly affording a scrambly route along the crest, or an easier option on the north side. Both ways are well trodden and lead to the trig pillar on the summit of Carnedd Ugain.

From Carnedd Ugain there is a short descent to join the route from Llanberis and the line of the Snowdon Mountain Railway for the equally short ascent by a constructed pathway to **Snowdon's summit**, adorned with a spanking new café.

The continuation to Y Lliwedd is not direct, but involves setting off as if heading for Rhyd Ddu, initially in a south-westerly direction down a rocky path, but only as far as a shapely finger of rock on the left that marks the top of the ascent via the Watkin Path (see Walk Three). A steep and loose

LOOKING **SOUTH-WEST**

descent leads to easier ground and a stony track to **Bwlch y Saethau**, the *Pass of the Arrows*; take great care on the upper section of this descent, especially if there are people ascending below you.

Bwlch y Saethau is said to be the battleground at which King Arthur was fatally wounded. Legend has it that Sir Bedivere carried his dying King to

On Crib Goch

Llyn Llydaw, casting the sword Excalibur into Glaslyn on the way. After placing his king on a barge to be taken away by the 'fair maids of the mountains', Bedivere climbed to a cave high in the crags of Y Lliwedd, where he and the Llanciau Eryri (Arthur's Men) lie sleeping even now, until their King should need them again.

Once the steep section is over you might consider climbing left, off the Watkin Path, and keeping as near as is comfortable to the drop into Cwm Dyli. This is much superior to plodding along the lower path, it goes to exactly the same place, and has fine views. The route passes the top of Cribau, a fine scrambly ridge descending to the outflow of Glaslyn below.

Press on to **Bwlch y Ciliau**, where the Watkin Path departs south-westerly into Cwm Llan, and here, from a large cairn, continue ahead (south-easterly), climbing again, to the twin summits of **Y Lliwedd**.

Arguments rage as to which of the two summits of **Y Lliwedd** is the higher, each appearing lower when viewed from the other. Modern surveying techniques settle the issue: Y Lliwedd West is 898 metres, Y Lliwedd East is 893 metres – although seeing may not be believing! The summits, either of them, have a tremendous feeling of height, being far enough away from Snowdon not to feel dominated by it, and give an excellent aerial view of the massive amphitheatre of Cwm Dyli.

From Y Lliwedd (East) it is a short descent to Y Lliwedd Bach, and then to a cairn at the top of the descent to **Llyn Llydaw**. Most walkers go this way, as it leads directly to the Miners' Track close by Llyn Llydaw. Now all that remains is to turn right along the track, and follow it back to Pen y Pass.

Purists, however, may want to take in **Gallt yr Wenallt**, the last nail in the horseshoe. The way to it, from close by the cairn, is by a path across undulating ground, agreeably pleasant underfoot after so much hard ground. From the summit of Gallt yr Wenallt descend due north with care, initially taking Llyn Teyrn as a rough guide. Cross the Afon Glaslyn and a water pipeline, and then climb to join the Miners' Track to complete the walk.

Y Lliwedd from Bwlch y Ciliau

The Rhyd Ddu Path
and the Snowdon Ranger

*F*ormerly known as the Beddgelert Path, the approach to Snowdon by the Rhyd Ddu Path is probably the least used. Yet it passes across outstanding mountain landscapes and, for those out late in the day, offers the prospect of incredible sunsets beyond bulky Moel Hebog and the undulating Nantlle Ridge. As a line of ascent, it is preferable to the Snowdon Ranger. You can judge for yourself, as the route continues over Snowdon and down the Snowdon Ranger, although it abandons the full descent in favour of a cross-country route that eliminates road walking.

The Route

Walk across the car park and continue alongside the railway track, and then turn right through a gate, crossing the railway line, to continue along a well-defined track. On your left is a ruined round tower that was the powder house for Ffridd Slate Quarry, now disused.

When the track divides, bear right, climbing gently as the track passes between the waste tip and the ruined buildings of the quarry, which closed in the 1860s. Cross a stile and soon you reach a gate/stile with views to your right of Llyn y Gadair and Y Garn in the distance. The track beyond the stile soon bends to the left, bringing into view **Llyn Cwellyn** in the valley to your left. Presently you reach another gate/stile with an easily missed sign on the rock opposite: 'Snowdon, first gate on left'. Just beyond this point, the path bears to the left. The path coming in from your right is an alternative start of the Rhyd Ddu path from Pitt's Head and Ffridd Uchaf, although parking

↑ The Snowdon Ranger Path snakes above Clogwyn Du'r Arddu to Snowdon summit

ROUTE INFORMATION

Distance	14km/8¾ miles
Height gain	970m/3182ft
Time	5–6 hours
Grade	energetic
Start point	Rhyd Ddu village SH571526

Getting there
Car park a little south of Rhyd Ddu village on the A4085 Beddgelert–Caernarfon road, adjacent to the Rhyd Ddu station

Maps
(Harvey Superwalker) Snowdonia and the Moelwynion; (Ordnance Survey) OL17 Snowdon/Yr Wyddfa

After-walk refreshment
Tea room and pub in Rhyd Ddu, and hotels, restaurants, pubs and cafés in Beddgelert

Old powder house at start of Rhyd-Ddu path

the path emerges onto the shoulder of Llechog. From here, you can see right across **Cwm Clogwyn** and through Bwlch Cwm Brwynog, flanked by Moel Cynghorion, on the left, and Clogwyn Du'r Arddu, and down towards Llanberis.

Continuing to your right, the path climbs the Llechog ridge through a harsh landscape, one that is very exposed to the prevailing wind. The landscape is dominated by frost-shattered rocks, and what little vegetation that is found here is low growing and stunted. Soon, you reach a wall meeting you on the right, from beside which there is a superb view into Cwm Clogwyn, housing three tiny lakes, **Llyn Nadroedd** (Lake of the Snakes), Llyn Coch (Red Lake) and **Llyn Glas** (Blue Lake). This wild and lovely

is very limited at this starting point. The track in front of you is the old miners' route to the slate quarries at Bwlch Cwm y Llan, below Yr Aran, and it is now used to reach Yr Aran, or Cwm Llan and the Watkin Path up Snowdon.

Pass through a gate and cross a stream. The path continues to climb gently, and gradually broadens. The landscape is now one of tangled heather and rock, through which the path leads to another stile with sheep pens to the left of the path. On your right is the wide expanse of **Cwm Caregog** bounded on the far side by Allt Maenderyn (Hill of the Bird Stone), a fine, narrow ridge used in Walk Three. The path soon becomes steeper and rougher underfoot.

The path crosses a stream, and climbs steeply until it reaches a wall. This section of the path is straightforward, but is bouldery and uneven. Through a gate in the wall,

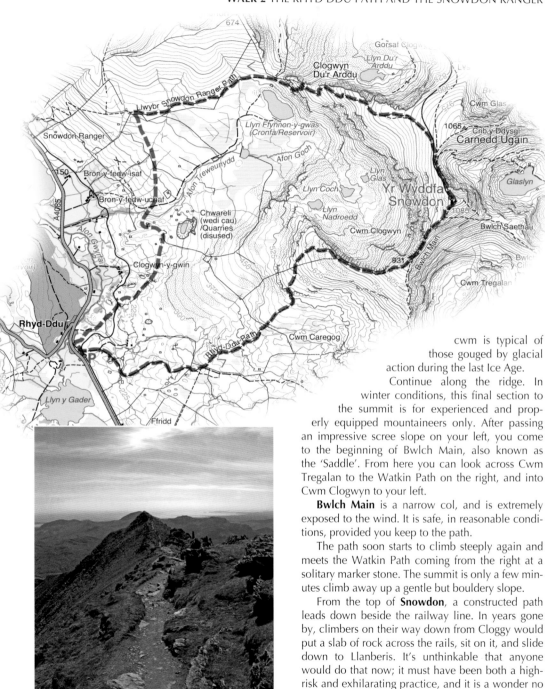

cwm is typical of those gouged by glacial action during the last Ice Age.

Continue along the ridge. In winter conditions, this final section to the summit is for experienced and properly equipped mountaineers only. After passing an impressive scree slope on your left, you come to the beginning of Bwlch Main, also known as the 'Saddle'. From here you can look across Cwm Tregalan to the Watkin Path on the right, and into Cwm Clogwyn to your left.

Bwlch Main is a narrow col, and is extremely exposed to the wind. It is safe, in reasonable conditions, provided you keep to the path.

The path soon starts to climb steeply again and meets the Watkin Path coming from the right at a solitary marker stone. The summit is only a few minutes climb away up a gentle but bouldery slope.

From the top of **Snowdon**, a constructed path leads down beside the railway line. In years gone by, climbers on their way down from Cloggy would put a slab of rock across the rails, sit on it, and slide down to Llanberis. It's unthinkable that anyone would do that now; it must have been both a high-risk and exhilarating practice, and it is a wonder no one was killed doing it. Very much a case of 'Don't try this at home!'

The Llanberis Path and the **Snowdon Ranger Path** are one at the top of Snowdon, and closely follow the railway track. On the way down you pass

Looking along the Allt Maenderyn ridge

a prominent marker stone on your right, where the Pyg Track descends for Pen y Pass. A short way further on, look for another marker stone over the other side of the railway on your left at the start of the Snowdon Ranger path. Follow this down above the cliffs of **Clogwyn Du'r Arddu** you reach the pass, Bwlch Cwm Brwynog, where you carry on along the path for a further 1.5km (1 mile).

> **Clogwyn Du'r Arddu** (the Black Cliff) is considered by many rock climbers to be among the finest cliffs in Britain, north facing and remote, and combining unrelenting steepness, seriousness and quality of rock. From the 1930s until 2000, 'Cloggy' maintained the record among the climbing fraternity of having the most difficult climbs in Britain, and many routes first climbed by the likes of the Abraham brothers, Joe Brown, Don Whillans, Colin Kirkus and Pete Crew are still high-ranking. To peer down the cliffs you need to leave the descending Snowdon Ranger Path, but do not do so if the wind is likely to be blowing from behind you – and stay well away from the very edge.

To head back to Rhyd Ddu you need to quit the Snowdon Ranger Path (although if you stick with it, you will eventually reach the A4085, and can turn left to walk back along this). For a more direct route, however, keep an eye open for a stile over a wall on the left (approximately at SH576553), just before the ground starts to fall away steeply again. Cross this stile into the moor beyond. The ongoing path is continuous but indistinct at times, aided by white marker posts that lead down to a stile in a fence, and then continue towards slate tips ahead. Pass round the right-hand edge of the tips, crossing a bridge over a stream, then up into the tips.

> These **tips** are fascinating and a famous Welsh poet, T H Parry Williams (1887–1975, who lived at Rhyd Ddu) wrote about how every piece of slate we are walking on has been through someone's hands.
>
> Parry Williams was the first poet to win the double of Chair and Crown at the National Eisteddfod of Wales, which he achieved at Wrexham in 1912 and repeated at Bangor in 1915.

When you emerge from the tips continue following markers over boggy ground until you reach and cross the railway and arrive back at the village car park.

The summit of Snowdon from Bwlch Main

The Watkin Path and Yr Aran

It was Sir Edward Watkin, a rich and influential railway owner and one of the brains behind the original idea to build a Channel tunnel, who directed the building of the Watkin Path, as a donkey track, at the end of the 19th century. Today it forms the most demanding route direct to the summit of Snowdon, and is here coupled with an optional add-on, embracing Yr Aran, a quite marvellous vantage point, and one that is often overlooked. However, tacking it on to this walk makes for a demanding day, one that should be contemplated only by strong walkers.

The Route

Set off from the car park at Pont Bethania by crossing the bridge and then the road to gain the signed Watkin Path, up steps and into light, broadleaved woodland that is a delight to encounter. The path brings you to an information panel just above **Hafod-y-llan**, which farms most of the land on this side of Snowdon, although centuries ago the valley would have been completely forested.

As you leave the woodland behind, so the valley widens and the path heads towards the lower slopes of Yr Aran. At a gate you enter the Yr Wyddfa National Nature Reserve, special for its arctic–alpine and montane plants.

The path climbs steadily on pitched paving until it intercepts a steep tramway belonging to quarry workings further up the cwm. Down to your right the **Afon Cwm Llan** puts on a fine display of cascades

Striding out along the Watkin Path

Distance	12.6km/8 miles; with Yr Aran 14.5km/9 miles
Height gain	1070m/3510ft; with Yr Aran 1320m/4330ft
Time	5–6 hours; with Yr Aran 6–7 hours
Grade	arduous/strenuous
Start point	National Park car park, Pont Bethania, Nantgwynant SH628507

Getting there
Nantgwynant; there is a small car park and adjacent toilets next to Pont Bethania

Maps
(Harvey Superwalker) Snowdonia and the Moelwynion; (Ordnance Survey) OL17 Snowdon/Yr Wyddfa

After-walk refreshment
Café near start, along the road to Beddgelert; pubs and cafés in Beddgelert; pubs at Pen y Gwryd, and Pen y Pass

as you approach an area of quarry buildings. One of these, Plas Cwmllan, enclosed by slate fencing, was the home of the manager of the slate quarry found a short distance further on. It was used as a Commando military target during the Second World War, and still bears the scars.

Press on past Plas Cwmllan, and soon reach a huge embedded rock on the left bearing a large stone plaque.

Tablet, Gladstone Rock

with a large cairn said to mark the site of the death of King Arthur. Indeed, the whole of the cwm below, Tregalan, is allegedly the scene of one of the king's many battles. Even older than Arthur's battles, the cwm displays fine lateral moraines – piles of grass-covered rocks and earth deposited by the retreating glaciers at the end of the last Ice Age. Yr Aran rises majestically on the other side, and beyond it Moel Hebog and the Glaslyn estuary.

From Bwlch y Saethau, the path starts to rise abruptly across the southern flank of Snowdon. The section between Bwlch y Saethau and the top of the climb, Bwlch Main, is very steep, unstable, dusty and worryingly loose when dry, and slippery when wet. In winter conditions, this route is the preserve only of experienced and well-equipped mountaineers. Not under any conditions should a deviation from the path be contemplated; it is far from the surest of routes, but it does head straight for a prominent finger of rock on Bwlch Main, an essential marker for anyone descending the Watkin Path.

This is **Gladstone Rock**, commemorating the visit in 1892 of W E Gladstone, then in his 84th year and Prime Minister for the fourth time. Here he addressed the People of Eryri on the topic of Justice in Wales.

The path continues clearly beyond Gladstone Rock, while prominent all around are the remains of the South Snowdon Slate Works, which began operation in 1840, but because of the expense of transporting slates to Porthmadog had to be closed in 1882. The large building on the left is the barracks, where the men slept through the week, returning to their homes only at weekends. Other ruins are dressing sheds and workshops. This wide cwm was used as location for the 1968 film *Carry on up the Khyber*.

Just past the barracks, the path starts to climb steeply, casting about to ease the gradient as much as possible until it reaches **Bwlch y Ciliau**, from where there is an exceptional view of Crib Goch and **Llyn Llydaw** below. There is a large cairn at Bwlch y Ciliau, and from it a path ascends, right, up Y Lliwedd. The Watkin Path, however, bears left, passing first across **Bwlch y Saethau**, once itself adorned

Once safely on **Bwlch Main**, turn right for a brief stony section up to the café and then the summit of **Snowdon** above that.

From the summit, retreat to Bwlch Main and the finger of rock, but then continue along a ridge path, initially in a south-westerly direction. This is excellent walking, but the ridge becomes narrow, and has a number of rocky sections. When the path forks, bear left, uphill, to experience more rocky ridge work along **Allt Maenderyn**. There are a few awkward, scrambly stretches along this steadily descending ridge, where hands, knees and bottoms will be called into play. This is no place to hurry, and can be very tiring.

35

LOOKING
NORTH-WEST

From Bwlch Cwm Llan, take to a slate gully that leads to and through a wall before skimming on down across grassy slopes. The descending path is continuous, if occasionally vague, but it does come down to intercept an old tramway used by the quarry, and along which horse-drawn trams took the slate to the top of a steep incline from where they were lowered to Pont Bethania.

On reaching the tramway, the route lies to the right, but it is worth taking a few moments to turn left towards **quarry buildings** in front of which lies what some have mistaken as a graveyard (SH611523). It is simply a random placement of slate slabs, of uncertain origin, although it is agreeable to think they may have been placed in commemoration of those who died working the quarries.

Eventually, you reach a ladder-stile spanning a fence, beyond which a final, rocky staircase of slate leads to **Bwlch Cwm y Llan**, and it is from here that those bound for Yr Aran will depart, upwards. Before deciding what to do, take a little time to inspect the old slate quarries.

The path for **Yr Aran** follows an old wall which, higher up, veers off to the left before turning to a south-westerly direction to climb to the summit, marked by a cairn and splendid views. From the top of Yr Aran, it is possible to head east alongside a wall, then leaving it as the wall turns to the south, by descending steeply, and without a path to guide you, in a northwards direction. It is somewhat safer, however, to retrace your steps to Bwlch Cwm Llan.

Return along the tramway, which passes through a few rock cuttings until it reaches the top of a clear path descending to the left, reaching the route of ascent not far from Plas Cwmllan. Now all you need to do is turn right, and retrace your steps to Nantgwynant.

Yr Aran from just above Bwlch Cwm Llan

The Pyg Track
and the Miners' Track

*W*alkers wanting to reach Snowdon's summit, who want neither the tedium of the ascent from
Llanberis, whether on foot or by train, nor the frights that Crib Goch and Crib y Ddysgl can
provoke, will opt for what has become a classic in its own right – up the Pyg and down the Miners'.
And there are many reasons why those venturing onto Snowdon for the first time will take pleasure
in this approach, not least the emerging prospect of mountains beyond mountains and the sheer
adrenalin rush that these rocky theatres generate.

The Route
The walk starts from the car park at **Pen y Pass**,
where the charge for parking is considerably more
than the old shilling (5p) once demanded. Ignore the
conspicuous track leading south from the car park,
this is the way you will return. Instead, start off west,
aiming for the pointed cone of Crib Goch seen in the
distance. If you can't see Crib Goch because of mist,
you may want to reconsider the day's plans.

The **Pyg Track**, contrary to a once-popular belief
that it took its name from the initials of the nearby
Pen y Gwryd Hotel, the haunt of Everest mountaineers in the 1950s, is actually named from the
high-level pass, Bwlch y Moch, the *Pass of the Pigs*,
immediately below the steep ascent to Crib Goch.

The track gains height in a series of stepped sections
that lie to the north of the long ridge leading to an

ROUTE INFORMATION

Distance	11½km/7 miles
Height gain	840m/2755ft
Time	4–5 hours
Grade	strenuous
Start point	Pen y Pass SH647555

Getting there
Pen y Pass car park, but note that this fills up early. Consider making use of the hourly Snowdon Sherpa shuttle bus from Llanberis or Nant Peris.

Maps
(Harvey Superwalker) Snowdonia and the Moelwynion; (Ordnance Survey) OL17 Snowdon/Yr Wyddfa

After-walk refreshment
Pen y Pass; Pen y Gwryd; Nant Peris; Llanberis

unnamed summit (perhaps we could be daring and call it Pen Bwlch y Moch, *The Peak of the Pass of the Pigs*, albeit with no justification).

At **Bwlch y Moch** the path forks. Go left, descending for a short while, to continue along the Pyg Track, and so begin a superb traverse of Crib Goch's lower slopes, yet sufficiently elevated to have a fine view of Llyn Llydaw and the towering vertical cliffs of Y Lliwedd, which were among the first crags in Wales to be explored by rock climbers. This traverse is to be appreciated; there is nothing quite like it in Wales, and every opportunity should be taken to embrace the scenery. When Snowdon bursts into view, hopefully it will be with a clarity that draws you on.

The **Pyg Track** is clear throughout its length, and substantially restored in its upper reaches. Along the way it cavorts with minor outcrops and later passes below the broken cliffs of Crib y Ddysgl, where the Miners' Track ascends from the left, rising through Cwm Dyli. The final escape is by the renowned zigzags, now pitch paved.

Snowdon and Llyn Llydaw

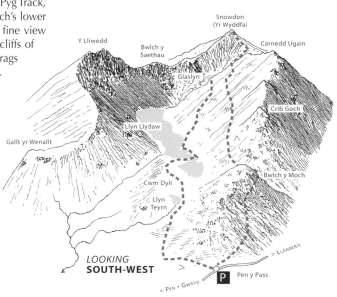

LOOKING
SOUTH-WEST

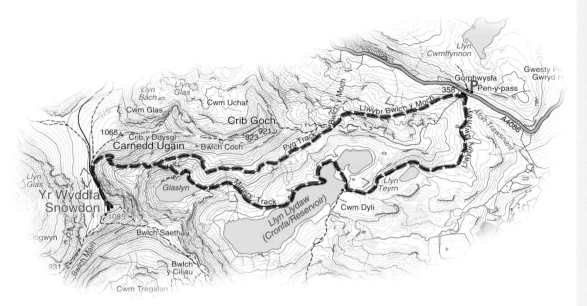

This used to be seriously tricky in winter conditions, and is no easier now when snow and ice abound. But in normal summer conditions, there is no difficulty popping up to the finger of rock that marks the top of the path, a key marker, incidentally, for the descent.

Now all that remains is to turn left (roughly south), and follow a broad trail up to the summit of **Snowdon**.

You make your descent by retracing your steps to the finger of rock above the zigzags, and the turning down onto the Pyg Track. Above **Glaslyn**, in an area of mining debris that often causes navigational confusion, a path descends steeply to the shores of the lake. There is a stone marker, a little over a metre high, that marks the best point of departure from the Pyg Track.

The Pyg Track in winter

Glaslyn, its water tinted by copper ore, was once known as **Llyn y Ffynnon Las**, the *Lake of the Green Fountain*, and is, so legend would have us believe, inhabited by a monster, an *afangc*, which used to live in a pool near Betws y Coed, where it frequently wreaked havoc among the locals. Tired of its ways, they finally moved it to Glaslyn, pulled by a team of oxen, one of which under severe strain lost an eye at Gwaun Lygad yr Ych, the *Field of the Ox's Eye*, on the slopes of Moel Siabod, by which way it was brought. The presence of the beast in Glaslyn's waters is said to be an explanation of why no bird will fly across the lake.

With the shores of the lake close by, and a substantial if rocky track now underfoot, you pass the outflow from Glaslyn, and continue the descent of the Miners' Track to mine buildings above the shoreline of **Llyn Llydaw**. The mines here were never very productive, and although supplied with new machinery in 1915, they closed down a year later.

Llyn Llydaw is divided by a causeway constructed in the 19th century. Formerly it was much lower than its modern-day counterpart and prone to flooding, necessitating a circuit of the north-eastern end of the lake to regain the path, or wading, a sometimes hazardous prospect not because of crocodiles or box jelly fish, but because to misjudge the depth in the middle could cause a seriously chilling sensation in one's nether regions.

One more lake awaits, **Llyn Teyrn**, the *Lake of the Ruler*, occupying a shallow hollow scooped out by a retreating glacier. It is believed to be so named because a local prince had the sole right to net fish there. On its shores are the ruins of barracks used by miners, and legend has it that they were occupied by miners from Brittany who fled at the outbreak of the Napoleonic Wars at the beginning of the 19th century.

Press on past the lake, and soon the track will swing around the end of the Pen Bwlch y Moch ridge and runs northwards to the top of Pen y Pass.

Moel Siabod, Llyn Llydaw and the Miners' Track

Moel Eilio Horseshoe

It is tempting to think of the four grassy hills that comprise the Moel Eilio Horseshoe as an alternative to Snowdon or the Glyders, something to do when the higher hills are in cloud. But in truth they have huge merit of their own, and should be on everyone's menu. Springy turf underfoot, leg-swinging freedom, not insignificant but not over-demanding undulations, a surprising display of minor cliffs, and ever-changing views make these hills an experience to linger over, especially on a warm day when all the world and his dog are bound elsewhere. Under snow, they make an excellent round on which to hone winter walking skills.

The Route

Leave Llanberis by walking up Ffordd Capel Goch, the road that leads to the youth hostel. At Pen y Bont, turn right into Fron Goch, and then, at the top of a rise, turn left towards the Plas Garnedd Care Centre. Once beyond the centre, the gated lane climbs steadily through farmland dotted with numerous derelict buildings. The final building, Maen-llwyd-isaf, with Moel Eilio and the valley of the Afon Goch rising on the left, is where the lane surfacing ends and a rough track takes you on upwards to a ladder-stile.

Once over the stile, bear left beside a wall. The track takes you past the site of Dinas Osian, an Iron Age settlement and hill fort, although there is little to see of it today. Continue to a gate across the track not far from the top of the ascent at **Bwlch y Groes**, and through the gate continue a little further as far as a branching grassy vehicle track (SH561598). Leave

↑ Moel Eilio and Foel Gron from Foel Goch

ROUTE INFORMATION

Distance	13.8km/8½ miles
Height gain	990m/3250ft
Time	4–5 hours
Grade	energetic
Start point	Llanberis

Getting there
There are multiple parking areas along the shores of Llyn Padarn, some offering the temptation to paddle when you should be elsewhere

Maps
(Harvey Superwalker) Snowdonia and the Moelwynion; (Ordnance Survey) OL17 Snowdon/Yr Wyddfa

After-walk refreshment
Plenty of refreshment opportunity in Llanberis (including the almost legendary Pete's Eats), but maybe call in at the 17th-century Pen y Ceunant Isaf licensed tea garden and café on the way down.

Snowdon Mountain Railway

the Bwlch y Groes path here, and climb easily onto the long and broad northern ridge of Moel Eilio, which is a delight to roam, the track soon merging with another that has climbed from Bwlch y Groes. The path gives lovely views to the west of the Lleyn Peninsula and Yr Eifl (The Rivals), swinging round across Caernarfon and across Anglesey to Holyhead Mountain.

Eventually, as you approach the top section of **Moel Eilio**, you encounter a fence. Walk alongside this, the path taking you finally to a ladder-stile not far from the summit. Over the stile, bear right beside the

Moel Cynghorion

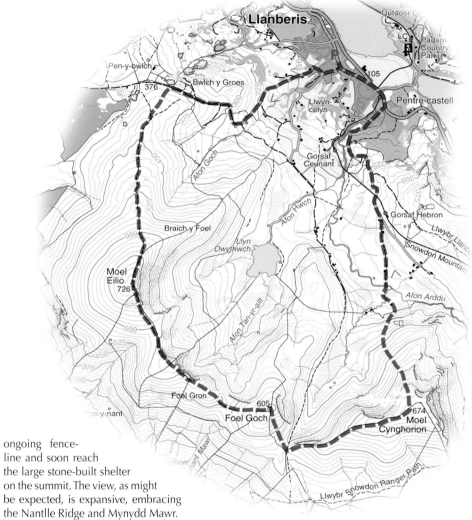

ongoing fence-
line and soon reach
the large stone-built shelter
on the summit. The view, as might
be expected, is expansive, embracing
the Nantlle Ridge and Mynydd Mawr.

The continuation from Moel Eilio follows a
fenceline descending steeply in roughly a south-
easterly direction. Follow the fence down to a stile
at a wall corner beyond which lie the twin summits
of **Foel Gron** and Foel Goch. From this summit there
is a stunning view of Cwm Dwythwch and its lake,
and then, after a dip, a final pull leads to a ladder-
stile near a fence corner on **Foel Goch**. The summit
is singularly undistinguished, other than by a tiny,
low-lying cairn (if you can find it).

Return to the ladder-stile, and then take to a
narrow path descending very steeply to Bwlch
Maesgwm, a high mountain pass, from where a
broad track (an ideal escape route if needed), heads
towards Llanberis.

At the pass, cross a
stile/gate and turn left beside a
fence and wall following a clear path rising in easy
stages to the top of **Moel Cynghorion** (The Hill of
the Councillors). The top of the mountain is flat and
grassy, and conceals a small, flattened cairn, as well
as a few small ponds.

The name **Moel Cynghorion** bears the legend that
when Edward I conquered Wales and started to
build his castles, he tried to trick the Welsh bards
into coming to an Eisteddfod, where he would
have killed them. But they got wind of his plot and
ran away to this lonely outpost; quite what they
did when they got here is not disclosed, however.

43

Cross a ladder-stile on the summit fence, and head off in a northerly direction. There is no path to follow, and progress is what you make of it, descending steep grassy slopes, but trending a little to the left lower down. The descent is not difficult, but does require attention to placement of feet. Your target is a ladder-stile (SH584574) due south of Helfa-fawr, a renovated building, neither of which is visible until the last moment.

Over the stile, keep to the right of the building to locate its rough access track, and then follow this out, soon crossing the **Afon Arddu**, with waters bright and sparkling. The track leads past derelict farm buildings, and on to Hebron Station, where you intercept a narrow lane that serves Hafodty Newydd.

All that remains is to follow the lane back to Llanberis, passing first under the course of the Snowdon Mountain Railway, and then crossing the end of the Llanberis Path to the summit. Before reaching Llanberis, you also pass Pen y Ceunant Isaf, a licensed café, ideally placed to entice thirsty walkers to rest a while, and open all year.

Continue down the lane to the edge of Llanberis, and finally arrive close by the Mountain Railway station, and the start of the walk.

On the summit of Moel Cynghorion, looking towards Snowdon

GLYDERAU

On the cantilever, Glyder Fach (Walk 6)

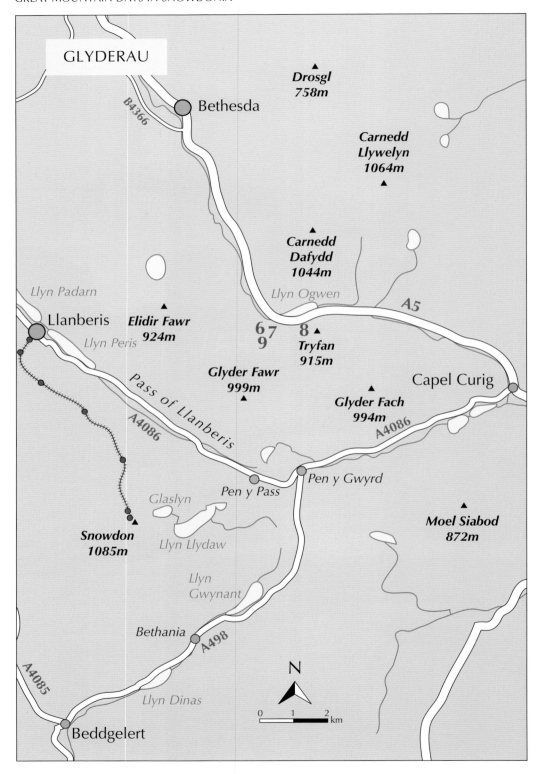

GLYDERAU

Drosgl
758m ▲

Carnedd
Llywelyn
1064m
▲

Bethesda ●

B4366

Carnedd
Dafydd
1044m ▲

Llyn Ogwen

A5

Llyn Padarn

Elidir Fawr
924m ▲

6 7   8 ▲
9   Tryfan
915m

Llanberis ●

Llyn Peris

Glyder Fawr
999m
▲

Capel Curig ●

Glyder Fach
994m ▲

Pass of Llanberis

A4086

A4086

Pen y Gwyrd ●

Pen y Pass ●

Moel Siabod
872m ▲

Glaslyn

Snowdon
1085m ▲

Llyn Llydaw

Llyn
Gwynant

Bethania ●

A498

A4085

Llyn Dinas

N

0   1   2 km

Beddgelert ●

GLYDERAU

Black's *Picturesque Guide to North Wales*, published in 1857, comments that 'in savage grandeur the Glyder is not surpassed by any scene in Wales'. A radical observation, but still quite valid. There is something about the Glyders, Glyderau in Welsh, that sets them apart from other mountain groups; there is certainly more visible rock here, strewn randomly in awesome heaps, and lying at jaunty angles, as if someone has tidied up all the loose shavings from mountains created elsewhere, and made them into one great pile until they could figure out what to do with them. This is true mountain ground, rugged and rocky arguably like no other in Britain outside the Isle of Skye, a place where the elemental force of nature is all but tangible.

Anyone travelling from Bangor down the A5 through Nant Ffrancon cannot fail to be awed by the high cwms and soaring rocks walls of the north Glyder ridge stretching from Carnedd y Filiast to Y Garn, by the disturbing atmosphere of the Devil's Kitchen and its singular gash of Twll Du, the Black Hole, or by the abruptness of the massive wall of Glyder Fach, which serves as a dominating bookend to the long valley. And then suddenly, as the road turns the corner, leaving Nant Ffrancon for Ogwen, the great cliffs of Tryfan hove into view; it is a breathtaking moment that has inspired hearts and tested resolve many times and with equal aplomb.

Tryfan moves you; it is the perfect mountain shape, the stuff of dreams, a sight you will never forget; a paradox, always the same, always different, taking on the light of the moment and playing tricks with it so that it becomes something quite magical. Arrive here from Capel Curig and the form of the mountain rises from the road in magisterial fashion, throwing down a challenge to everyone, a place where the careless, those who do not show it the respect it deserves, can so easily come to grief.

The name 'Glyder' has baffled people for many years as to its meaning, but the generally accepted translation is that it means a 'pile', or 'heap', after the array of tumbled boulders on the summits.

The mountains, rising at their highest to almost 1000 metres, seem to be bound on all sides by steep cliffs, and although this impression eases in the south, along Nantgwryd, better known perhaps as the Dyffryn valley, the severity resumes on the descent of the Llanberis Pass, along which there is a formidable array of cliffs.

Debris, if you can call it that, lies by the road – the **Cromlech Boulders**, believed to have fallen from the clean-cut angular crags of Dinas Cromlech above. Beneath the boulders, it is said, used to live a gruesome, child-devouring hag, Canthrig Bwt. For many years she was well known among the surrounding farms, and not thought to have brought harm to any children, until a dog was seen to be eating a child's hand, from which a finger was identified as belonging to a boy who had recently gone missing. The hag was lured from her cave, and beheaded.

Along the southern edge of the range lies the isolated Dyffryn Mymbyr farm sometime home of Esmé Firbank-Kirby. In 1935, she was running riding stables when she met and soon married Thomas Firbank, who had just purchased the 2500-acre mountain farm of Dyffryn Mymbyr. Esmé instantly threw herself into the role of farmer's wife, and shared her husband's zeal for the powerful landscapes of Snowdonia. Those early years at Dyffryn were later immortalised by Thomas in his best-selling novel *I Bought a Mountain*. After the outbreak of the Second World War, Thomas, like so many young men, went to fight, and although he survived the war and earned great distinction, he never returned to the farm. Life then was desperately hard for Esmé, but soon after the war she met and married Major Peter Kirby. From then on, Esmé was an ardent conservationist, becoming the founder of the Snowdonia National Park Society, and, later, the Esmé Kirby Snowdonia Trust. She died in 1999, at Dyffryn Mymbyr, and her remains lie buried on her beloved mountain.

Sadly, the northern end of this compact range has been despoiled, mainly by the extraction of slate both at Llanberis and near Bethesda. More recently, but less intrusively, the mountains have been used for a hydroelectric scheme involving the low-lying Llyn Peris and a high glacial lake, Marchlyn Mawr, which fluctuate in their daily process of providing power.

The mountain massif is crossed by one long route, the Miners' Track. It starts from behind Pen y Gwryd and slants up to a boggy plateau near Llyn Caseg-fraith. The route then slips in a north-westerly direction across the head of Cwm Tryfan to cross Bwlch Tryfan and skitter downwards, past Llyn Bochlwyd to Ogwen. The route is the product of the days when hardy miners crossed the mountains every week between their homes in Bethesda to the ill-fated mines of Snowdon.

The Glyders are not a huge group, in reality just one long ridge, kinked in the middle, and with bits stuck on the sides. You could walk from Capel Curig to Bethesda or Llanberis along the ridge in a full day, but in this instance the individual parts offer better walking than the whole, not least because then you have left yourself something for another day.

Llyn Bochlwyd with Y Garn and Foel Goch in the background (Walk 6)

The Glyders
by the Bristly Ridge

*T*he ascent of the Bristly Ridge is one of the highlights of hillwalking in Wales. Technically, it ranks
as a scrambling route, but one on which only the most timid are likely to find anything to test
their nerve. There are no insurmountable difficulties, although in spite of encircling rock walls there
are a few route-finding challenges that may invoke a little casting about and less than elegant poses.
But the overall sensation is one of invigoration and excitement. And this is only the precursor to a
splendid high-level traverse of two massive summits. Strong walkers may consider including the
ascent of Tryfan as a prelude to this walk (see Walk 8).

The Route

Herbert Carr in *The Mountains of Snowdonia* commented that 'the Glyders are true mountain ground, and the wanderer must not look for smooth paths upon their craggy ridges.' The Miners' Track, along which this walk begins, is no exception to this, as it finds a way through such weaknesses as there are between Ogwen and Pen y Gwryd. This ancient highway is a relic of the days when hardy quarrymen crossed these rough and broken slopes every week on the journey from their homes at Bethesda to the mines beneath Snowdon.

At Ogwen, the Miners' Track is routed around buildings near the youth hostel, but, having crossed a usually turbulent issuing stream, it joins the traditional route to the Cwm Idwal Nature Reserve. After only a few hundred metres, the Cwm Idwal paths swing to the right, and we continue along the

↑ *Cwm Idwal*

Distance	8.5km/5¼ miles
Height gain	845m/2772ft
Time	4–5 hours
Grade	arduous
Start point	Ogwen (SH648604)

Getting there
Car park at Ogwen; fills quickly, but there are more roadside car parks close by

Maps
(Harvey Superwalker) Snowdonia The Glyderau and the Carneddau; (Ordnance Survey) OL17 Snowdon/Yr Wyddfa

After-walk refreshment
Café at Ogwen, and pubs in Capel Curig (to the east) and Bethesda (to the north)

scrambling). Work a way up to the base of the cliffs of the Bristly Ridge, to enter a narrow gully that is not easy to spot from below, but distinctive enough on reaching it.

From the bottom of the gully the route upwards is well marked, twisting and turning through a maze of rock walls that make it impossible to give meaningful directions. Towards the top of the ridge, the route moves to the right a little before finally pulling upwards to a small plateau at the top. Now it is just a simple stroll, ahead and then slightly left, to a prominent jumble of rocks, perched atop of which is the Cantilever, an immense balanced rock estimated to weigh more than seventy tons. The actual summit of **Glyder Fach** is nearby, an even greater jumble of boulders and slabby rocks that render momentarily thoughtful any assault on the very summit. In spite of its evident size, this summit of Glyder Fach is surprisingly easily missed in poor visibility.

Miners' Track, striking across boggy ground to the falls issuing from unseen Llyn Bochlwyd, and to the right of the shapely Bochlwyd Buttress, identified by its elongated H-shaped crack. A brief steep section leads up to the hollow of Cwm Bochlwyd, and **Llyn Bochlwyd** resting below imposing cliffs.

Beyond the lake, a well-marked path climbs steadily towards a low point on the eastern skyline, Bwlch Tryfan. Just below the bwlch, the path forks, the left branch climbing energetically towards Tryfan's south ridge. The Miners' Track keeps to the right and weaves an easy way through broken downfall beneath the bwlch.

Bwlch Tryfan, crossed by a wall and two ladder-stiles, is an imposing place, with the vast hollow of Cwm Tryfan ahead, across which the Miners' Track continues. Tryfan rises to the left and the Bristly Ridge rears steeply on the right. Below the Bristly Ridge, a stretch of broken rockfall has a number of well-worn paths labouring upwards (the obvious scree gully to the left is an alternative for anyone having second thoughts about

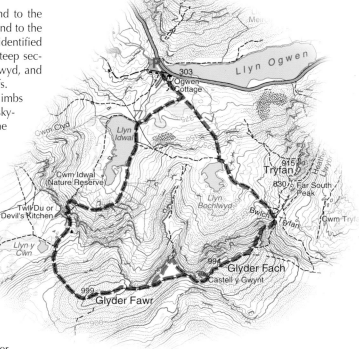

← *Tryfan south ridge, from the Bristly Ridge*

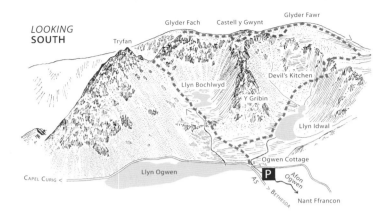

In his novel *Two Years Ago* (1857), author **Charles Kingsley** despatches his hero onto Glyder Fach by moonlight on an ill-fated expedition that nevertheless wrought from the author evocative prose rare for its day, describing the summit plateau as 'that enormous desolation, the dead bones of the eldest born of time', and the area around the Cantilever as 'a line of obelisks like giants crouching side by side'. Such description confirms, should it ever have been doubted, that Kingsley stood on Glyder Fach's summit.

The onward route lies around the northern side of Glyder Fach, but appears to be blocked a short way on by a gnarled array of rocky teeth and splintered turrets as big as a house, and resonant of war zone aftermath. Known as **Castell y Gwynt, '**Castle of the Wind', this strange configuration is not so difficult to cross as might be imagined, although it will still require thought, but there is a clear, rocky path descending to its left and around it. On the other side, a well-trodden trail blazes left towards Glyder Fawr, from the dignified-sounding Bwlch y Ddwy

Castell y Gwynt (The Castle of the Winds), and Glyder Fach

Glyder. Here it was that Showell 'Pip' Styles, inspirational writer and mountaineer, says he saw the only ghost he had ever seen on a mountain, a tale he recounts in *The Mountains of North Wales*.

From Bwlch y Ddwy Glyder you can take the obvious route, but there is a rather more attention-grabbing variant which, facing towards Glyder Fawr, bears off to the right, ascending gently to the top of **Y Gribin** (an emergency way down if needed). From here, with its fine retrospective view of Glyder Fach's cliffs, it is a straightforward stroll across to the higher mountain.

> Thomas Pennant says of **Glyder Fawr**: 'The elements seem to have warred against this mountain, rains have washed away the soil, lightnings have rent its surface, and the winds make it the constant object of their fury.' The battle still goes on, and this is no place to be when the winter furies are roaring.

Compared with Glyder Fach, the summit of the **Glyder Fawr** is something of a disappointment, a token gesture almost. Beyond this modest pile,

a path sets off in a north-westerly direction, but then curves northwards as it begins its descent to **Llyn y Cwn** – a convex slope of scree and rock that can be treacherous under the snows of winter, when an ice axe and crampons are vital. Even on a good day, careful placement of feet is needed all the way down. It is often with some relief that the bottom is reached, and the path to the right, heading for the top of the Devil's Kitchen, is joined.

Twll Du, the Black Hole, is more properly the narrow cleft that splits the cliffs above Cwm Idwal, while it is the entire upper part of the cwm that bears the name Devil's Kitchen, so-called because sailors passing along the Menai Straits to the north would gaze southwards into the dark mass of mountains and see the swirling mist, which they likened to steam rising from the Devil's cauldron. Pennant describes Twll Du as a 'dreadful aperture', and in certain wind conditions the cleft is said to produce weird sounds.

The path down into upper **Cwm Idwal** has been rebuilt in fairly recent times, and presents a clear descent through a maze of tumbled boulders and outcrops; a short out-and-back diversion is needed

← *Retrospective from Glyder Fawr to Glyder Fach*

to reach the foot of Twll Du. And then it is all rockily downwards, taking to a path that bears right to pass below the Idwal Slabs, a perfect place on which to learn the rudiments of rock climbing.

The stretch of rocky ground from Twll Du downwards will greatly interest **botanists**, who may just find here the Snowdon Lily (*Lloydia serotina*). Thomas Pennant was not too thrilled with Cwm Idwal, describing it as 'a fit place to inspire murderous thoughts, environed with horrible precipices, shading a lake, lodged in its bottom...no bird dare fly over its damned water'.

Finally, a good path runs out alongside **Llyn Idwal** to the outflow of the lake, there bearing right to descend gently and rejoin the outward route.

Pen yr Ole Wen from Cwm Idwal

Y Garn to Elidir Fawr and Carnedd y Filiast

*T*he ridge that forms the western boundary of Nant Ffrancon is relatively infrequently visited, *although footpath restoration work on Y Garn makes it more readily accessible. Even so, the traverse of the ridge, from Y Garn to Carnedd y Filiast and including Elidir Fawr, is really quite special, posing few technical problems other than deciding how to return to the start. What follows is a basic route around which a number of possibilities are draped.*

The Route

The first objective is Y Garn, a very shapely mountain extending its arms towards Ogwen in open invitation, while encircling a wild cwm, Cwm Clyd, in which repose two small lakes, known by the singular name, Llyn Clyd.

From Ogwen take the Miners' Track, which weaves around buildings, and soon crosses a busy stream before joining the traditional route to the **Cwm Idwal** Nature Reserve.

Cwm Idwal is a Site of Special Scientific Interest (SSSI) and the first Nature Reserve in Wales, designated in 1954. The area around the lake has considerable interesting geology and botany, while the Idwal slabs and the cliffs around the head of the cwm are hugely popular with rock climbers.

This is one of the best places to see Arctic plants once common during inter-glacial periods, like moss campion and alpine saxifrages, including tufted saxifrage (*Saxifraga cespitosa*)

↑ Y Garn

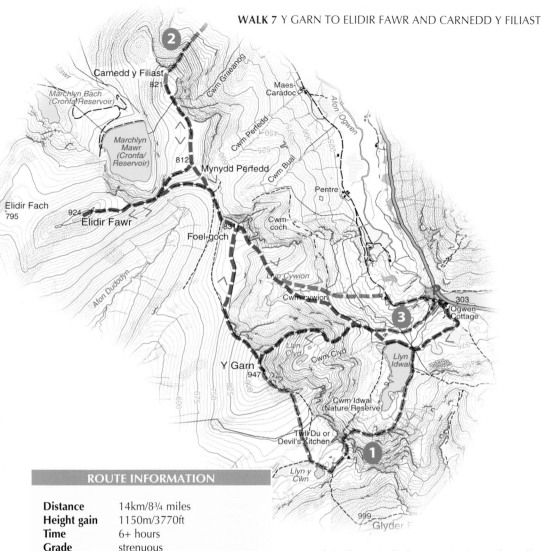

ROUTE INFORMATION

Distance	14km/8¾ miles
Height gain	1150m/3770ft
Time	6+ hours
Grade	strenuous
Start point	Ogwen, near youth hostel (SH649603)

Getting there
The car park at Ogwen; fills quickly, but there are more roadside car parks along the A5

Maps
(Harvey Superwalker) The Glyderau and the Carneddau; (Ordnance Survey) OL17 Snowdon/Yr Wyddfa

After-walk refreshment
Café at Ogwen, and pubs in Capel Curig (to the east) and Bethesda (to the north)

and *Saxifraga nivalis* that grow in the cracks and crevices. The Snowdon lily (*Lloydia Serotina*), a protected species, also inhabits the cwm, a plant found only in Britain, but which has never had a wide British distribution.

After only a few hundred metres, the Cwm Idwal paths swings to the right, and leads unerringly to the north-eastern shore of **Llyn Idwal**. Now circle to the right to cross a double-gated footbridge and continue onto a rough stony path that heads around the lake. You are not going to stay on this path for much longer; there is a more direct route from Ogwen, but this roundabout approach, which invigorates hearts, lungs and legs is preferred. Before reaching the stream issuing from **Cwm Clyd** you need to bear right across rough ground, targeting the north-east arm of Y Garn

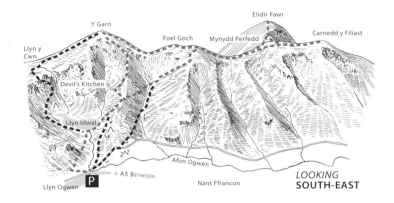

LOOKING
SOUTH-EAST

and soon joining a clear and well-trodden path. The ascent is quite special, and provides many opportunities to take in the surrounding mountains.

The top of the ridge is marked by a cairn on a small plateau, although this is not the summit of the mountain, for which you will need to climb a little further, to the south.

Beyond **Y Garn** the ridge undulates northwards, with the bulk of Elidir Fawr prominent on the left. An easy descent leads to the grassy col above Cwm Cywion, and the start of a gentle rise, first over a small plateau and then upwards to the cairn on the summit of **Foel Goch**. From the summit there is a fine view across Nant Ffrancon to Pen yr Ole Wen and the distant Carneddau. Perhaps more usefully, as you traverse from Y Garn to Foel-goch you might like to examine the layout of **Cwm Cywion**. This affords the most likely line of descent, but it is untracked, and various possible lines exist.

A straightforward descent leads northwards from Foel-goch to Bwlch y Brecan, across which there is what is thought to be an old packhorse route linking Nant Ffrancon and Nant Peris. From Bwlch y Brecan a well-trodden path skirts Mynydd Perfedd, and swings westwards climbing ruggedly to the rocky top of **Elidir Fawr** and a fine view northwards over **Marchlyn Mawr**.

Y Garn

Marchlyn Mawr is a dammed lake used as part of the **Dinorwic Pumped Storage Scheme**, the largest pumped storage hydroelectric scheme in Europe at the time of its construction. The lake formerly held about 2.5 million cubic metres behind a natural moraine dam some 40m high. The modern dam was constructed on the rock sill of the cwm (valley), incorporating the moraine. It raised the water level by 33m to create a reservoir capacity of 9.2 million cubic metres with live storage of 6.7 million cubic metres.

From Elidir Fawr, return towards Bwlch y Brecan, but peel off left, avoiding needless descent and re-ascent, to gain **Mynydd Perfedd** and then on to **Carnedd y Filiast**, the most northerly summit of the group.

To return to Ogwen you need to backtrack along the main ridge as far as Foel-goch. The north-east ridge is not recommended in descent, as it involves scrambling. Instead, opt for the southeast ridge, Y Llymllwyd on some maps. There is no path to speak off, at least no sustained path. The line of least resistance drops into **Cwm Cywion**, and then tracks diagonally in a south-easterly direction to pass below Pinnacle Crag, after which you round the end of Y Garn's north-eastern arm to rejoin the outward route. The exact route you will take depends entirely on your own judgement of rugged terrain and your ability to cross it, but that's all part of the fun. It is arduous at times, but the setting is quite superb – this is route-finding in the raw, but, unless you really mess up, is without serious consequences if you make a mistake.

You can, of course, simply go back down the Y Garn ridge you came up.

Alternatives:

1. The ascent to Y Garn can also be achieved by taking the path along the east side of Llyn Idwal, passing the Idwal Slabs, and climbing a constructed staircase, below then left of Twll Du, to gain the little hollow containing Llyn y Cwn. From there you strike northwards

Twll Du (The Black Hole), Devil's Kitchen

following a well-trodden route up a smoothly rounded slope to the top of Y Garn.

2. From Carnedd y Filiast, you can descend directly to the Nant Ffrancon by using the north-east ridge. This faces you with a walk back along the minor road on the west side of the valley.

3. The descent from Foel-goch can be varied by making more directly for the valley, reaching the minor road a little to the north of Yr Hafod. This involves finding a way through walls, which is one of the reasons why studying the terrain was a good idea earlier in the walk.

Tryfan

*T*ryfan has been called 'a small, Gothic cathedral of a mountain which seizes upon our imagination so as almost to exaggerate the effect of its own shapeliness', and, more prosaically, the 'second of the hills which stood on the left'. This last tribute came from George Borrow, who spent time travelling around Wales in 1854. Such an airy-fairy description is typical of Borrow, who just as summarily dismissed Gallt yr Ogof as the first hill on the left, and Carnedd Dafydd as 'a huge long mountain on the right' – somewhat under-endowed in the waxing lyrical department, you might think.

Earlier, the Reverend W Bingley undertook 'A Tour round North Wales during the Summer of 1798' and actually got to the summit of Tryfan in what must be the first recorded ascent of the mountain. Even earlier still, Thomas Pennant gazed down on Tryfan from the top of the Bristly Ridge on the Glyders in 1781, observing 'in the midst of the vale below rises a singular mountain Trevaen, assuming on this side a pyramidal form, naked and very rugged'.

Whatever may be said of it, Tryfan is a remarkable mountain; one that captures the eye of travellers approaching from Capel Curig, and rather smacks you abruptly in the face as you turn the corner of Nant Ffrancon into Ogwen if coming from Bethesda.

↑ *Tryfan from Llyn y Caseg-fraith*

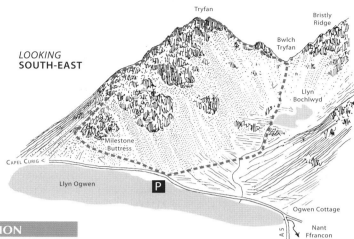

LOOKING
SOUTH-EAST

ROUTE INFORMATION

Distance	3.75km/2½ miles
Height gain	585m/1920ft
Time	3–3½ hours
Grade	arduous
Start point	SH659602

Getting there
Parking area on A5, 1km east of Ogwen Cottage; there are other parking areas nearby

Maps
(Harvey Superwalker) Snowdonia: The Glyderau and the Carneddau; (Ordnance Survey) OL17 Snowdon/Yr Wyddfa

After-walk refreshment
Refreshment kiosk at Ogwen Cottage; pubs in Capel Curig and Bethesda

The Route
From the parking area, go through a metal kissing-gate at the eastern end to thread a way through a jumble of boulders, then climbing steadily below the prominent rock climbing arena of Milestone Buttress, finally to reach a ladder-stile over a wall.

Milestone Buttress was the setting for a novel by Glyn Carr, **Death on Milestone Buttress**, published in 1951, which relates how a Shakespearean actor, Ambercrombie Lewker, turns detective when a member of his climbing party is killed on what was supposed to be an easy route on a mountain in Wales.

Beyond the wall, a well-marked path ascends steeply for a while, first across loose and broken ground until it arrives at a rock- and heather-covered shoulder. This is where you now begin to tackle the true North Ridge.

Walkers who are competent and comfortable on rock require little in the way of description: 'up' is probably instruction enough, and it will take you on an enthralling journey, wandering among rock walls and buttresses, an altogether entertaining ascent.

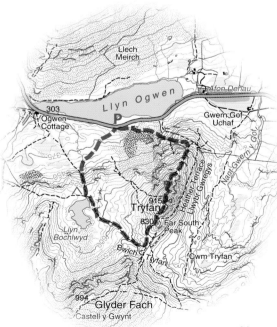

61

Those who are rather less at home on rock need not fear, however, that Tryfan is barred to them, although it is fair to say that the ascent is unlikely to be accomplished confidently (if at all) with one's hands in one's pockets!

At the heathery shoulder, you need to turn your attention to the ridge, which resembles an impenetrable barrier of rock from this point of view. But after a brief dallying with scree, a way through does become apparent, and has been marked by countless thousands of feet (including my own on at least 25 occasions). The route, as a result, is eroded in places, and can be problematical in winter conditions, when an altogether different level of mountaineering expertise is called for. Generally, you stick to the centre of the ridge, and soon arrive at a small platform with a large cairn known, since it is the meeting point of a number of routes (the Heather Terrace departs from here), as Piccadilly Circus.

Continue directly upwards and eventually the path arrives at a small, quartz-covered plateau to the right of which stands a finger of rock known as The Cannon, a feature you can actually pick out from the car park below. Unless you are happy on rock,

do not be tempted to climb onto it; getting up is one thing, getting down quite another.

A path to the left at this point leads upwards to another small plateau and a rock wall at the base of which there is a tumble of massive boulders and a finely pointed pinnacle not dissimilar to The Cannon below. The wall may seem impassable, but after negotiating the boulders it affords a not-too-difficult direct ascent to the top of a steep gully. A slightly easier way bears left before tackling the boulders, through a small gap just before the wall, making a short descent and re-ascent on an obvious path that leads round a corner into the gully itself. A scramble over blocks, including a few awkward limb movements, takes you to the top of the gully.

Now a short scramble upwards leads across a more level array of boulders to a short descent to the top of another, this time wider, gully. Almost there now, and a final pull around the Central Buttress sees you clambering to the top of the mountain.

The **summit of Tryfan** is crowned by two huge boulders known as Adam and Eve (although which is which has never really been clear). Many

The Cannon, Tryfan

Tryfan from Llyn y Caseg-fraith

years ago, the practice evolved of somehow getting yourself onto the top of one of the boulders and 'stepping' from one to the other. But firstly, unless you have enormously long legs, it is certainly no 'step', and the resultant leap doesn't have an awful lot of runway to land on, what there is boasting significant drops on both sides. Common sense suggests that you simply reach up and pat the top with your hand: at least some small part of you will have conquered Tryfan.

Getting back to Ogwen was never going to be easy, and is best accomplished by heading down the South Ridge, itself not without a few tricky moments. But it is short, and the popular way has become etched in the rocks: the key is to avoid trying to descend away from the ridge too soon. What you should be aiming to do is head for the narrow neck of land, **Bwlch Tryfan**, linking the mountain with the Glyders beyond. This is crossed by a wall.

From the bwlch, turn right (west) and follow a clear path down to **Llyn Bochlwyd**, the banks of which are a superb place to chill out after the ascent and before quitting the mountains altogether. Beyond the lake, the path drops more steeply, and will eventually take you down to Ogwen Cottage – this is a longer but generally easier option (you have to walk back eastwards along the road to reach the starting point). But just as the path starts to descend from the lake, you will notice a prominent rock buttress on the right: this is Bochlwyd Buttress, a popular and comparatively easy rock gymnast's playground; many is the time I've climbed on here and watched RAF pilots whizzing through Ogwen and into Nant Ffrancon *below* me!

Cross the stream flowing from Llyn Bochlwyd, and pass well below the Buttress following a sometimes tenuous path across boggy and bouldery terrain to return to the car park.

On the summit of Tryfan

Bwlch Tryfan, Y Foel Goch, Gallt yr Ogof and Cefn y Capel

*T*ryfan and the two Glyders are not the only summits of worth in the compact group of mountains bounded by the Pass of Llanberis and that of Ogwen. East of Glyder Fach an ill-defined ridge continues to Capel Curig, and along its length provides excellent walking, much less rugged than the higher summits but no less appealing. Beginning at Ogwen, this walk dogs the footsteps of quarrymen to Bwlch Tryfan and around the cwm beyond, before parting company and taking to easier ground. You can call it a day on reaching Capel Curig, or take the preferred route back, an interesting line that parallels the A5 but occasionally lacks its firmness as it deals with numerous streams and boggy ground.

The Route

Behind the buildings at Ogwen, a clear path scampers up to cross the busy stream issuing from Llyn Idwal, and presses on in a south-easterly direction. When this main track swings to the right, bound for Idwal, leave it and take to a less pronounced route heading towards a prominent buttress (Bochlwyd Buttress) to the left of a waterfall.

A clamber beside the falls leads to a bouldery crossing of the issuing stream before finally taking to the path rising above the waters of **Llyn Bochlwyd**. Already rocky, the path surges on upwards to stiles

↑ *Tryfan peers over the top of Y Foel Goch*

ROUTE INFORMATION

Distance	16.5km/10¼ miles
Height gain	840m/2755ft
Time	6+ hours
Grade	moderate
Start point	Ogwen (SH648604)

Getting there
Car park at Ogwen; this fills quickly, but there are more roadside car parks close by

Maps
(Harvey Superwalker) Snowdonia: The Glyderau and the Carneddau; (Ordnance Survey) OL17 Snowdon/Yr Wyddfa

After-walk refreshment
Café at Ogwen, and pubs in Capel Curig (to the east) and Bethesda (to the north)

spanning a wall at **Bwlch Tryfan**, with the eponymous mountain to the left, and the seemingly impenetrable crags of the lower Bristly Ridge on your right. This is a wild and inspiring spot, rugged and satisfying. Beyond, a clear path skims below Glyder Fach's north-east face, the headwall of Cwm Tryfan. The setting is majestic, offering fine views across the Ogwen valley to the high summits of the Carneddau. Finally, the track emerges on a plateau containing, to the left, **Llyn y Caseg-fraith** (The Lake of the Piebald Mare).

Thus far you have followed the **Miners' Track**, which continues to Pen y Gwryd and then up into the heart of the Snowdon massif, and the lake offers a reasonable moment for a breather and to consider those who have gone before you. When the Snowdon copper mines operated, between 1810 and 1916, miners would walk from Bethesda along this route to and from their homes at weekends, in all seasons. The distance is about 20km (12 miles), but distance alone gives no indication of how demanding the walk might have been in the worst of winter conditions.

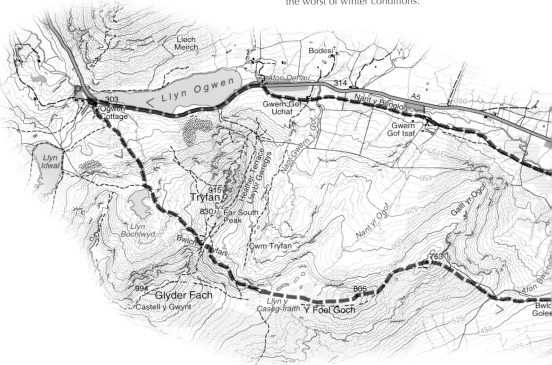

The Bristly Ridge from Llyn y Caseg-fraith

Beyond Llyn y Caseg-fraith lies **Y Foel Goch**. Quite how this became 'Y Foel Goch' is unclear. When the author first tramped these hills in the 1970s, it was, as Showell Styles describes, 'Point 2,639 feet – an unnamed summit', although by the time *The Mountains of Wales* was published (1985) it was, by common consensus, known as the 'Nameless Peak', and everyone was happy with that. Who decided they had to meddle with things is not clear: 'Nameless Peak' was a fine name!

Tryfan from Llyn y Caseg-fraith

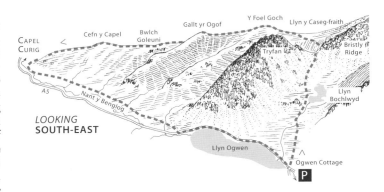

Grassy Y Foel Goch has a cairn to mark its highest point, and the intervening ground to the lower, but more substantial, **Gallt yr Ogof**, presents no difficulties. Beyond that lies only the long, lovely, low-lying ridge of **Cefn y Capel** before a final descent to the edge of **Capel Curig**. Here, just 200m north of refreshments in Capel Curig, should you need them, you meet and should follow a lane running northwards above the true right bank of the **Afon Llugwy**, along **Nant y Benglog**. This used to be the old road along which mail was carried in stagecoaches from London to Holyhead, bound for Ireland.

The track ultimately links two farms, both with campsites – **Gwern Gof Isaf** and **Gwern Gof Uchaf** – after the last of which the track finally emerges onto the A5, leaving you less than 2km (1 mile) back to Ogwen.

The **view** you gain of Tryfan as you walk this route back to Ogwen is one of the all-time classic images not only of Snowdonia but of mountain ranges throughout Britain.

Y Foel Goch and Gallt yr Wenallt (in the background Tryfan, Pen yr Ole Wen and Carnedd Dafydd)

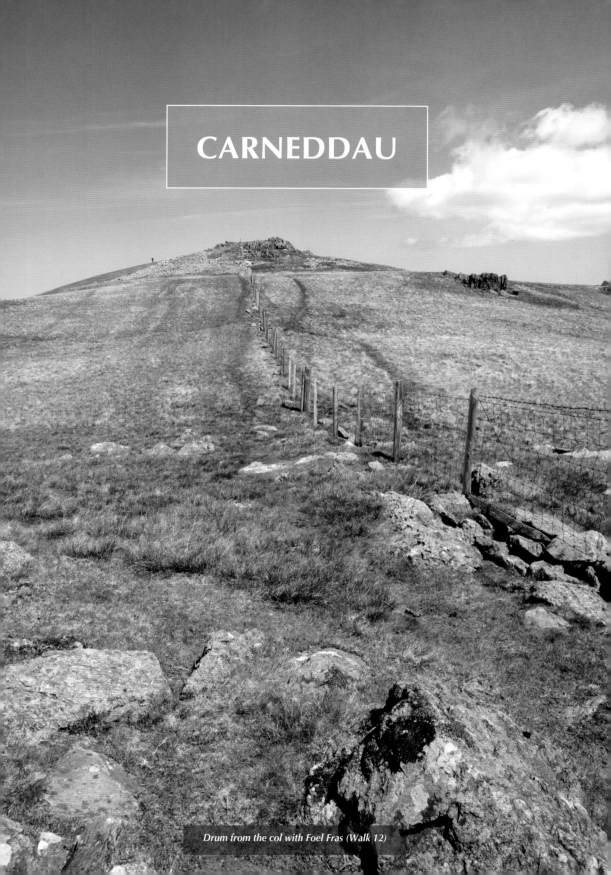

CARNEDDAU

Drum from the col with Foel Fras (Walk 12)

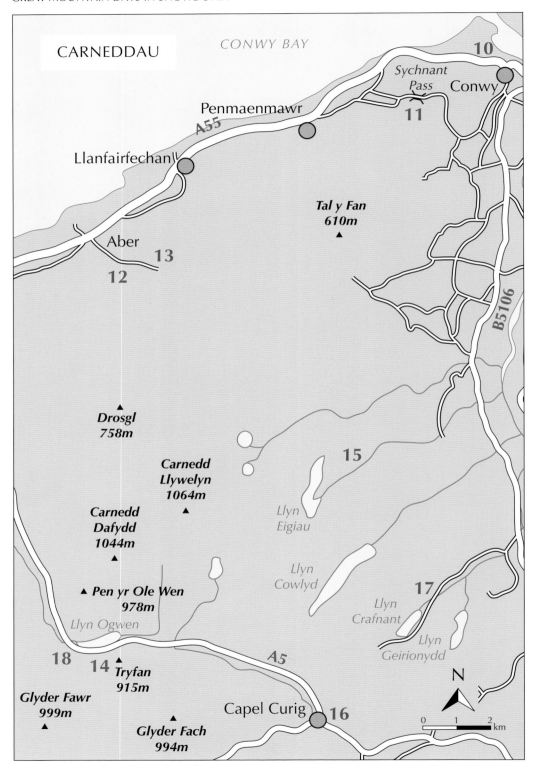

CARNEDDAU

CONWY BAY

10

Sychnant Pass
Conwy

Penmaenmawr

A55

11

Llanfairfechan

Tal y Fan
610m
▲

Aber
13

12

Drosgl
758m
▲

Carnedd
Llywelyn
1064m
▲

Llyn
Eigiau

15

Carnedd
Dafydd
1044m
▲

Llyn
Cowlyd

Llyn
Crafnant

17

▲ Pen yr Ole Wen
978m

Llyn Ogwen

Llyn
Geirionydd

18   14 ▲
Tryfan
915m

A5

N

Glyder Fawr
999m
▲

Capel Curig

16

▲
Glyder Fach
994m

0   1   2
km

B5106

CARNEDDAU

There is no wilder place in Britain, outside the Cairngorms, than the high tops of the Carneddau. This near-Arctic range is essentially one huge whaleback ridge running roughly north-east to south-west, yet with enough high ground to spare to cast off numerous sprouting shoots that convert a simple and elegant design into a sprawling convolution of tops and valleys, lakes, busy streams and rivers. And yet, sad but true, on Carnedd Uchaf/ Carnedd Gwenllian, amid the serried rock spears stacked in readiness for a war against the elements, you are in one of only two places in Snowdonia that is more than three miles from a road – the other is among the Rhinogydd.

Like some great fortress, the moat of which is the Afon Conwy, the Carneddau have thwarted the attentions of invaders since Anglo-Saxon times. For millennia, the borderlands of Wales, known as the Marches, were the preserve of outlaws and robbers sufficient in skill, number and temerity to prevent invading forces from reaching the mountains of the Arans and the Arenigs. The north coast of this land yielded a fine marching route along which came the Roman legions, the Saxon raiding parties and

Norman warlords intent on making themselves masters of Wales, but if these unwanted outsiders could reach the fortress wall, it remained difficult to get across it; you have only to drive the A55 today to see how abruptly the rock walls plummet to the sea. It is an untroubled journey these days, but as recently as 1720 coaches with travellers bound for Ireland had to be dismantled and carried onward in pieces with the attendant risk of archers lurking on every crag top. Prehistoric man knew the hill pass that is today the Bwlch y Ddeufaen, for his remains scatter the surrounding hills. But it was the Romans who rediscovered this weakness, marching from their fort at Canovium (Caerhun) in the Conwy valley to reach a terminus at Abergwyngregyn, the 'River-mouth of the White Shells', where easier ground was finally gained. Today, Aber (as it is commonly called) is a neat and attractive village, but it is a settlement of considerable antiquity and pre-conquest significance previously known as Aber Garth Celyn, which effectively controlled the ancient crossing point of the Lafan Sands to Anglesey. From the 12th to the 13th centuries, Garth Celyn was the home of the royal princes of Wales.

↑ *Bera Mawr from Bera Bach (Walk 12)*

Among the mountains above you can be striding across a seemingly limitless plateau of springy turf one minute, and fighting for your life in a blizzard the next. And yet there are so few vantage points from which the mountains, singularly or collectively, take on a commanding profile. One exception is Yr Elen, a summit that commemorates Eleanor de Montfort, wife of Prince Llywelyn. Seen from the vicinity of Carnedd Uchaf/Carnedd Gwenllian, it is shapely and imposing. But elsewhere, the central thrust of the Carneddau is composed of rounded flanks rising to stony tops. Relief from this sameness comes, however, in the south-east of the range beyond the vast, uninhabited, lark-loud void of Cwm Eigiau, from which rises the distinctive Pen Llithrig y Wrach. Further away, offering a repertoire of hummocks, craggy upthrusts and perverse undulations, Creigiau Gleision's lowly heights provide entertainment of the highest order before the landscape slips by myriad lakes and woodlands to the tourist hub of Betws y Coed.

Extremes of wind and temperature on the Carneddau mean that few plants survive. Yet species like stiff sedge and dwarf willow are virtually confined to high ground, the latter being locally common in montane heath communities such as are found on and around Carnedd Dafydd. Among these high mountains the summit heath is at the southern extremity of its distribution in the UK and is a protected habitat.

With a measure of good fortune, walkers visiting the eastern Carneddau during May, when crane flies and other flighted insects hatch from the hundreds of tiny pools, will be treated to the sight of thousands of herring and lesser black-backed gulls whirling around and feeding on them. At other times keep an eye open for chough, dotterel, peregrine and merlin.

And across these wide-ranging hills, especially in the north-east, it is unusual not to encounter Welsh mountain ponies (Merlod y Carneddau). This hardy breed has a history dating to Celtic times. Henry VIII is said to have ordered their destruction because they were unable to carry a knight in full armour. Luckily they survived, and during the 19th century were used to pull carts in the Welsh mines and quarries. Each year, usually in November, the ponies are brought down from the hills for an annual check-up, but they remain among the wildest animals in Britain, freely roaming the hills and among the finest of free-range companions on a long walk among the folds of the Carneddau.

↑ *Wild ponies, Carneddau*

Conwy Mountain

*C*onwy Mountain (Mynydd y Dref), tucked neatly into the top right-hand corner of Snowdonia
*National Park, may be ascended easily and speedily from the Sychnant Pass above the coastal
settlement of Dwygyfylchi. But to wring every ounce of pleasure from this fine, elongated ridge and its
great views of Conwy Bay, Great Orme and the eastern mountains of Snowdonia, this walk begins in the
ancient town of Conwy, reaching the Sychnant Pass at the halfway stage. Strong walkers would have no
difficulty combining this walk with Walk 11 over Tal y Fan for a long and hugely pleasurable day.*

The Route

You need to leave Conwy, seemingly heading in the
wrong direction, by walking onto the quayside, there
turning left and soon passing the Smallest House in
Britain, Quay House, which measures a mere 3.05m
x 1.8m, and has been lived in since the 16th century.

> **Conwy** is an ancient market town, its castle built
> by Edward I between 1283 and 1289 as part of his
> conquest of Wales. The nearby suspension bridge

is the handiwork of the ever-industrious Thomas
Telford, who completed the construction in 1826,
replacing the ferry that plied across the Afon Conwy
at this point. The adjacent tubular railway bridge
is the work of Robert Stephenson, built along the
Chester to Holyhead railway line in 1849.

Continue along the quayside and out through the
town wall, as far as a road junction. Here, bear right
onto the North Wales Path, a 60-mile jaunt from

↑ Approaching the summit of Conwy Mountain 73

ROUTE INFORMATION

Distance   9.5km/6 miles
Height gain   370m/1215ft
Time   3 hours
Grade   moderate
Start point   SH783775

Getting there
Conwy town centre; there are numerous car parks, all Pay and Display

Maps
(Ordnance Survey) OL17 Snowdon/Yr Wyddfa

After-walk refreshment
Numerous cafés, snack bars and pubs in Conwy

The walls of Conwy

Bangor to Prestatyn. This soon becomes a surfaced path leading along the water's edge. Follow the path to its conclusion at another road junction, and there turn left to walk out to meet the A547 close by a convenient pedestrian crossing. Cross into the road opposite, go over the bridge spanning the railway line, then press on along a walled track to a surfaced lane and then a road junction.

At the junction, turn right, climbing gently past houses, and when the rising track levels and then forks, branch right to a ladder-stile giving onto Conwy Mountain. The path now climbs through bracken, flanked by beech and gorse, and climbs energetically for a while with improving views to the south and east. At a waymark pole, leave the North Wales Path by branching right to intercept a wide, grassy path along the spine of the mountain; turn left along this and continue climbing easily, following, as closely as possible, the actual crest of the mountain. Always sticking to

the high ground, and ignoring deviating paths, you come finally to the top of the mountain.

The top of **Conwy Mountain** is occupied by Neolithic hut circles and Castell Caer Seion (sometimes Castell Caer Lleion), an Iron Age stone-walled hill fort. The many remains and excavations show that this was an extensive site. Today you can still pick out the remains of over 50 hut circles and platforms, with a citadel and outposts.

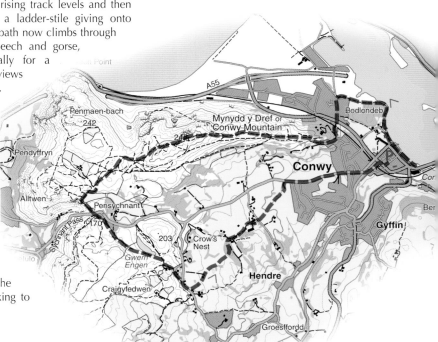

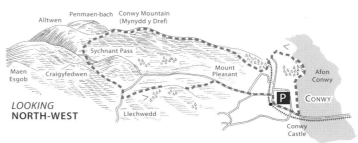

LOOKING
NORTH-WEST

Cross the top of the mountain, gradually descending through a scattering of low hills at the western end, progressively moving to the landward side of the mountain. The path comes down to meet a broad track at a North Wales Path waymark. Keep forward and make another short ascent before the path drops to a ford and stepping stones not far from Pen-pyra farm.

Having crossed the farm access, either go forward onto a broad grassy track traversing a low shoulder, or simply turn left along the access track. Both routes shortly rejoin, and the path is then followed to the top of **Sychnant Pass** (Bwlch Sychnant).

Cross the road at the pass and climb to a gate in a wall beyond which a gently rising path runs beside a wall, climbing into the Pensychnant Nature Reserve. Just as the path passes beneath powerlines, it divides. Branch left onto a narrow path crossing a hill shoulder, and parallel with a wall. Soon the path descends to a wall corner. Over this, go forward to a small group of lakes (**Gwern Engen**), and then keep on in the same direction to reach another rough track. Turn right to a junction near a group of buildings, and then bear left, to descend steeply to a narrow lane.

Turn right and pass Ty Coch farm, and at Y Bwthyn, the next house, leave the lane by turning left through a gate onto an enclosed path that shortly breaks out into a field. Stride across this towards a vehicle track, cross it, and go through a gate. Now follow an obvious route across fields linked by gates, finally targeting a tree in a fence corner not far from a small wooded hill, and then keep on to reach another lane.

Turn right and follow the lane past Oakwood Park Hall to a T-junction. Turn right, briefly, and then go left at a signpost, and across fields to a gate. Through this bear left along the field margin to reach the **Sychnant Pass road**. Now all that remains is to turn right and follow the road back to Conwy.

Conwy Castle from Conwy Mountain

Tal y Fan

*P*rehistory abounds on Tal y Fan. The whole of the Carneddau have been roamed from the earliest times, and isolated Tal y Fan supports its share of the prehistoric and Roman legacy. In terms of ruggedness, Tal y Fan does not rate highly. It is a little too close to civilisation to carry any hallmarks of mountain independence, but its myriad ways will test the best navigator. As a starting point for an exploration of Snowdonia, it is as good as any, less demanding than most, and enough of a taster to arouse an appetite for more. Here you can wander among lost civilisations, and make your mind up about Snowdonia at the same time.

The Route

Cross the road at the top of Sychnant Pass and go up to a gate, beyond which a track, here part of the North Wales Path, curves round the end of a ridge. Walk only for about 200m, and then take an obvious track turning abruptly to the right and climbing onto higher ground. At a waymark, go left onto a green trail for about 300m, and, on reaching overhead powerlines, bear right to strike across heather moorland to a wall and stile.

Over the stile, descend a little to cross the western slopes of **Maen Esgob**, and then abandon the North

Wales Path by turning left through a pronounced pass between low-lying hills following a stony track and passing a small lake. Cross the little col ahead to meet a wall on your left. Now turn right following a grassy track for 1.5km (1 mile) with a wall. Later, veer to the right crossing the eastern flanks of **Cefn Maen Amor**. The track climbs to a huge standing stone below quarries. Past this, when the track divides keep to the right, over a low col.

Maintain much the same direction now, and after about 400m pass a ruined building as you cross the northern slopes of Tal y Fan before bearing

ROUTE INFORMATION

Distance	15.5km/9¾ miles
Height gain	640m (2100ft)
Time	5 hours
Grade	moderate
Start point	Sychnant Pass (SH749770)

Getting there
There is limited parking space at the top of the Sychnant Pass

Maps
(Ordnance Survey) OL17 Snowdon/Yr Wyddfa

After-walk refreshment
Numerous snack bars, cafés and pubs in Conwy; pubs and hotels in Dwygyfylchi.

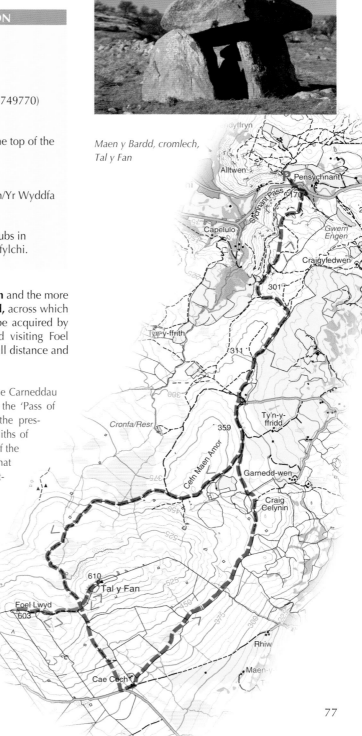

Maen y Bardd, cromlech, Tal y Fan

southwards to a col between **Tal y Fan** and the more westerly and slightly lower **Foel Lwyd,** across which there is a wall. Both summits may be acquired by simple diversions from the col, and visiting Foel Lwyd will nominally add to the overall distance and height gain.

Between Tal y Fan and the rest of the Carneddau lies the gap of **Bwlch y Ddeufaen**, the 'Pass of the Two Stones', so named from the presence there of two prehistoric monoliths of uncertain date, standing to the east of the highest point of the Roman road that passes through the gap. There is little evidence of the original Roman road today, but it is known that the Romans used this high pass as a means of access to the westerly parts of the North Wales coast from their fort at Caerhun in the Vale of Conwy.

From the col continue down an obvious and waymarked track with stiles until you reach a lane. Turn left onto the lane, but after only 100m, branch left for another 100m and then cross a stile and ascend

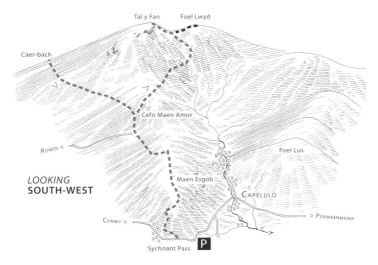

LOOKING
SOUTH-WEST

Walk around to the right of Caer-bach and then bear left beside a collapsed wall, heading for **Craig Celynin**. A good, terraced path passes along the western side of Craig Celynin, and from its north-western edge you can cross rough pasture to a wall corner, with a gap (SH744736). Once through the wall gap, turn right, alongside a wall, and follow it until you rejoin your outward route on the flanks of Cefn Maen Amor.

Now simply retrace your outward route, although the whole area is such a delight to explore, and there are so many pathways, that you may want to wander off before returning to your starting point.

towards **Cae Coch farm**. Before reaching the farm, turn right to follow a track with a wall on your right. This leads to another stile by a gate and continues above a wall. Now follow a track to Caer-bach (SH744730).

Caer-bach is a small hill fort on a rounded hillock with two lines of defence circles round the hillock, the outer of which consists of an earthen bank and an external ditch.

On the summit of Tal y Fan →

Tal y Fan from Drum

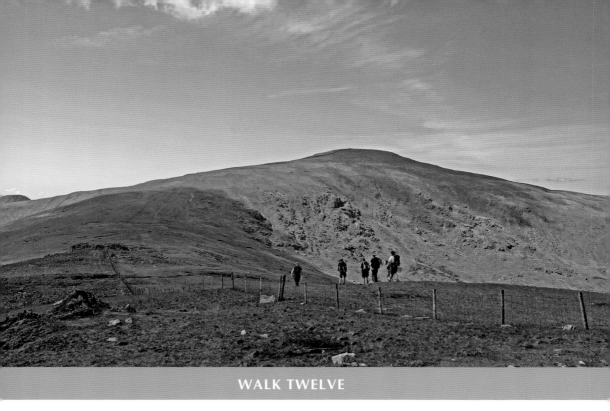

Drum, Foel Fras,
Carnedd Uchaf, Drosgl and the Aber falls

*T*he Carneddau are the first of the mountains of Snowdonia that visitors see as they approach
from the east; soft-moulded domes rising beyond the Dyffryn Conwy, enticing but seeming to
lack the rocky grandeur of summits further to the west. Yet it is easy to overlook (or forget) just what
marvellous walking country these grassy, but not entirely grassy, mountains offer, as this walk from
near Abergwyngregyn reveals. The walk to the highest point, Foel Fras, not much under 1000m in
height, is remarkably easy, which makes it all the more agreeable. But the present walk has a fairly
significant sting in the tail when, above the Aber falls, the going becomes very demanding. For
reasons that will become obvious, walking poles, spare socks and maybe even a towel will prove to
be useful additions to your rucksack.

The Route
Cross the bridge and follow the lane ahead (ignore
the turning on the right to a second car park), climbing steadily. The hedgerows are bright in spring with
red campion, Welsh poppies, valerian, lesser stitch-
wort and creeping buttercup. The lane climbs easily
through ever-improving scenery to an upper car park
directly below the slopes of Foel Dduarth.

Press on past the car park, through a gate, and
onto a stony track that soon swings to the left and
climbs easily to meet a wall. A more direct route
from the car park crosses a metal ladder-stile and
leads up beside the wall. Continue beside the wall
for a short distance further to reach overhead powerlines, where the track forks, the main track now
bearing right (east). Stay along the main track, with

↑ *Foel Fras from Drum*

ROUTE INFORMATION

Distance	18km/11¼ miles
Height gain	1035m/3395ft
Time	6+ hours
Grade	energetic
Start point	Bont Newydd, Aber (SH662720).

Getting there
Bont Newydd, Aber, reached by a minor, ramped road through the village. There are car parks on both sides of the bridge (Pay and Display)

Maps
Harvey: Superwalker Snowdonia: The Glyderau and the Carneddau; (Ordnance Survey) OL17 Snowdon/Yr Wyddfa

After-walk refreshment
There is a pub in Aber village, but otherwise Llanfairfechan or Penmaenmawr.

the grassy slopes of **Foel Dduarth** and **Foel Ganol** rising on the right, and a lovely sweep of rough pasture flowing down to the coast. There is a great view across the Traeth Lafan to the eastern tip of Anglesey and Puffin Island.

The track makes a marvellous traverse of the moorland, heading ultimately for Bwlch y Ddeufaen, and without significant ascent. Wander easily along the track until just after crossing a ridge descending northwards from **Yr Orsedd**, the track divides at a signpost (SH693722). Here, branch right for Drum, and now climbing more steeply across a landscape frequented by feral ponies and carpeted with bilberries and heather.

The track you are following is a gem because it is at an agreeable angle and leads directly to the top of **Drum**, a summit crowned by a large stone shelter, and enjoying an excellent view across Anglesey to far-away Holyhead Mountain.

The summit of **Drum** goes by the name Carnedd Penydorth Goch, a title that hints at more than the immediately obvious. This is the site of a Bronze Age platform, roughly circular and about 18m

Foel Fras (left) and Llwytmor

(60ft) in diameter, with a marked terrace on the east side. The modern cairn/shelter is slightly west of the centre.

The continuation to Foel Fras is guided by a fence-line, and later a wall as it approaches the summit. On Drum the stony track effectively ends, and a grassy path takes over. Between Drum and Foel Fras

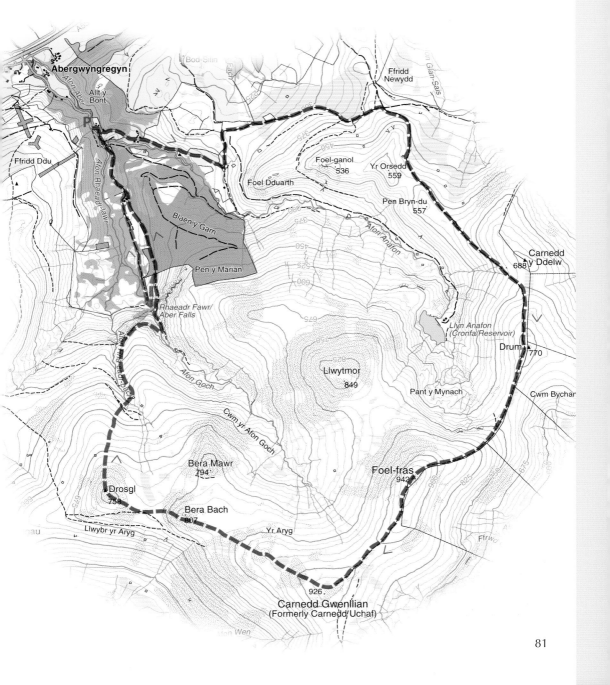

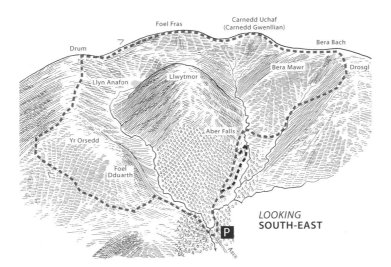

LOOKING
SOUTH-EAST

a mildly boggy col is crossed on a stepping-stone causeway before engaging low gear for the steady haul up onto Foel Fras.

After so much grass it will come as a surprise that the summit of **Foel Fras** is quite so rocky, a great rash of boulders in the middle of which is perched a trig pillar. But this spread of rock is tightly contained, and soon, as you continue beside the wall, you are back on grass until you reach a clear track heading in a south-westerly direction towards Garnedd Uchaf. This minor top is a little off-route for anyone headed for Foel Grach and Carnedd Llywelyn which looms to the south, so you may have it entirely to yourself.

> Compared with those around it, **Carnedd Uchaf**, a cluster of boulders and rocks, is low-lying and insignificant. In September 2009, it endured a name change instigated by the Princess Gwenllian Society, to Carnedd Uchaf/Carnedd Gwenllian, as a tribute to Princess Gwenllian (1282-1337), the only daughter of Prince Llywelyn ap Gruffudd and Eleanor de Montfort. Eleanor died in childbirth (June 1282), and Llywelyn was slain in battle in December of that year. To ensure the abolition of the line of Welsh princes, Gwenllian was abducted and imprisoned by Edward I in a nunnery at Sempringham in Lincolnshire, where she died 54 years later.

Carnedd Uchaf/Carnedd Gwenllian marks a turning point for this walk, for it is from here that the return leg begins. The up-thrusting rocks of this summit,

however, make an excellent shelter in which to enjoy a breather, and to take in the dramatic profile not so much of Carnedd Llywelyn but of its satellite, Yr Elen. The summit also marks the last chance to backtrack the easy way to Aber, by retracing your steps. Anyone uneasy about pathless terrain, narrow paths on steep slopes or crossing a fast-flowing stream should retreat.

From Carnedd Uchaf/ Carnedd Gwenllian, looking towards the northwest, two rocky piles are almost in direct line. The first of these is **Yr Aryg**, and once you clear the rocky top of Carnedd Uchaf/Carnedd Gwenllian, a grassy path bears in that direction. As you reach Yr Aryg, you get a better view of the next, Bera Bach, and, off to the right, the great pile of rock that is Bera Mawr. Mawr means 'big', and, in the case of Bera Mawr, refers to the greater mass of rock that forms the summit compared with the higher summit of Bera Bach.

Find a way through the rock of Yr Aryg and then descent easily to a broad col where the ongoing path divides three ways (SH676675): one strikes off to **Bera Mawr**, one goes forward to **Bera Bach**, and the other bears to the left. The middle one of these is arguably the best option, heading for the rocky top but, unless the urge is upon you and you want to scramble across its top, keep a little to the left where you will encounter something of a rock tower. Keep above the tower, and as you pass it so you find that the path continues downwards to another broad, grassy col below Drosgl.

As you arrive at the col, a more substantial track is reached, but leave this at SH667678 for a narrow path climbing up onto **Drosgl**, the summit of which is crowned by a huge pile of boulders, a Bronze Age burial cairn and the now almost expected rash of rocks.

From here on, the going becomes more demanding, and largely without paths of any note. The main route leads you down into a valley that few walkers visit. It is really quite splendid, but does call for focus as you are crossing terrain that combines huge swathes of bilberry and knee-deep heather with half-concealed rocks.

From the top of Drosgl set off in a northerly direction, heading down a broad grassy ridge where a line of cairns suggests, wishfully, that a path exists. For the moment you are on delightful springy turf. As you descend so a shallow valley comes into view on the right – beyond this is a more pronounced valley, that of Afon Goch below Llwytmor. It is the shallow valley, that of the **Afon Rhaeadr-bach**, you are heading for, and it helps to cross its stream as high as possible. Getting down to stream level brings you into conflict with the first spread of heather, bilberry and tussock grass across which attention to the placement of feet will aid a safe passage.

Once across the stream, turn left and follow its course, while keeping a safe distance above it. It is all quite delightful, but a long way from regular routes. Lower down you will notice a path dropping to the stream from the left, and this is a path that has crossed the northern slope of Drosgl at a lower point, and which would serve just as well for reaching the stream should you opt to press on down the easier ground of the north ridge. You are heading for this path, but, as you reach it, you find that on your side of the stream its sense of purpose evaporates.

The stream rushes headlong into a rocky gully where it suddenly becomes Aber's lesser-known waterfall, **Rhaeadr-bach**. You cannot descend the gully or the waterfall, so continue towards the edge of the steep drop down which the falls plummet. As you near the top of the falls (unseen), you should keep an eye open for a narrow path across bilberry slopes that branches right and undulates across the very edge of the drop until finally it emerges at a point high above the valley of the Afon Goch.

Now, before pressing on, a little forward planning is needed. To your left, beyond the Afon Goch, is a spread of screes that you have to cross. Paths lead to the screes, but it does no harm to gain a general idea of what is going to be encountered. More directly below, bilberry slopes drop to the **Afon Goch**, and this busy stream you have to cross. A high vantage point enables you to get a fix on where this may be possible; there is no clear crossing point, and, in any case, this varies on an almost daily basis. However, the water is invariably fast-flowing and a pair of walking poles will help your stability in crossing. The further upstream you choose, the greater the likelihood of success.

Few people manage to cross dry-shod, and so the time-honoured practice of removing socks and replacing boots to protect your bare feet makes the

Aber Falls (Rhaeadr Fawr)

crossing a little easier, even if you end up with boots full of water. Now that towel and spare socks will come into play.

Once across the stream, climb to a path, and then follow this down towards the top of the main Aber falls; in places the path dances around rocky outcrops, but is clear throughout and leads to the edge of the scree downfall. A good path crosses the scree, and you should resist the temptation to descend the screes – they were unstable when the author descended them thirty years ago, and they have not improved.

Once across the scree, the path continues to a ladder-stile at the edge of woodland. Here you have the choice of swinging left and descending to the main valley path, and the chance of a close encounter with the falls, to which a path leads. Or, cross the stile, and take to the cool shade of the plantation.

You quit the trees at a gate, from which the ongoing path skims along below the plantation boundary. Eventually, the descending path meets the main track. Turn right along this, back towards Bont Newydd. At a metal gate you have the choice of going left through a narrow gate and onto a woodland path that will lead you directly back to the car park, or of going through the larger gate to pass the second car park and then out to the road used at the start of the walk just by Bont Newydd.

If you opted for the lower path, clear and broad throughout, then you will pass Tirwedd Dyffryn, what looks like a pile of stones, but which proved to be the walls of a roundhouse later adapted into a kiln for drying corn and probably dating from the Iron Age. The orange-lichened standing stone is thought to have been in place for between 4000 and 6000 years.

The valley of the Afon Rhaeadr-bach

Llyn Anafon
and the eastern Carneddau

*B*y long tradition, the people of Llanfairfechan held the right to fish Llyn Anafon and its river, so it was always a place of popular resort. No less so now, although many walkers prefer the surrounding heights to the simple walk up the service track to the lake. But what makes Llyn Anafon so inviting is the long arm of low hills that embrace it, hills that are more often neglected than appreciated as walkers head for the heights. This walk offers a short day's alternative to higher fare, although it does still involve a significant amount of height gain from the lake to the ridge above.

The Route
Pass through the gate adjacent to the car park and take to the stony track beyond. The hill immediately facing you is **Foel Dduarth**, and the valley to the right that of the **Afon Anafon**. To access the valley, turn left with the stony track for a short distance, and you will see a clear, broad service track crossing the hill slope. You can climb to this at any time, passing the ruins of a small homestead on the way. Now all that is required is to follow the track all the way to **Llyn Anafon**. Smooth-sided, steep mountain sides completely embrace the walk, and tend to shelter it from prevailing winds; they also make it a sun trap at certain times of the year.

↑ *Drum from the col with Foel Fras*

ROUTE INFORMATION

Distance	10km/6¼ miles
Height gain	690m/2265ft
Time	3–4 hours
Grade	moderate
Start point	SH675716

Getting there
Car park at the end of a narrow lane rising from the village of Abergwyngregyn

Maps
Harvey Superwalker Snowdonia: The Glyderau and the Carneddau; (Ordnance Survey) OL17 Snowdon/Yr Wyddfa

After-walk refreshment
There is a pub and café in Aber village, but otherwise Llanfairfechan or Penmaenmawr

In 1930 a dam was built across **Llyn Anafon**'s outflow to create a reservoir for nearby coastal villages, but this was decommissioned many years ago, since when water levels have fluctuated. A leak in the dam also meant that for a time the margins of the lake were a hazardous quagmire in which sheep became bogged down. When the water levels are low, this is still a hazard, and children should be kept well away from the water's edge.

For a remarkably easy day among the hills you can simply make a post-picnic retreat from the lake, an option that will give a round walk of 8km (5 miles), with 342m (1120ft) of height gain.

A much more demanding, but also more gratifying option is to climb to the broad grassy ridge of Drum above. This involves a pull in a south-easterly direction of 220m (720ft), mainly on grass and bilberry slopes over a distance of 1km (half a mile). There is no path, but the climb is nothing like so arduous as might be imagined, and succumbs to a relaxed plod. Your aim is to strike the ridge just south of Drum (at about

↑ *Llyn Anafon nestles in a hollow below Llwytmor*

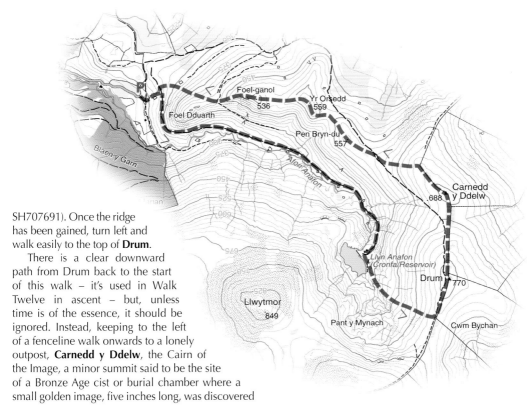

SH707691). Once the ridge has been gained, turn left and walk easily to the top of **Drum**.

There is a clear downward path from Drum back to the start of this walk – it's used in Walk Twelve in ascent – but, unless time is of the essence, it should be ignored. Instead, keeping to the left of a fenceline walk onwards to a lonely outpost, **Carnedd y Ddelw**, the Cairn of the Image, a minor summit said to be the site of a Bronze Age cist or burial chamber where a small golden image, five inches long, was discovered

Yr Orsedd, Foel Ganol and Foel Dduarth from Pen Bryn-du

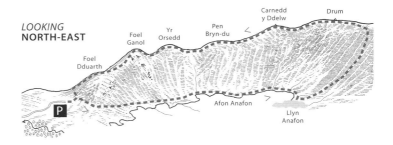

LOOKING
NORTH-EAST

in the 18th century. There is an excellent view from here down to the Bwlch y Ddeufaen and across to Foel Lwyd and Tal y Fan.

Cross the top of Carnedd y Ddelw following a fenceline to a fence corner, and from there descending through heather and bilberries to intercept that main broad track at SH700709. Continuing to ignore the track, cross onto a narrow path that guides you through a brief interlude of marshy ground and up onto **Pen Bryn-du**, a minor top crowned by a lovely cairn of quartz rocks. What follows now is quite delicious, leading first by a grassy path to **Yr Orsedd**,

which turns out to possess a surprisingly narrow crest. Follow the path across the top and down the other side to climb up onto **Foel Ganol**.

Beyond Foel Ganol lies **Foel Dduarth** and you can easily climb to its top, but continuing along the ridge from there only leads into a steep, craggy and impassable descent. The key is the low col between the two 'foels', from where you can bear right to join a grassy ramp across the north slope of Foel Dduarth, descending springy turf to within striking distance of the stony track. At any time you can descend to the track and follow it back to the car park at the start.

Foel Ganol from the summit of Yr Orsedd

Pen yr Ole Wen, Carnedd Dafydd, Carnedd Llywelyn and Pen yr Helgi Du

*F*rom Pont Pen y Benglog, the point where the Ogwen valley doglegs northwards as the Nant Ffrancon, Pen yr Ole Wen rises like a colossus, throwing down a challenge most walkers find easy to resist, judging by the small number you ever see heading upwards. The prospect is awesome, daunting, unthinkable, as your eyes trace a tenuous path threading a way ever higher before disappearing over the skyline at what, optimistically, you hope is the summit. Why would anyone go this way, when there is an easier way via Tal y Llyn Ogwen and Ffynnon Lloer?

The Route

The wisdom of parking east of Pont Pen y Benglog will become painfully apparent if you try hitting the slopes of Pen yr Ole Wen without being sufficiently warmed up. From the car park, the easy walk to the outflow of **Llyn Ogwen** at Rhaeadr Ogwen gets the blood flowing in readiness.

Near the telephone box at the side of the A5, pass through a gap in the wall on the opposite side of the road and pick a way through the tumble of rock and broken outcrops to gain a more conspicuous path heading up the mountainside. The 675m (2215ft) of ascent may seem brutal, but it has the advantage of directness over the alternative route by Tal y Llyn Ogwen. It is hard work, but once the top of **Pen yr Ole Wen** is reached, then there is nothing further to deter you: but be aware, the apparent 'summit' lip viewed from below is just that – apparent.

Pen yr Ole Wen from Tryfan

The actual summit lies further back, although the steepness is now much less.

Having garnered Pen yr Ole Wen, regained your breath and stopped your leg muscles from twanging, it is time to take in the onward route, and it is stunning, just reward for the effort. Although it will not all become obvious until you reach Carnedd Llywelyn, Pen yr Ole Wen is the south-western terminus of 16km (10 miles) of convoluted ridge that forms the central backbone of the Carneddau.

From the cairn on Pen yr Ole Wen continue around the upper rim of Cwm Ffynnon Lloer to the minor intermediate top, **Carnedd Fach**, and then on to **Carnedd Dafydd**, a summit thought to be named after the penultimate independent Prince of Wales.

Distance	16km/10 miles
Height gain	1170m/3840ft
Time	6+ hours
Grade	arduous
Start point	SH659602

Getting there
Parking area on A5, 1km east of Ogwen Cottage; there are other parking areas nearby

Maps
(Harvey Superwalker) Snowdonia: The Glyderau and the Carneddau; (Ordnance Survey) OL17 Snowdon/Yr Wyddfa

After-walk refreshment
Refreshment kiosk at Ogwen Cottage; pubs and cafés in Capel Curig and Bethesda

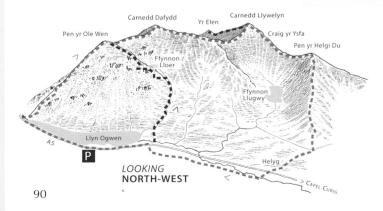

LOOKING
NORTH-WEST

Extremes of wind and temperature on the summits of the Carneddau (and elsewhere in Snowdonia) mean that few **plants** can survive. Nevertheless, species such as stiff sedge and dwarf willow occur on high ground. The latter species is locally common in montane heath communities such as are found on and around Carnedd Dafydd. This is the southern extremity of the distribution of summit heath in the UK and is protected under the Habitats Directive, Conservation (Natural Habitats &c.) Regulations 1994, so although this is Access Land it really isn't a good idea to stray too far from the path, in the interests of conservation.

From Carnedd Dafydd, the stretch to the highest summit, Carnedd Llywelyn, is especially rewarding, taking an airy stroll across the top of **Ysgolion Duon**, the Black Ladders, a popular rock climbers' playground, with extensive views down Cwm Llafar to distant Anglesey and Puffin Island. After Ysgolion Duon, the ridge narrows considerably as it crosses **Bwlch Cyfryr-drum**, before you climb to the rocky plateau of **Carnedd Llywelyn**.

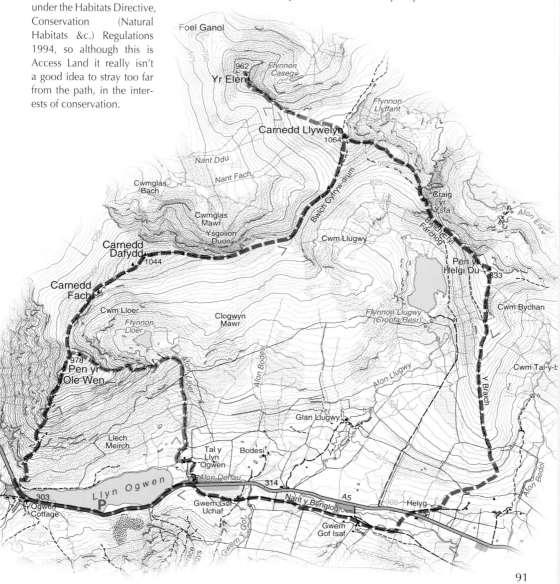

Ffynnon Llugwy, Craig yr Ysfa and Carnedd Llywelyn

There is a fine sense of achievement on reaching **Carnedd Llywelyn**. The rocky summit, typical of Carneddau tops, is an almost sterile place, and from it locating the radiating ridges is fraught with difficulty in poor visibility, as the author discovered in the 1970s, although that's quite another story, and one best forgotten. But the distant views of surrounding summits is quite special, and a warm day offers reason enough to linger among the rocks and let the world go by.

The spelling of the name is mildly puzzling. Carnedd Llewelyn is the form used by the Ordnance Survey, although Harveys use Llywelyn. It is this latter spelling that is in common use in Wales; it is a Welsh personal name, and always spelt with a 'y', although the forms 'Llywelyn' and 'Llewellyn' are both found in older English-language sources.

An optional extra available from the top of Carnedd Llywelyn is to visit **Yr Elen**. It is something of a lonely outpost, but it is a quite superb location, and seldom visited. The mountain is linked to the higher summit by a narrow ridge high above Ffynnon Caseg, but is best seen from the north-east. The summit is a lovely place, relaxing and refreshing.

From Carnedd Llywelyn, the concluding stages begin in a south-easterly direction, heading steadily downwards to pass above **Craig yr Ysfa**, a dramatic cliff on which climbers find their sport. The Saddle (**Bwlch Eryl Farchog**) is a tight but brief arête, reached from the top of Craig yr Ysfa by a brief rocky scramble downwards, after which the path continues to

the steep pull onto Pen yr Helgi Du. There is an easy opt out from the Saddle, should it be needed; a descending path on the right, initially steep, but then easing lower down and running out to meet a reservoir service road, which can be followed all the way down to the A5.

The haul onto **Pen yr Helgi Du** can be awkward, and involves a little easy scrambling, but is not unduly difficult. As you progress southwards from its spacious summit so the lovely whaleback ridge of **Y Braich** entices you onwards, a path running down its length to cross a leat by a footbridge. Cross the leat, and turn right until you reach the service road, and turn down it to the A5.

Helyg is a Climbers' Club hut and is a keystone in the history of British climbing. It was the first climbing hut in the UK, and was used as a base by the pioneers of British climbing in the 1920s for their early ascents, particularly on Lliwedd and Tryfan. Later it was used as a training base for the 1953 Everest expedition.

On reaching the A5, turn right and then left into the grounds of **Gwern Gof Isaf** farm. As you approach the farm buildings you can turn right to join the old stagecoach route that ran through the valley. This improved path can now be followed back towards Ogwen, rejoining the A5 opposite the turning up to **Tal y Llyn Ogwen**, from where it is but a short walk back to the start.

Alternative start: Walkers seeking to avoid the steepness of the *direttisima* of Pen yr Ole Wen can go by way of Tal y Llyn Ogwen, taking the track to the farm and then across fields and on to the open hillside, keeping close to the line of the Afon Lloer and crossing it in the early stages of the climb. As you approach Ffynnon Lloer so you can bear left (west) to gain the spur thrown down by Pen yr Ole Wen, through the rocks of which it is easy enough to find a way, with the gradient easing as you approach the summit. Of course, while this approach avoids the steep start, the distance is a little further and the height gain to the top of Pen yr Ole Wen reduced by not so much as one centimetre.

Cwm Eigiau Horseshoe

*S*tarting *in a remote and little-visited area of the Carneddau, this grand circuit of Cwm Eigiau ranks
as one of the classic walks of Wales, boasting soaring ridges, narrow arêtes, high mountains and
stunning landscapes. Amid beech, oak, hawthorn, blackthorn, bracken and ancient field systems,
the walk launches from a valley floor that was once mined and inhabited by folk who long since gave
up the unequal struggle against the elements and poor soil. Today, this isolated mountain upland is
as empty as it has been since prehistoric man roamed its vastness, set keenly against a backdrop of
mountain summits that rival Snowdon in altitude but without the clamour of pounding feet.*

The Route

From the parking area follow the straight, stony
track on the south to **Hafod-y-rhiw**, beyond which
you can take to a path climbing onto the end of the
broad ridge descending from **Pen Llithrig y Wrach**,
the Slippery Hill of the Witch. A long and rough haul
now takes you up to this shapely summit, marked by
a large collapsed cairn. To the south-east the ground
falls very steeply to Llyn Cowlyd, and then rises just as
abruptly to the long bumpy ridge of Creigiau Gleision.

The way onward from Pen Llithrig y Wrach, however, lies down a mainly grassy ridge to cross Bwlch
y Tri Marchog, the 'Pass of the Three Horsemen',
a place where three ancient boundaries met, and
where clan chiefs may well have convened to settle
disputes. Who they were is not recorded, but they
left behind a name that lingers on, linking the modern with distant times.

A short, steep climb leads up to the spacious top of
Pen yr Helgi Du, the summit marked by a small cairn.

↑ *Cwm Eigiau and Pen Llithrig y Wrach*

ROUTE INFORMATION

Distance	16.5km/10¼ miles
Height gain	1075m/3525ft
Time	6–7 hours
Grade	arduous
Start point	SH732663

Getting there
Parking area at the end of gated minor lane from Tal y Bont in the Vale of Conwy. Leave the B5106 just south of Y Bedol pub, and drive very carefully

Maps
Harvey Superwalker Snowdonia: The Glyderau and the Carneddau; (Ordnance Survey) OL17 Snowdon/Yr Wyddfa

After-walk refreshment
In addition to Y Bedol in Tal-y-Bont, there are various pubs, hotels along the Conwy valley, notably at Llanrwst, Trefriw, Dolgarrog and Tal y Cafn

A few steps from the cairn, however, invokes a striking change: below, seen for the first time, are the sombre waters of **Ffynnon Llugwy**, while on the opposite side of the ridge lie the ruins of the Cwm Eigiau slate quarries. Nearer to hand, the ridge plunges abruptly to a knife edge arête, The Saddle (**Bwlch Eryl Farchog**), beyond which rise the cliffs of Craig yr Ysfa.

Craig yr Ysfa is one of the three largest rock faces in Wales, on which the first climbing route was Great Gully, ascended by J Archer Thomson and a party of climbers in 1900, and still a popular gully climb.

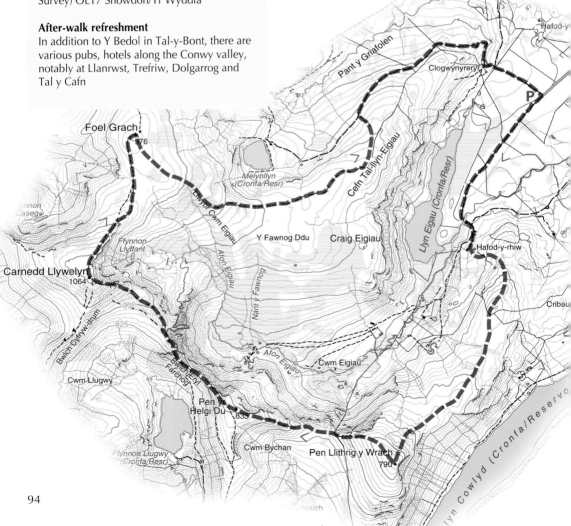

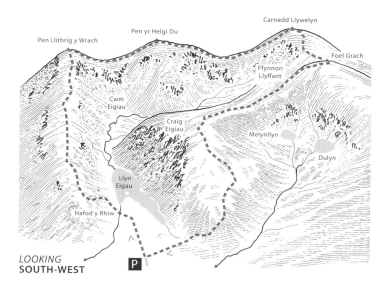

The descent to The Saddle proves to be quite short, but it is steep and hands (and maybe bottoms) will be needed. The continuation to **Carnedd Llywelyn** more or less follows the rim of upper Cwm Eigiau, beginning with a little mild scrambling. Once beyond Craig yr Ysfa, it is a steady and easy pull on a clear path to the top of the mountain, a large plateau from where the onward route to Foel Grach requires a little thought: being higher than surrounding mountains, Carnedd Llywelyn prevents a view of its nearest neighbours.

LOOKING
SOUTH-WEST

Carnedd Llywelyn (sometimes Llewelyn) is the highest summit in the Carneddau, and surpassed in England and Wales only by Snowdon and its adjacent peak, Carnedd Ugain. The name means 'Llywelyn's cairn', and it is a widely held view that Carnedd Llywelyn was named after Llywelyn ap Gruffudd ap Llywelyn (c1223–1282), the last independent Prince of Wales. An alternative view holds that the peak is named after Llywelyn the Great, or Llywelyn ap Iorwerth (c1173–1240), who held court at Aber on the North Wales coast and used the top of the mountain as an observation post. That the mountain might be named after the last prince of Wales has credence as it sits besides Carnedd Dafydd, thought to be named after his

The final stages up to Carnedd Llywelyn from Craig yr Ysfa

brother, and Yr Elen, which commemorates his wife, Eleanor, who died giving birth to their only child, Gwenllian. In September 2009, a geographically minor top, Carnedd Uchaf, within sight of the other mountains, was renamed Carnedd Uchaf/Carnedd Gwenllian as a tribute to the princess.

The final pull to Carnedd Llywelyn; Pen yr Helgi Du and Pen Llithrig y Wrach in the background

Once the correct direction is located – and in mist this will require compass work – set off for **Foel Grach**, roughly in a north-easterly direction. The way poses no problems being down easy slopes, and allows a brief diversion, right, to investigate a conspicuous rock tower that turns out to be the remains of a circular burial mound. Some stories claim this as the burial place of Tristan, of Arthurian legend. More probably, given the wealth of similar sites in this vast area, it dates from the Bronze Age.

From Foel Grach you need to descend steeply in a south-easterly direction, and without much of a path, to gain the long ridge that curls round **Melynllyn**.

The walled enclosures of a **Bronze Age** settlement near Dulyn Reservoir are well seen from this descending ridge, and may tempt you to reflect for a while on mountain life as it must have been when protective clothing, boots, mobile phones and the facility of returning home to a warm bath and hot food were non-existent.

Trend right down the ridge, unless you want the negotiate steep and wet ground to visit Melynllyn itself, and later take rather easier ground to intercept a service track that will steer you back to the start.

Creigiau Gleision and Pen Llithrig y Wrach from Moel Siabod

Creigiau Gleision
and Llyn Cowlyd

*S*eparated from the rest of the Carneddau by Llyn Cowlyd, Snowdonia's deepest lake, Creigiau
Gleision is rather a secluded summit. But its proximity to Capel Curig and the rugged terrain that
surrounds it is wonderful compensation for the isolation, and makes it popular with hillwalkers who
like the ups and downs of mountain life. The mountain itself is a double-topped affair, and getting at
it involves dealing with a number of minor bumps and tops along the way; all very entertaining, and
providing an insight into rather less rounded, grassy country than is encountered elsewhere among
the Carneddau. A visit to Llyn Cowlyd is simply the icing on the cake, while the final romp back to
Capel Curig across the moors just flies by.

The Route
Walk out to the main road and cross the A5 to a stile/
gate beside St Curig's church, now a B&B.

Much of **Capel Curig**'s history revolves around
highways, from Roman incursions to packhorse
trails and stagecoach routes that brought the first
fare-paying visitors to the area. The earliest visitors
were botanists, but it wasn't long before adven-
turous Georgians and Victorians came in search
of enlightenment. That they might be accommo-
dated handsomely, Richard Penrhyn, Bethesda
quarry owner, built the Capel Curig Inn in 1800
(later the Royal), the first stylish hotel in the area

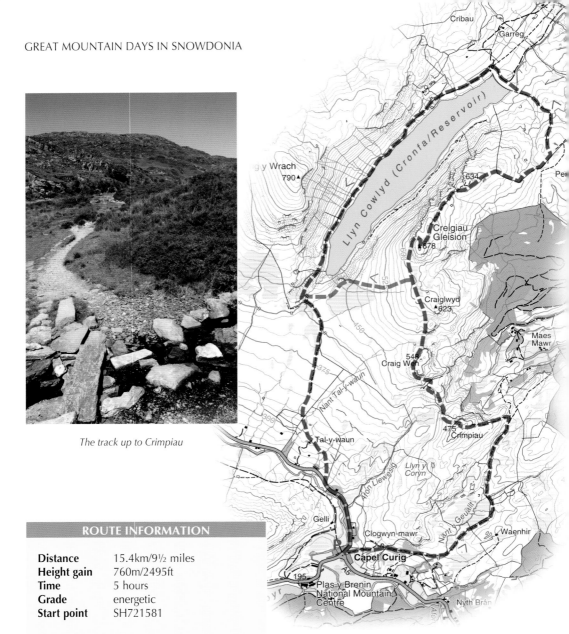

The track up to Crimpiau

Distance	15.4km/9½ miles
Height gain	760m/2495ft
Time	5 hours
Grade	energetic
Start point	SH721581

Getting there
Car park up narrow lane and behind Joe Brown's shop in Capel Curig

Maps
(Harvey Superwalker) Snowdonia:The Glyderau and the Carneddau; (Ordnance Survey) OL17 Snowdon/Yr Wyddfa

After-walk refreshment
Café and hotels in Capel Curig

and specifically intended to serve the tourist trade. George Borrow thought it 'a magnificent edifice', and it is now part of the Plas y Brenin centre.

Take to a gently rising path across a large enclosure, soon passing a rock feature known as 'The Pinnacles', used by Plas y Brenin for training. At a stile and gate you enter a stretch of light, broadleaved woodland along the base of **Clogwyn Mawr**, where you may find a few specimens of wood sorrel, an ancient woodland indicator species, and a pointer to this area having been substantially covered by trees in the

Creigiau Gleision and the head of Crafnant

past. When you leave the woodland behind you continue to a ladder-stile-gate across a fence, from where there is an lovely retrospective view to the Snowdon Horseshoe and across the valley to Moel Siabod.

On reaching a footbridge, the path divides; bear left, with the long craggy ridge of Crimpiau off to your left. The scenery here is rugged and unkempt in a fashionable kind of way, with rock outcrops and small buttresses punctuating a landscape of heather and bilberry. But it is a delight to explore, which the ongoing path does with great aplomb.

Follow the track, which is straightforward and gradually starts to climb, and keep on as far as a high point just where the track divides (SH738596). Here, branch left, and almost immediately left again onto a clear path ascending on the left towards Crimpiau. Soon there is a stunning view of your ultimate objective, Creigiau Gleision, viewed across the gulf of upper Crafnant. Press on to the top of **Crimpiau**, and then take the path descending steeply on the other side to a small col amid a convoluted landscape of hummocks, hollows and glacial moraine.

Cross the col, and then resume the path up onto **Craig Wen** without the necessity to actually climb to the summit of this minor outlier. The path, continuous throughout this walk, passes around Craig Wen, and crosses a boggy section before setting foot on **Creigiau Gleision**. The path circles around the summit, although you can make a direct ascent at any point.

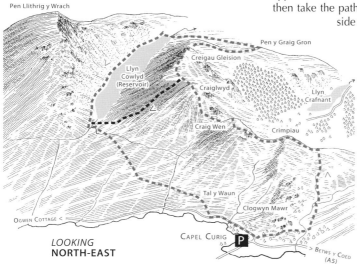

Pen Llithrig y Wrach

Pen y Graig Gron

Creigiau Gleision

Llyn Cowlyd (Reservoir)

Craiglwyd

Llyn Crafnant

Craig Wen

Crimpiau

Tal y Waun

Clogwyn Mawr

OGWEN COTTAGE <

CAPEL CURIG P

LOOKING
NORTH-EAST

> BETWS Y COED (A5)

99

But the circling path eventually turns back to reach the large cairn on the top of the mountain.

The view to the north is consumed by the bulk of Pen Llithrig y Wrach below which Llyn Cowlyd waits. Press on along the top of Creigiau Gleision, a grassy path leading from the top in a north-easterly direction to a minor, unnamed, summit, and then onwards to intercept an ancient fenceline just beyond a small pool. Rather than attempt a direct line to the dam of Llyn Cowlyd, it is better to follow the path beside the fenceline, and then, near **Pen y Graig Gron** and another small pool, you can turn northwards to descend a wide gully through deep heather to reach the dam.

Beyond the dam you reach a good path that now streaks south-westwards above the reservoir, and is a most delightful romp, finally rising to a concrete footbridge spanning a stream flowing down to Llyn Cowlyd. Do not cross the bridge, but keep right, beside the stream, to a ladder-stile and a wooden footbridge (SH717609). Cross this bridge and so gain a broad track that initially follows a fenceline, but then breaks free to race down across moorland slopes.

There are fine views along the Ogwen valley and of Gallt yr Ogof and Tryfan. At a ladder-stile/gate you quit Access Land, and follow a good path down to **Tal y Waun** bunkhouse. Maintain the same direction, now parallel with a small stream, until the path finally comes down to reach the A5 at a ladder-stile/gate. Cross the road and go left, back to Capel Curig, the exact distance remaining being displayed on an ancient milestone – 3 furlongs.

Alternative: Walkers wanting a shorter walk can backtrack from the summit of Creigiau Gleision a little, until you are free of the rocks, and then head downwards across the heather, bilberry and tussock slopes of Llethr Gwyn, aiming for a small bilberry platform that offers a splendid view down the length of Llyn Cowlyd, and then pressing on through deep heather to the concrete footbridge at the inflow to the reservoir. You need to cross the footbridge to join the main route.

There is a continuous path down from Creigiau Gleision, but it is not easy to find and it is arguably better to fashion your own route, mindful of where and how you are placing your feet in the deep vegetation. This shortened version will give a walk of 11.5km (7 miles), with much the same amount of height gain as the main walk.

Llyn Geirionydd
and Llyn Crafnant

*M*aking the most of an exquisite confusion of woodlands, hummocky hills, lakes, rivers and wildness, this walk, albeit indisputably in 'mountainous' terrain, underscores the point that you do not have to clamber up to a mountain top in order to appreciate what the mountains of Snowdonia have to offer. The two valleys that house Llyn Geirionydd and Llyn Crafnant have long been popular, and deservedly so. Although this walk begins beside the Afon Crafnant, it heads first into the neighbouring valley before finding a way through woodlands to join an old track from Capel Curig across the uplands to Llyn Crafnant.

The Route

Leave the car park and turn left down the road, back in the direction of Trefriw, soon walking alongside tree-lined **Afon Crafnant**. Continue for about 800m, as far as a footpath sign on the right (SH763624), just before a cottage (Hendre Isaf). Here, turn right onto a descending track that leads to a concrete bridge spanning the river. On reaching the bridge, turn left at the side of the river to a narrow pedestrian bridge nearby and over this go forward beside a fence following a path through bracken to reach a mining area with ruined buildings and spoil. This is the Klondyke Mill, and the way through is not clear.

↑ *Llyn Crafnant*

ROUTE INFORMATION

Distance	13.7km/8½ miles
Height gain	570m (1879ft)
Time	5 hours
Grade	moderate
Start point	SH756618

Getting there
There is a large car park (Pay and Display; toilets) north-east of the outflow from Llyn Crafnant, reached along a very narrow road from Trefriw, and signed for Llyn Crafnant

Maps
(Harvey Superwalker) Snowdonia: The Glyderau and the Carneddau; (Ordnance Survey) OL17 Snowdon/Yr Wyddfa

After-walk refreshment
Cafés, pubs and hotel in Trefriw. Lakeside café at Llyn Crafnant (open Easter until late summer)

Klondyke Mill was powered by water from the river flowing from Llyn Geirionydd, and apart from processing its own metals (which never amounted to much) also received lead and zinc ore from the Pandora mine on the shores of Geirionydd. The route of the tramway from that mine ran partly along the route of the lakeside road (which did not exist at the time).

Climb up onto the spoil heaps and then look for a narrow path into woodland on the far right-hand side. The path is continuous and climbs steadily if not always clearly, passing around the north-eastern end of **Mynydd Deulyn**, the Mountain of the Two Lakes, and joining one of the Trefriw Trails (No 5), a series of short walks from the village, where any ambiguity about the route now ends. Cross a nearby ladder-stile, from which the path continues to climb to become a broad, grassy path across a low shoulder where **Llyn Geirionydd** comes into view. Keep forward on an obvious path, soon passing a large monument. Go past the monument and down towards the water's edge, where you find a path running between and wall and the lake.

Main photo: *The monument, Llyn Geirionydd;* **Inset:** *Rock detail, Llyn Geirionydd*

Llyn Geirionydd has a number of literary associations, not least with Taliesin (c534–c599), a Brythonic poet of Sub-Roman Britain whose work has possibly survived in a Middle Welsh manuscript, the *Book of Taliesin*. Taliesin was a renowned bard who is believed to have sung at the courts of at least three Celtic British kings, and was the earliest poet of the Welsh language. He lived on the shores of Llyn Geirionydd, where many claim he is buried. The Red Book of Hergest XVII, one of the most important medieval Welsh language manuscripts, contains the line: 'I being Taliesin, from the borders of the lake of Geirionydd.'

The lakeside path passes the base of an old mine, after which you climb into a brief skirmish with tree roots before returning to the water's edge. At the far end of the lake pass Ty Newydd, and then cross a stile giving onto a broad track. Here, bear right, following a broad trail as it rises into woodland. The main stands of pine are set back from the trail and fronted by sensitively planted broad-leaved trees, so there is no sense of enclosure, and the walking is very agreeable.

When you reach a junction at SH755601, where the track divides, go left over a step-stile beside a gate, continuing to follow a broad track, but one that now escapes the trees. At another stile you return to a wooded area through which you descend to pass **Llyn Bychan**, a glorious little lake, its dark silky waters fringed by golden reeds and dotted with white water lilies.

Where the track divides at the first turning on the right after Llyn Bychan (SH751584), swing right into a section of woodland that is now much more enclosed for a while, but is no less agreeable. The track climbs steadily, and then suddenly, as you round a bend, Moel Siabod springs into view, framed by trees.

You leave the woodland at SH738579, and here cross a ladder-stile giving onto a path enclosed between a wall and fence, with fine views of Moel

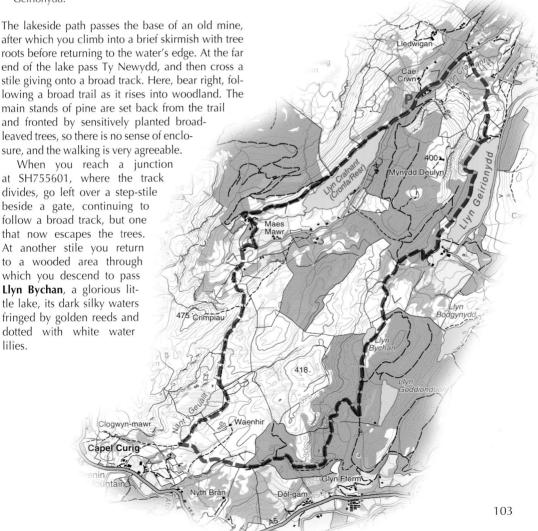

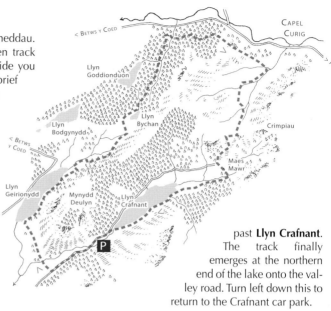

Siabod the Glyderau and the Carneddau. The path turns out to be an old sunken track bounded by tumbledown walls that guide you to a step/stile in a fence giving into a brief bout of mainly willow woodland before you emerge onto Access Land, across which the path takes a way-marked route, with the long ridge Crimpiau on your right.

When you intercept a broad track, continue across it, still following a waymarked route along which wooden footbridges span drainage channels. Finally, the path arrives at a bridge at SH732581. Do not cross the bridge, but turn immediately right to begin the return to Llyn Crafnant. This section of path is used in Walk 16, and it ambles very agreeably through a rocky landscape, steadily working its way up to a high point where the track divides. Branch left, and pass the point where the path for **Crimpiau** turns away.

Keep forward here, through an obvious gap ahead to begin the descent to Crafnant. The path eases down through a rugged gorge flanked by rock outcrops, bracken and heather.

When this opens up, Creigiau Gleision appears ahead, along with a **stunning view** of Llyn Crafnant, arguably one of the most breathtaking views in Snowdonia, and worthy of a pilgrimage.

The path descends steeply for a while to a ladder-stile close by Blaen-y-nant. Take the grassy path leading to the cottage, walk past it and then turn right down a rough access track. After about 100m, as you reach a large ash tree on the left (SH739603) as the track swings to the right, leave it for a grassy path descending through bracken to another cottage, Tan y Manod. Go left on a broad track in front of the cottage, pass another cottage and continue as far as a gate at Hendre, just after which you cross a stream by a footbridge, and climb up into woodland.

Walk up through the woodland for a short distance until, just after a ladder-stile, you intercept a broad track at a waymark. Here, turn right, descending eventually through waterside woodland as it eases

past **Llyn Crafnant**. The track finally emerges at the northern end of the lake onto the valley road. Turn left down this to return to the Crafnant car park.

Crafnant takes its name from 'craf', an old Welsh word for garlic, and 'nant', a stream or valley, an association that is headily evident when the garlic is in bloom. The lake is a reservoir, and dammed at its northern end in 1874, but the dam is barely visible as the outflow plunges down steeply from it. At the outflow end of the lake is an obelisk, erected in 1896 by the inhabitants of Llanrwst which commemorates 'The gift to that town of this lake' by one Richard James. Areas around the lake were used for location shots in the 1981 fantasy movie *Dragonslayer*, and the lake also appeared briefly in the 1966 film *Morgan: A Suitable Case for Treatment*.

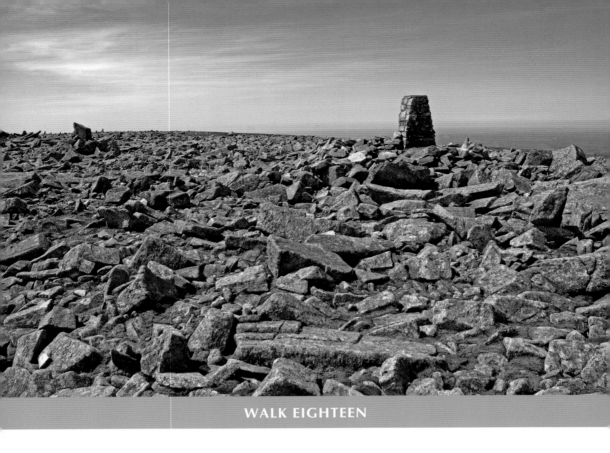

The Carneddau:
End-to-end

*A*s linear walks go, the traverse of the Carneddau is a beast of considerable magnitude, and not something that can be undertaken lightly, or other than in perfect conditions and even then only by strong and experienced walkers. There are escape routes, should they be needed, and the chance to truncate the walk in a few places if you want to tackle something a little less demanding, and can arrange transport to collect you. But overall, if you do make it end-to-end, you will know you've been for a walk. Logistically, it is something of a problem, as there is little flowing water along the length of the walk, so whatever you need to drink you will have to carry. Thankfully, all the hard work is at the beginning, and then things do start to ease significantly.

The Route

The walk begins with the steep ascent of **Pen yr Ole Wen**, as described in Walk 14. It is a demanding start to the day, but you have to gain height somewhere, and this crams a lot of ascent into a relatively short horizontal distance: cruel but efficient.

Near the telephone box at the side of the A5, look for a gap in the wall on the opposite side of the road and then pick a way through the tumble of rock and broken outcrops to gain a more conspicuous path heading up the mountainside. Only one word of route description is needed: up! From below, you think you can see the top of the mountain, but this

↑ *The summit of Foel Fras*

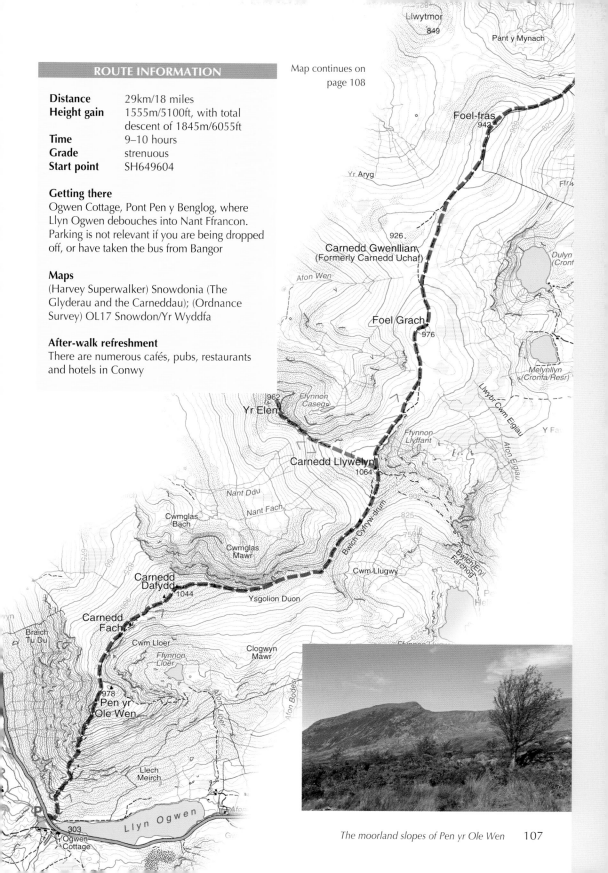

Map continues on
page 108

ROUTE INFORMATION

Distance	29km/18 miles
Height gain	1555m/5100ft, with total descent of 1845m/6055ft
Time	9–10 hours
Grade	strenuous
Start point	SH649604

Getting there
Ogwen Cottage, Pont Pen y Benglog, where
Llyn Ogwen debouches into Nant Ffrancon.
Parking is not relevant if you are being dropped
off, or have taken the bus from Bangor

Maps
(Harvey Superwalker) Snowdonia (The
Glyderau and the Carneddau); (Ordnance
Survey) OL17 Snowdon/Yr Wyddfa

After-walk refreshment
There are numerous cafés, pubs, restaurants
and hotels in Conwy

The moorland slopes of Pen yr Ole Wen   107

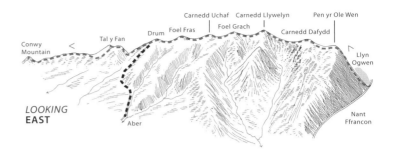

Conwy Mountain · Tal y Fan · Drum · Foel Fras · Carnedd Uchaf · Foel Grach · Carnedd Llywelyn · Carnedd Dafydd · Pen yr Ole Wen · Llyn Ogwen · Nant Ffrancon · Aber

LOOKING
EAST

is a wicked sham, as the real summit lies some way further back. Once you reach it, and your eyes have started to focus again through the red mist, the view that reveals itself will gladden your heart, and spur you on, curving almost majestically around the top of **Cwm Lloer**.

The way to **Carnedd Dafydd** and above the rock climbers' playground of **Ysgolion Duon** is well trodden, and takes you to a final pull up to **Carnedd Llywelyn**. This ascent to the highest summit of the day does end the uphill work for the day, at least that of any note. So you may be tempted to dash out to **Yr Elen**, reached by a splendid arête

running in a north-westerly direction and back. Realistically, this extension, worthy as it is, should be contemplated only if you intend to end the walk at Aber or the Bwlch y Ddeufaen, as the out-and-back additions to distance and height gain may be one straw too many if you plan on going all the way to Conwy.

North-east of Carnedd Llywelyn, a good path runs out to **Foel Grach**, with its bothy/refuge, and then on to bypass **Carnedd Uchaf/Carnedd Gwenllian**, beyond which you head for the end of a wall that accompanies you across the rash of boulders that is the summit cap of **Foel Fras**, reached by a gentle walk uphill. Off

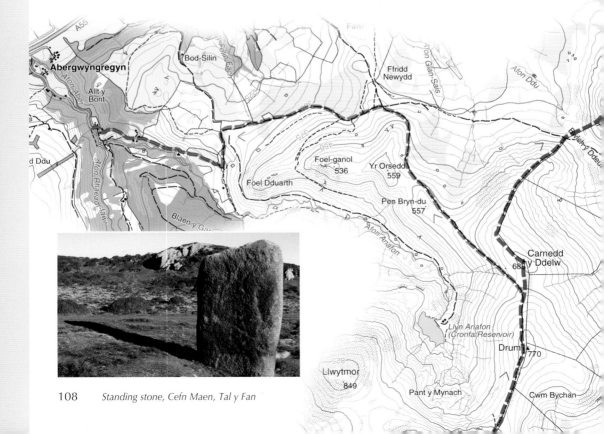

Standing stone, Cefn Maen, Tal y Fan

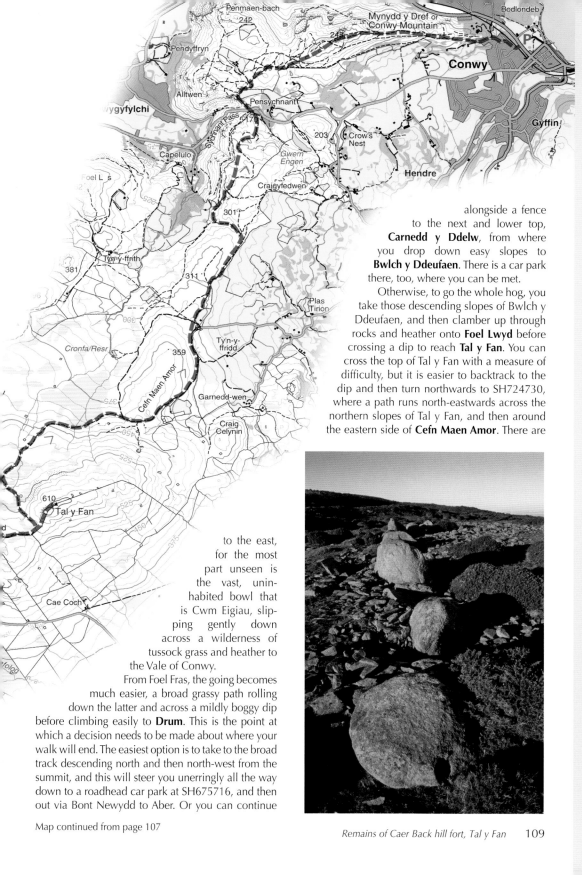

alongside a fence to the next and lower top, **Carnedd y Ddelw**, from where you drop down easy slopes to **Bwlch y Ddeufaen**. There is a car park there, too, where you can be met.

Otherwise, to go the whole hog, you take those descending slopes of Bwlch y Ddeufaen, and then clamber up through rocks and heather onto **Foel Lwyd** before crossing a dip to reach **Tal y Fan**. You can cross the top of Tal y Fan with a measure of difficulty, but it is easier to backtrack to the dip and then turn northwards to SH724730, where a path runs north-eastwards across the northern slopes of Tal y Fan, and then around the eastern side of **Cefn Maen Amor**. There are

to the east, for the most part unseen is the vast, uninhabited bowl that is Cwm Eigiau, slipping gently down across a wilderness of tussock grass and heather to the Vale of Conwy.

From Foel Fras, the going becomes much easier, a broad grassy path rolling down the latter and across a mildly boggy dip before climbing easily to **Drum**. This is the point at which a decision needs to be made about where your walk will end. The easiest option is to take to the broad track descending north and then north-west from the summit, and this will steer you unerringly all the way down to a roadhead car park at SH675716, and then out via Bont Newydd to Aber. Or you can continue

Map continued from page 107

Remains of Caer Back hill fort, Tal y Fan

quite a few paths and tracks in the next stretch to the top of the Sychnant Pass, so it helps to be careful with navigation, and to look for a low gap between hills to gain the North Wales Path, and follow this to **Pensychnant**.

Cross the pass, and climb on the other side, first by a lane towards Alltwen, but soon leaving this to head north-east and then east to the top of **Conwy Mountain**. The long ridge descending to Conwy is a delight, charging downhill with Conwy Castle beckoning ahead. When the mountain ground ends on reaching a minor road, it is simply a question of picking your way through the streets to the quayside or your pick-up point. It is a reasonable guess that you will be in need of a cuppa, or something stronger.

Looking down the Sychnant Pass

The Great Orme and Conwy from Conwy Mountain

EIFIONYDD

Nantgwynant and Moel Hebog (Walk 21)

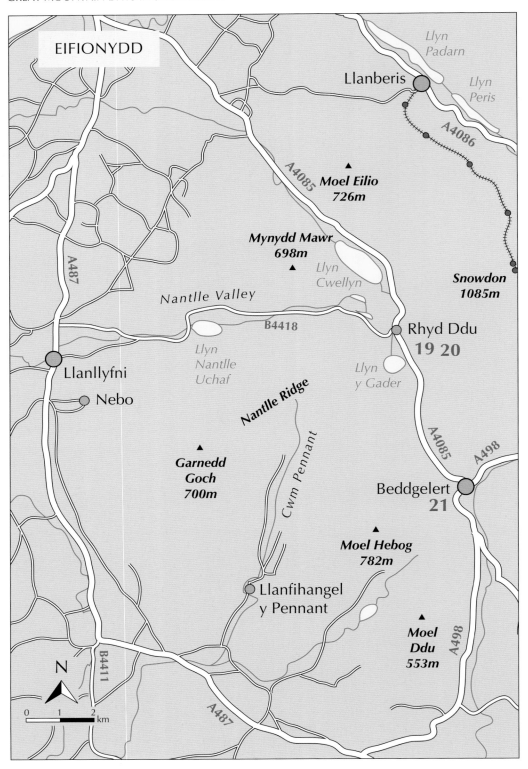

EIFIONYDD

Llyn Padarn

Llanberis

Llyn Peris

A4086

A4085

Moel Eilio
726m

Mynydd Mawr
698m

Llyn Cwellyn

Snowdon
1085m

Nantlle Valley

B4418

Rhyd Ddu
19 20

Llyn Nantlle Uchaf

Llyn y Gader

Llanllyfni

Nebo

Nantlle Ridge

Cwm Pennant

A4085

A498

Garnedd Goch
700m

Beddgelert
21

Moel Hebog
782m

Llanfihangel y Pennant

Moel Ddu
553m

A498

N

B4411

A487

0   1   2 km

A487

EIFIONYDD

Of all the groupings used in this book, it is a fair bet that few will know of Eifionydd. This is one of only two names of the old Welsh cantrefs and commotes that survived to be used by tourists and mountaineers in North Wales. This ancient commote was the northern half of the minor kingdom, or cantref, of Dunoding, within the larger kingdom of Gwynedd. Today, although the name is in common use locally, beyond the region it is arguably unheard of.

From a hillwalker's perspective, Eifionydd embraces a self-contained group of eight principal tops and a handful of minor ones, presided over by Moel Hebog. Strictly speaking, Eifionydd ends in the north at the Nantlle valley, but a judicious application of author's license has extended it to include the huge, bulky mountain Mynydd Mawr. Apart from this independent outlier, the remaining mountains form themselves into a rough T, the top, horizontal stroke taking the form of the Nantlle ridge, one of the finest ridge walks in Wales, while the down stroke crosses an old corpse road between Cwm Pennant and Rhyd

Ddu and continues south, gaining height in a series of undulations until it tops out at Moel Hebog.

To the east of this line runs Nant Colwyn, flowing south to Beddgelert along an ancient thoroughfare. To the west, completely unsuspected by the majority of visitors to the area, is Cwm Pennant, an exquisite dale, scenically magnificent, but with, dare it be said, more of the flavour of the English Lake District about it than a Welsh cwm. Yet Cwm Pennant is characteristic of an older North Wales, one of which little remains, a land of quiet hills, lonely pastures bleating with sound in springtime, a place more *andante* than *allegro*, more Vaughan Williams than Richard Strauss.

The tranquillity of Cwm Pennant is left untouched by these walks, which opt to circle around it and savour the view downwards, perhaps recalling days when what few mountain passes there were echoed to the sound of drovers and shepherds moving their herds and flocks beneath skies once cruised by eagles. Is that where the Hill of the Hawk, Moel Hebog, gets its name?

↑ *On the summit of Y Garn (Nantlle) (Walk 20)*

Y Garn and Mynydd Drws y Coed from Rhyd Ddu; the start of the Nantlle ridge (Walk 20)

Idle, but wholly unfounded, speculation might lead one to question whether the remoteness of Cwm Pennant was the resting place sought by 'that great magician' Owain Glyndwr, a man who holds a foremost place among Welsh heroes. On the east face of Moel yr Ogof is a large cave-like cleft, still called Ogof Owain Glyndwr, and said to be one of his many hiding places, in which he 'dwelt...for six months'. So, it is perhaps not so far-fetched to suppose, given the fact that no one knows what became of him, that he may have slipped over the hills into the seclusion of Pennant and spent the rest of his life among the shepherds. Glyndwr epitomises the Welsh nationalist movement because his rebellion in the early 15th century was the last Welsh bid to re-assert political independence. It was not to be, but the memory of the great man lives on, not only in his cave, but in the name of the route he took to get to it, and so escape his pursuers: in climbing circles it remains 'Glyndwr's Gully. 250 feet. First ascent: Owain Glyndwr, c1400.'

Mynydd Mawr

I *solated Mynydd Mawr, viewed from Anglesey, assumes the form of a recumbent elephant, but from all other directions it is simply a big mountain, as its name suggests. Mynydd Mawr does not readily lend itself to circular walks, and although linear walks can be fashioned across its grassy slopes, this simple romp up and down by the same route is perfectly suited to an uncomplicated and leisurely day, albeit one that will take its toll on dodgy knees.*

The Route

Walk to the northern edge of the car park and, opposite a railway crossing point, take a broad track to the left between cottages to walk out to the village road. Turn right and walk as far as the turning for Nantlle, there turning left. Just after the speed de-restriction sign, leave the road by branching right onto a broad trail (SH569529) into the northern arm of the **Beddgelert Forest**.

Follow the trail pleasantly through the plantation, with none of the close oppressiveness generally associated with commercial forest, until you reach an area where the forest has been cleared. Down below, Planwydd Farm sits by the road (from where an alternative start begins), and suddenly **Llyn Cwellyn** eases into view against a backdrop of the soft-moulded Moel Eilio and its acolytes.

A path climbs from Planwydd Farm, rising to meet the forest trail at SH563541. Here the ongoing path, as it now is, divides. Climb left, taking the higher of two paths, up through the remaining plantation to arrive at a ladder-stile spanning a fence at the top boundary of the plantation. Ahead now all is Nantlle valley, the Nantlle Ridge and the steep

↑ Y Garn (Nantlle Ridge) and Clogwynygarreg

ROUTE INFORMATION

Distance	10km/6½ miles
Height gain	550m/1805ft
Time	3–4 hours
Grade	moderate
Start point	SH571526

Getting there
The path starts from the car park a little
south of Rhyd Ddu village on the A4085
Beddgelert–Caernarfon road, adjacent to the
Rhyd Ddu station on the Welsh Highland
Railway

Maps
(Ordnance Survey) OL17 Snowdon/Yr Wyddfa

After-walk refreshment
Ty Mawr tea room and the Cwellyn Arms pub
in Rhyd Ddu; pubs and cafés in Beddgelert

The final slopes onto Mynydd Mawr from Foel Rudd

slopes of Mynydd Mawr along which the cracked
and rugose crags of Craig y Bera are starting to take
form. In the foreground **Clogwynygarreg**, a volcanic
plug or *roche moutonnée* (who knows for certain?),
is dashingly dramatic, rising above the obviously
drained area that once housed Llyn Bwlch y Moch.
To the south, looking towards distant Moel Hebog,
lies the fabled **Llyn y Dywarchen**.

Llyn y Dywarchen was remarked upon by Gerald
of Wales in his *Journey through Wales* as possessing a floating island. In time, this marvel of physical geography became legend, although, with the
unchallenged faith of a cleric, Gerald offered a
rational explanation: 'It is possible that a section
of the bank was broken off in times long past and
that, bound together in a natural way by the roots
of the willows and other shrubs which grow there,
it has since become larger by alluvial deposits. It
is continually driven from one bank to another
by the violent winds.' Subsequent travellers, up

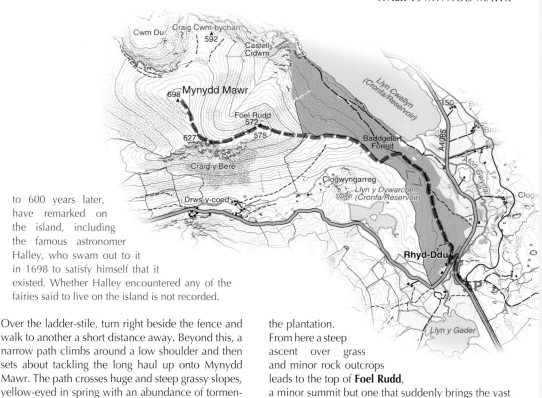

to 600 years later, have remarked on the island, including the famous astronomer Halley, who swam out to it in 1698 to satisfy himself that it existed. Whether Halley encountered any of the fairies said to live on the island is not recorded.

Over the ladder-stile, turn right beside the fence and walk to another a short distance away. Beyond this, a narrow path climbs around a low shoulder and then sets about tackling the long haul up onto Mynydd Mawr. The path crosses huge and steep grassy slopes, yellow-eyed in spring with an abundance of tormentil, and rises to another stile close by the top edge of the plantation. From here a steep ascent over grass and minor rock outcrops leads to the top of **Foel Rudd**, a minor summit but one that suddenly brings the vast hollow of bilberry-filled **Cwm Planwydd** into view;

Craig y Bera, Mynydd Mawr

it is quite a stunning moment, with Mynydd Mawr rising smoothly on the other side.

All the steepness now is over, and the final stretch is outstanding, a delicious amble along a clear path that whizzes around above the topmost rocks of **Craig y Bera**, steadily making its way to the top of the mountain, reached over close-clipped turf interspersed with small scatters of rock, although the highest ground is covered by a beanie of stone and boulders, marked by three shelters and a large cairn on the highest point.

As you approach the summit of **Mynydd Mawr**, especially in poor visibility, make a mental note of the line of your approach, as the return path is not instantly visible from the top.

Throughout the walk the undulations of the Nantlle Ridge have remained in **view** to the south, and these inviting hills now lie across the skyline like a fine frescoed flourish of Nature's artwork. Northwards the view spans Anglesey, while to the north-west you gaze over the Moel Eilio group to Elidir Fawr and the higher Carneddau beyond.

Once satisfied with your visit to Mynydd Mawr, simply retrace your steps and hope that your knees hold out.

The summit of Mynydd Mawr

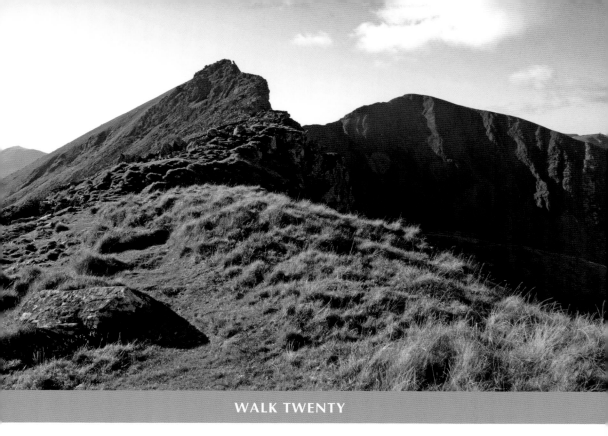

The Nantlle Ridge

In the whole of North Wales, the Nantlle ridge is surpassed in unadulterated ridge-walking pleasure by only the Snowdon Horseshoe. The dubious talisman of height gives Snowdon a degree of magnetism, but for superb walking without the drama and the crowds, nothing beats the Nantlle ridge. Of course, being a linear walk, you have to resolve the logistics of getting back to the start, if such is your need, although an enthralling day can be made of a walk just as far as Mynydd Tal y Mignedd, and then walking back.

The Route

Directly opposite the car park, a gate gives access to a slate path across a field, leading to a stream flowing from Llyn y Gader. On reaching the stream, follow path to footbridge, and then a stile, beyond which you reach the access road to a cottage, Tal y Llyn. Cross this access and take to a narrow path through rushes and across rough pasture until you rejoin the access and can follow it out to the B4418. Here, immediately turn left through a gate and take a footpath to another gate from where the ascent begins in earnest.

The way on to **Y Garn**, and the start of the ridge, is clear enough, a steeply rising path gouged into slatey runnels in places. Higher up, the path leads to a ladder-stile over a wall, beyond which you soon reach the top of Y Garn. The hard work is rewarded by a dramatic view of the cliffs of Craig y Bera on the southern slopes of Mynydd Mawr, and of the lush pastures of the Nantlle valley below. In fact, images of Mynydd Mawr and its crags feature throughout most of the walk, beckoning impatiently as if to say 'You should be over here, not over there.'

↑ *Mynydd Drws y Coed and Trum y Ddysgl*

119

ROUTE INFORMATION

Distance	13km/8 miles
Height gain	1025m/3360ft
Time	5–6 hours
Grade	energetic
Start point	SH571526

Getting there

Car park a little south of Rhyd Ddu village on the A4085 Beddgelert–Caernarfon road at the South Snowdon Station of the Welsh Highland Railway

Maps

(Ordnance Survey) OL17 Snowdon/Yr Wyddfa

After-walk refreshment

Ty Mawr tea room and the Cwellyn Arms pub in Rhyd Ddu; pubs and cafés in Beddgelert

Y Garn and the start of the Nantlle ridge

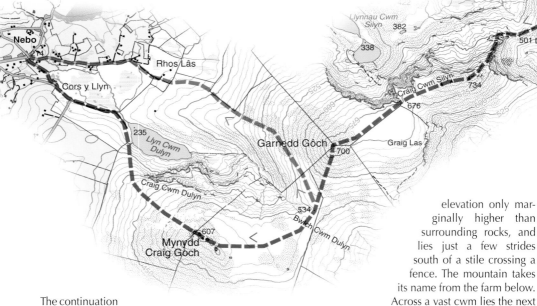

The continuation to Mynydd Drws y Coed, of which Y Garn is simply a northerly extension, soon turns from grass to rock, becoming steep and narrow in places, but is nowhere unduly difficult, though hands will be needed for balance in a few places. The summit of **Mynydd Drws y Coed** is a grassy elevation only marginally higher than surrounding rocks, and lies just a few strides south of a stile crossing a fence. The mountain takes its name from the farm below. Across a vast cwm lies the next summit, **Trum y Ddysgl**, the 'Ridge of the Dish', and takes its name from the shape of its northern cliffs when viewed from the valley. The mountain has outstanding structure, possessing two fine arêtes, glacial cwms and an abundance of rock. The summit, a delightful, elongated grassy ridge, breezy and

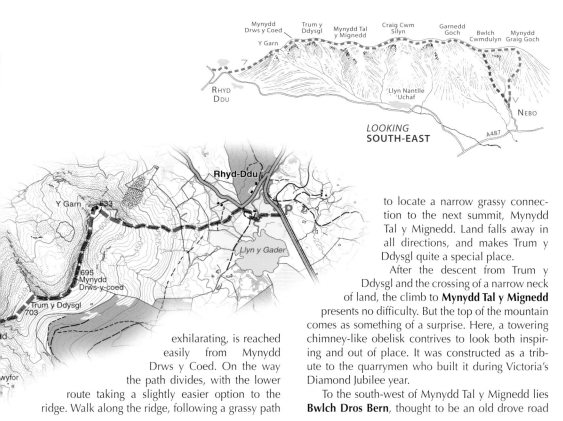

Mynydd Drws y Coed
Y Garn
Trum y Ddysgl
Mynydd Tal y Mignedd
Craig Cwm Silyn
Garnedd Goch
Bwlch Cwmdulyn
Mynydd Graig Goch

RHYD DDU

Llyn Nantlle Uchaf

NEBO

A487

LOOKING
SOUTH-EAST

Rhyd-Ddu

Y Garn 633

Llyn y Gader

695 Mynydd Drws-y-coed

Trum y Ddysgl 703

exhilarating, is reached easily from Mynydd Drws y Coed. On the way the path divides, with the lower route taking a slightly easier option to the ridge. Walk along the ridge, following a grassy path to locate a narrow grassy connection to the next summit, Mynydd Tal y Mignedd. Land falls away in all directions, and makes Trum y Ddysgl quite a special place.

After the descent from Trum y Ddysgl and the crossing of a narrow neck of land, the climb to **Mynydd Tal y Mignedd** presents no difficulty. But the top of the mountain comes as something of a surprise. Here, a towering chimney-like obelisk contrives to look both inspiring and out of place. It was constructed as a tribute to the quarrymen who built it during Victoria's Diamond Jubilee year.

To the south-west of Mynydd Tal y Mignedd lies **Bwlch Dros Bern**, thought to be an old drove road

Trum y Ddysgl viewed from the summit of Mynydd Drws y Coed

Busy day on Mynydd Tal y Mignedd

from Cwm Pennant to Nantlle, by which route the Pennant shepherds took their sheep to the market in Caernarfon, although it is difficult to find traces of the cross-route these days. The descent to the pass is at first in a southerly direction, by the line of a fence, and then south-west.

Bwlch Dros Bern seems to mark a change in character: to the east, the four summits are narrow and twisting, and mostly grassy, while to the west, the remaining three summits are broader, more rocky and less serpentine.

From the pass there is a rocky ascent to the wider summit of **Craig Cwm Silyn** at the centre of the ridge, its summit lost in a rash of boulders, and the highest point of the Nantlle ridge.

The continuation westwards to **Garnedd Goch** is a straightforward walk, a diversion from which, to the northern edge of Craig Cwm Silyn, will reveal the Great Slab, a popular playground with rock climbers, poised above the twin turquoise lakes in Cwm Silyn below. Onward, the route soon joins a stone wall leading to the summit of Garnedd Goch.

The final summit along the ridge is **Mynydd Craig Goch**, a weird place of castellated and gnarled rocks overlooking the sea and the Lleyn peninsula. In 2008, Mynydd Craig Goch came of age, when, following resurveying, it was proven that the mountain achieved a height of 609.75m, and so exceeded, by 0.49 feet, the long-held criterion for status as a mountain – 2000 feet!

To reach Mynydd Craig Goch, the 'new' Welsh mountain, from Garnedd Goch, descend steeply by a wall until you can conveniently cross it, and then follow another wall to the col between the two mountains, **Bwlch Cwmdulyn**. The continuation from the bwlch is not direct, and heads first in a southerly direction before taking to gently rising ground westwards.

From the summit, descend in a north-westerly direction to the outflow of Llyn Cwm Dulyn, and then by lanes to Nebo, or wherever you are being picked up. Possibly easier would be to backtrack to Bwlch Cwmdulyn and follow a path across the western flank of Garnedd Goch down towards **Cors y Llyn**, and so to Nebo.

The linking col between Mynydd Tal y Mignedd and Trum y Ddysgl

Moel Hebog,
Moel yr Ogof and Moel Lefn

*T*he distinctive Moel Hebog, the Hill of the Hawk, presides over the touristy grey-stone village *of Beddgelert, which is a perfect starting point to follow in the footsteps of visitors of yesteryear who came from far and wide to enjoy the views from its summit. North of Hebog, two lower summits, cocky little rough-and-ready siblings, invite you to stay on the hills rather than skedaddle back the way you came, and while finding a way back through Beddgelert Forest may pose a few problems of route-finding, the abiding sensation will be of having experienced a great day in the hills.*

The Route

The key to this walk is a bridge spanning the river in Nant Colwyn, on the A4085 Beddgelert to Caernarfon road about 500m from the centre of the village.

Beddgelert is reputedly named after a story of how Llywelyn the Great mistakenly killed his favourite hound in the belief that it had attacked his child, when in reality it had attacked and slain a wolf.

But it is now believed that there is no substance to the Gelert legend, and that it was actually fostered with an eye to the main chance by local innkeeper, David Pritchard, during the 19th century. The village is probably named after an early Christian leader called Celert (or Cilert) who settled here early in the 8th century.

One of the particular delights of the area has been the re-opening as a heritage narrow-gauge

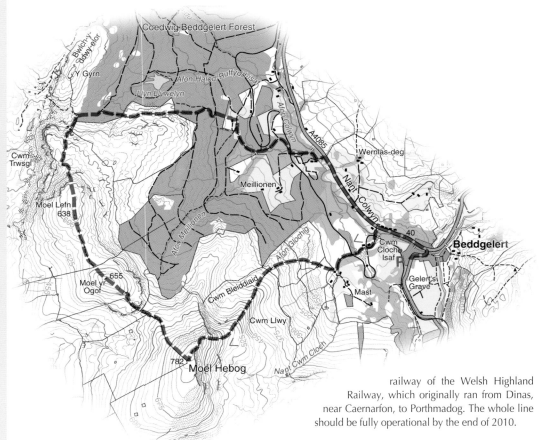

ROUTE INFORMATION

Distance	12.5km/8 miles
Height gain	945m/3100ft
Time	4–5 hours
Grade	energetic
Start point	SH587481

Getting there
Along the A498 Aberglaslyn road, there is
a large car park not far from the Royal Goat
Hotel

Maps
(Harvey Superwalker) Snowdon and the
Moelwynion; (Ordnance Survey) OL17
Snowdon/Yr Wyddfa

After-walk refreshment
Numerous cafés, restaurants, pubs and hotels
in Beddgelert

railway of the Welsh Highland
Railway, which originally ran from Dinas,
near Caernarfon, to Porthmadog. The whole line
should be fully operational by the end of 2010.

Cross the bridge over the **Colwyn** and take the track
beneath the restored railway line, past a couple
of farmhouses and through woods to reach a barn
(SH581479). Immediately after the barn go through
a gate, and follow the ongoing path, which is well-
defined and with attendant route markers.

A short distance further on, the climbing starts,
and it is a steep and energetic haul all the way to
the summit of Moel Hebog. The path continues up
an ill-defined ridge and swings to the left, below
the spectacular crags, Y Diffwys, after which there
is some mild scrambling. The path becomes rocky
and the route is marked by small cairns that deline-
ate a way up through the crags to a grassy shoulder,
which in turn leads to another short rocky stretch
and the summit plateau. The summit of **Moel Hebog**
is marked by a trig pillar near a stone wall.

There is something unreal about the retrospective
view of Yr Aran and Snowdon that opens up as
you climb **Moel Hebog**. It is nothing more than
the fact that the mountains are being seen from

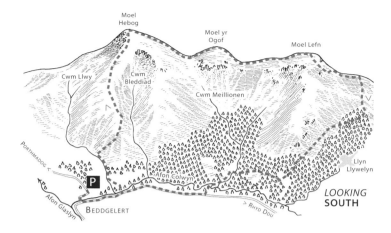

an unfamiliar angle, but for a moment your mind struggles to identify the mountains. The view across Aberglaslyn reaches to Cnicht and the Moelwynion, which contrive to restrict further views to the south.

From the summit of Moel Hebog the next leg of the walk descends steeply north following the wall to the impressive rocky assemblage at the foot of Moel yr Ogof. From here it is a short but steep climb to the top of Moel yr Ogof. This is a small, compact mountain with interesting rocky outcrops on its summit, among which fossils may still be found.

Moel yr Ogof, the 'Hill of the Cave', commemorates the ubiquitous Owain Glyndwr who was compelled to seek refuge in a cave, still to be found by a route up through the Beddgelert Forest. Glyndwr (c1354/1359–c1416) has remained a notable figure in the popular culture of both Wales and England, portrayed in Shakespeare's play *Henry IV, Part 1* (as

Moel Hebog from Nantgwynant

Nantgwynant and Moel Hebog

Owen Glendower) as a wild and exotic man ruled by magic and emotion. In 1400, Glyndwr instigated the Welsh Revolt against the rule of Henry IV, and although initially successful, the uprising was eventually put down. Glyndwr was last seen in 1412, and was never captured, nor tempted by Royal Pardons and never betrayed. His final years remain a complete mystery. Glyndwr is to Wales what Bonnie Prince Charlie is to Scotland, the rightful heir forced to run for his life.

Leaving Moel yr Ogof head north again descending to a col before climbing once more onto the summit of **Moel Lefn**.

Moel Lefn is separated from the splendid walking country of the Nantlle ridge by a narrow pass, **Bwlch y Ddwy Elor**, the Pass of the Two Biers, signifying that this is an old corpse road from Cwm Pennant to Rhyd Ddu.

Descend northwards from Moel Lefn to a forest stile at SH554495. The return route through the forest is far from clear, but succumbs to thoughtful navigation. The forest is in popular use, and there are many walkers' trails and cycling routes, which can be confusing. But the general direction is east.

Cross the stile into the forest, and when you come to a forest trail follow it left for less than 200m to a waymark. After about 250m, leave the forest over another stile to cross an open area of bog, boulders and heather. Re-enter the plantation at yet another stile, and eventually reach a forest trail at SH567497. Now the simplest direction is to follow forest trails south and then east until you reach the campsite at SH577491. The route through the lower part of the forest has been slightly affected by the re-opening of the railway. From the campsite, walk out to the main road, turn right and soon return to your starting point in Beddgelert.

SIABOD
AND THE
MOELWYNION

The final slopes up to Cnicht summit (Walk 24)

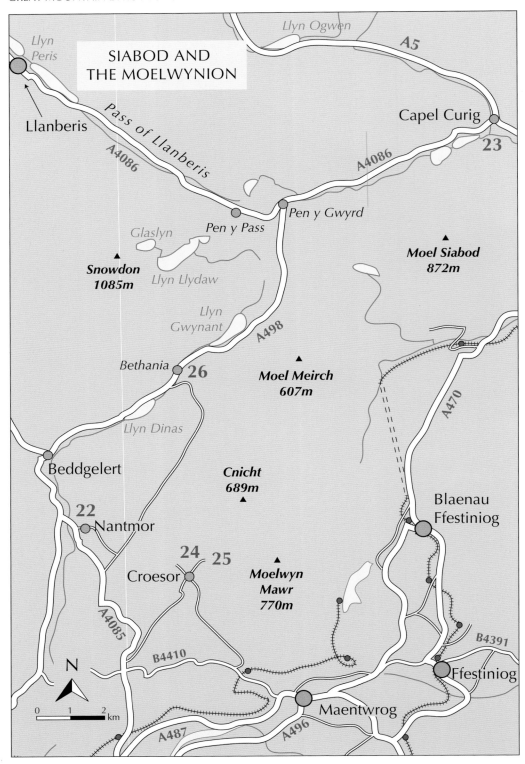

SIABOD AND
THE MOELWYNION

Llyn Ogwen

A5

Llyn Peris

Llanberis

Pass of Llanberis

A4086

Capel Curig

A4086

23

Pen y Gwyrd

Glaslyn

Pen y Pass

Moel Siabod
872m

Snowdon
1085m

Llyn Llydaw

Llyn Gwynant

A498

Bethania

26

Moel Meirch
607m

A470

Llyn Dinas

Beddgelert

Cnicht
689m

Blaenau
Ffestiniog

22

Nantmor

24

25

Croesor

Moelwyn
Mawr
770m

A4085

B4391

B4410

Ffestiniog

N

0   1   2 km

A487

A496

Maentwrog

SIABOD AND THE MOELWYNION

In the days before the re-organisation of local government in 1974, the Moelwyns were in Merionydd; now they are part of Gwynedd, not that there is anything wrong with Gwynedd – it is, after all, the name of an ancient kingdom that lasted from Roman times until the 13th century – it's just that Sir Feirionydd has a pleasing ring about it. As an aside, Merionethshire (the Anglicised version) made a brief re-appearance in the 1990s when a further carve up of districts created 'Caernarfonshire and Merionethshire' as a principal area, whereupon one of the first acts of the new council was to rebrand itself as 'Gwynedd'.

What distinguishes Merioneth is that it contains more high upland in proportion to its area than any of the other ancient shires of Wales. Its mountains are certainly different. You have only to compare the hills north and south of Nantgwynant to see that. To the north lies the Snowdon massif, bearing the juggernauts of Snowdonia's catalogue of mountains,

while to the south all that fearsome rock and steep, rocky slopes gives way to a landscape that is much more rugged and broken, more fecund and diverse, and certainly much lower in height. Here the hills have greater variety – in their shape and form, their colour, their myriad lakes, few of which are other than idyllic. There is, too, a tang of wildness which can leave you bewildered, in the original sense of the word – lost in a wilderness – and space and peace and lakes whose dazzling reflections leave you wondering at times where the water ends and the sky begins, reminiscent of the Outer Hebrides of Scotland.

Despite having in its midst two of the most enjoyable summits in Snowdonia, Moel Siabod and Cnicht, the Moelwynion as a whole are relatively unvisited. Siabod is a little remote to be wholly embraced within the Moelwynion, to which it is linked by a long stretch of bog and heather, but the agents of convenience impose some sort of order on the book.

↑ *Cwm Bychan (Walk 22)*

Snowdon and Y Lliwedd from Moel Meirch (Walk 26)

At the extreme western end of this vast area lies the spectacular gorge of the Aberglaslyn Pass, just south of the village of Beddgelert.

The landscape of the Moelwynion is a contradiction: rugged and demanding, and yet relaxing, long on eventually and short on now, offering numerous days when finding some sheltered cranny and hunkering down with no sense of urgency while you put the world to rights is all that matters. Lakes abound; you can count 15 from the summit of Moelwyn Mawr, and yet because of the complex geology, they sit a different heights, dotted randomly about the place, some looking perilously close to tipping over the edge and spilling away.

And then there is the industry, or what remains of it. The scars of slate quarrying are everywhere, but only to the east, where Blaenau Ffestiniog, that great hole in the National Park, sits amid ramparts of spoil, is the scenery marred to any extent.

In 1798, the Rev John Evans crossed the Moelwyn and lamented that he saw no sign of man making any effort to improve the land. He was appalled by 'the dreary aspect and awful desolation', where there was 'no vestige of a dwelling, no mark of a human footstep'. Of course, the slate industry changed all that, but now that has had its day, leaving behind a quiet emptiness that walkers have come to value as precious.

Near the head of Cwm Bychan, looking across to Y Lliwedd (Walk 22) →

Aberglaslyn,
Llyn Dinas and Cwm Bychan

*T*he village of Beddgelert flanks the confluence of the Afon Glaslyn, flowing through Nantgwynant, and the Afon Colwyn, which rises on the south-western slopes of Snowdon. Beddgelert today is a popular tourist destination (see Walk 21), and for this reason the walk begins not from the busy village but from Nantmor, to the south of the Aberglaslyn Pass, which has the added advantage of allowing you to chill out in the scenic splendour of Cwm Bychan only minutes from the end of the walk. It was possible, until 2000, to walk along the trackbed of the Welsh Highland Railway, between Nantmor and Beddgelert, but with the re-opening of the railway this is no longer possible. The alternative is a marvellous rocky passageway through the gorge, following a fisherman's path that hugs the river with an intensity that is to be admired. This walk is the shortest in the book, and does not visit a mountain summit, but it crams so much in and is always possible, even when the surrounding summits have their heads in cloud.

The Route

Beside the toilet block a gate gives onto a path going left for Pont Aberglaslyn, climbing through bracken and into light woodland above the road. Continue as far as the bridge, but do not cross it. Instead, take to an undulating fisherman's path, rocky and rooty, on the right along the true left bank of the Afon Glaslyn. Proximity to the river, and the fact that it is

↑ *Llyn Dinas*

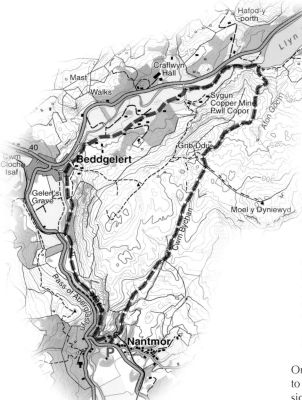

passing through a narrow defile with steep sides cloaked in vegetation, conditions that are much favoured by starry saxifrage, means that the path is often slippery. This route through the **Pass of Aberglaslyn** is of considerable beauty, but its finer points are best appreciated while standing still rather than marching onward.

Perhaps surprisingly, as recently as the early 19th century, the **Afon Glaslyn** was navigable at high tide by small boats as far as Pont Aberglaslyn. In the sixth century a monastery existed here, succeeded in the 12th century by an Augustinian priory. The Middle Ages were a period when Beddgelert, cloistered among high mountains, was seen as a welcome resting place before travelling further, and the route from the coast via Beddgelert to Caernarfon or Bangor via Llyn Cwellyn was preferable to the long trek round the Lleyn Peninsula.

On the way through the gorge, you pass the entrance to an old mine tunnel; this is flooded for some considerable distance and yields nothing of interest and

ROUTE INFORMATION

Distance	8.5km/5¼ miles
Height gain	540m/1770ft
Time	3 hours
Grade	moderate
Start point	SH597462

Getting there
Wooded car park (Pay and Display) with toilets off the A4085, which leaves the A498 just after it exits the Aberglaslyn gorge, south of Beddgelert

Maps
(Harvey Superwalker) Snowdon and the Moelwynion; (Ordnance Survey) OL17 Snowdon/Yr Wyddfa

After-walk refreshment
Numerous cafés, restaurants, pubs and hotels in Beddgelert

The Afon Glaslyn and distant Moel Hebog from Llyn Dinas

133

LOOKING
NORTH-EAST

gorge and the way onward to Beddgelert opens up, running parallel with the railway. Beside the path stands a particularly fine specimen of a tall yellow-flowered plant known as Great Mullein, and also as Aaron's Rod.

Eventually you reach a point where you need to cross the railway. Continue beyond, without crossing the nearby footbridge spanning the river, and instead walk easily onward along a surfaced path to **Beddgelert**. As you reach the edge of the village, do not cross the nearby footbridge, but keep right, walking between the river and the village green to pass the end of a terrace of cottages. Cross a lane at the next bridge, and then continue through a kissing-gate to follow a gravel path, which leads to a ladder-stile giving on to a narrow lane.

much of unhappy consequence if you venture too far. Poke your nose inside to satisfy curiosity, but go no further.

A short way further on, following repairs to this fisherman's path, a short section has had iron hand holds fixed into a rock; then you are through the

Turn right, and walk along the lane to the Victorian **Sygun Copper Mine**, closed in 1903 but re-opened as a tourist attraction in 1986. As you approach the mine, leave the lane by branching left through bracken and in front of a cottage to reach the metalled access lane to the mine. Turn left through a wide wall gap and walk down towards a nearby bridge. Don't cross the bridge but bear right along a riparian path that leads agreeably on to reach the shore of Llyn Dinas.

The village green, Beddgelert

On the way you pass below **Dinas Emrys**, a rocky, wooded hillock which has lent its name to nearby Llyn Dinas and given rise to the enduring legend of the Red Dragon, the emblem of Wales. The hill is no more than an Iron Age hill fort that post-dates Roman times, but its roots lie deep within Arthurian legend, according to which, when the warlord Vortigern fled to Wales to escape Anglo-Saxon invaders, he chose this near-impregnable hill as the site for his royal retreat. Every day Vortigern's men worked at erecting defensive towers; but each morning they returned to find their efforts destroyed. This continued until Vortigern was advised to seek the help of a young boy born of a virgin mother. The King sent his soldiers out to find such a lad; the boy they found was named Myrddin Emrys (Merlin Ambrosius).

Following the advice of his counsellors, Vortigern planned to kill the boy to appease the supernatural powers preventing him from completing his fortress. But, perhaps not surprisingly, Merlin scorned the advice, and explained that the hill concealed a hidden pool containing two dragons, and how the White Dragon of the Saxons, although winning the battle for the moment, would be defeated by the Red Dragon. In time, the fort was named Emrys Wledig (Ambrosius Aurelianus), hence Dinas Emrys. Of course, there are many more legends surrounding this hill, and the people who sought to live there, but only this one explains the Red Dragon of Wales.

Pass through a gate to reach the shores of **Llyn Dinas**, and bear immediately right onto a stepped, stony path, rising through a spread of bracken, heather and bilberry. After a steep ascent, the gradient eases as the path enters a vast hummocky hollow of considerable enchantment. Follow the path, level for a while, and then climbing again to reach a three-way signpost, close by the spill from copper mine workings.

Turn left at the signpost for Aberglaslyn, following a path through rich banks of bell heather that leads to a ladder-stile spanning a fence. Cross the stile and now go forward and down into neatly framed **Cwm Bychan**. What follows is pure delight, a lovely natural garden from which not even the gaunt remains of a cableway associated with the copper mines detract; if anything they add a poignancy.

It was in hidden **Cwm Bychan** that scenes from the 1958 film *The Inn of the Sixth Happiness*, starring Ingrid Bergman, were filmed. The film was the true story of Gladys Aylward (1902–1970), who became a missionary to China during the years leading up to World War II. Llyn Dinas, Ogwen and Nant Ffrancon also featured in the film.

Lower down you enter woodland, with ample opportunity to divert to the stream, but as you pass into a woodland clearing, a bridge supporting the railway line invites you through. On the other side, a few strides return you to the car park at Nantmor.

← *Looking down into Cwm Bychan*

Moel Siabod

L ying so close to higher and more extensive ranges of mountains, and dogged by the disadvantage of being an isolated mountain that is difficult to link with any other, you might expect Moel Siabod to be neglected. Far from it; this is a superb viewpoint and has an excellent line of ascent that is rugged and refreshing amid so many acres of undulating boggy moorland. Lacking an especially pleasing profile when viewed, say, from Snowdon, Moel Siabod presents a most shapely aspect to Capel Curig, and that is the allure.

The Route

Leave the car park and turn right, walking towards Capel Curig, and soon reaching a small viewing platform in the wall on the left that gives a splendid outlook over the always dramatic Afon Llugwy. Walk on a little further and take the first turning on the left, a narrow lane, to cross **Pont Cyfyng**. Over the bridge, ignore the footpath on the right, and continue instead to reach the first building of this small community, and there branch right across a cattle grid and onto a surfaced lane, signposted for Moel Siabod.

When the rising, surfaced lane swings sharply to the right, leave it for a slaty gravel path on the left that climbs across a low shoulder above a farm and through rock outcrops to join another broad track. Turn left to a ladder-stile-gate beyond which the broad track continues, almost immediately bringing the peaked profile of Moel Siabod into view.

Keep following a track up onto rough moorland, always aiming for the mountain. At a gate and stile you enter Access Land with an old track that once served the quarries leading arrow-straight towards

↑ *The east ridge of Moel Siabod (the descent uses the prominent green gully to the right of centre)*

ROUTE INFORMATION

Distance	9km/5½ miles
Height gain	760m/2495ft
Time	4–5 hours
Grade	energetic
Start point	Bryn Glô car park (SH737570), on A5.

Getting there
A convenient, free car park south-east of Capel Curig along the A5, with stunning views of the tempestuous Afon Llugwy

Maps
(Harvey Superwalker) Snowdon and the Moelwynion; (Ordnance Survey) OL17 Snowdon/Yr Wyddfa and OL18 Harlech, Porthmadog and Bala

After-walk refreshment
Cafés, pubs and hotels in Capel Curig

The Afon Llugwy, near Capel Curig

your target. As the track starts to level, you come to another gate-stile. (Off to the right at this point is another ladder-stile, your target on the return leg.)

The ongoing track heads for a quarry, runs on to pass a small dammed lake then climbs through quarry workings, mildly unsightly but quite fascinating and encouraging a respect for the toughness of the men that worked these isolated places. Further on, a quarry lake, fed by two waterfalls, is quite a surprise. The path passes to the left and climbs above the waterfalls continuing as a stony but often wet path to a low col where the fine ridge of Daear Ddu and **Llyn y Foel** ease into view.

Studded with islands, **Llyn y Foel** is a neat circle of water – if you're not very good at drawing circles – with a small stony dam at the eastern end. Jim Perrin, writing in *Visions of Snowdonia*, identifies this lake as Llyn Llygad yr Ych, the Lake of the Ox's Eye. This links to the legend that the lake was formed when the eye of an ox came out under the exertion of dragging a monster – an *afangc* – from Betws y Coed, over the watershed to Glaslyn directly below Snowdon. Herbert Carr tells the same story in *The Mountains*

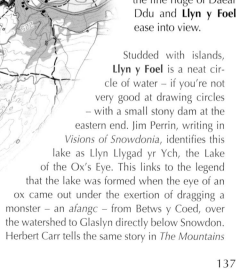

137

Moel Siabod

Llyn y Foel

LOOKING WEST

Afon Llugwy

Pont Cyfyng

P

of Snowdonia, but relates how the creature was dragged over a pass between Moel Siabod and Carnedd y Cribau, Bwlch Rhiw'r Ychen (Bwlch Rhiw-yr-Ychain in the book). It was, according to Carr, the strain of crossing the pass that caused the ox to lose its eye, pointing rather more to one of the Llynnau Diwaunedd being the legendary Llyn Llygad yr Ych rather than Llyn y Foel.

Descend to cross marshy ground at the western end of Llyn y Foel. An alternative circling path clings to dry ground for a little longer but this route leads to a clear path that sets about the ascent of Daear Ddu. This is an excellent ridge, one that offers both a difficult line, for those happy to figure things out for themselves, and also a well-trodden route that dodges around, through, up and over numerous boulders and ledges. Both are excellent and most enjoyable, and pop you out at the top of **Moel Siabod** close by the trig pillar, which sits on a little plinth amid a rocky landscape.

There is little in print about the derivation of the name **Moel Siabod**, or more correctly Carnedd Moel Siabod, although the mountain is one of just a few mentioned on John Evans' map of 1795, where the spelling is rendered as 'Shiabod'. There is a suggestion that 'Si' before a vowel denotes a word borrowed from the English, as in *siop*. But there is no certainty

The ridge of Daear Ddu leading to the summit of Moel Siabod

Quarry pool, Moel Siabod

about the name, which may come from the Middle English *schabbed*, meaning 'scabbed'.

Not far from the trig pillar is a large stone shelter. To begin the descent, walk to this. Moel Siabod has a fine rocky ridge rippling away in a north-easterly direction, and that is the way to go, although not necessarily along the crest of the descending ridge, as this is awkward in a few places.

Keep to the left of the ridge, following an indistinct path and studiously ignoring a very prominent track that descends towards Capel Curig (see alternative finish). Your objective is a pair of ladder-stiles over a fence at SH711554. Cross the fenceline here and continue below a downfall of boulders following a narrow grassy path and soon passing a bubbling spring of clear water.

After a fairly gentle initial descent the ground steepens and the track used at the start of the walk now comes into view. A little further on the gradient steepens even more, calling for care in the placement of feet when the path goes down a stony gully. Once beyond the gully, the descent continues as a broad grassy ramp sloping down the end of the ridge.

At the bottom of the descent you cross a collapsed wall and press on in the same direction a little further across rough ground to a ladder-stile. Over this you soon join the outward track at SH724563, and can now savour the enchanting descent facing into the verdant loveliness of the valleys ahead, above which rise the craggy tops of Creigiau Gleision and Pen Llithrig y Wrach. Simply follow your outward route back to Pont Cyfyng.

Alternative finish: On the descent from the summit of Moel Siabod you can bear left (east of north), taking a broad path, which doesn't start at the top of the mountain but a little way down it. This is an old pony track along which Victorian visitors used to ride to the top of the mountain. It leads down into woodland to the south of Plas y Brenin, and at a couple of points – the last being just before you cross the river – you can turn to the east through woodland to emerge at the river's edge, where you can turn right, alongside the river to the footpath noticed at the start of the walk close by Pont Cyfyng.

Cnicht
and Cwm Croesor

*T*here is a sharp, conical symmetry about Cnicht when seen from the south-west, and a dramatic
*presence as it rises above Cwm Croesor. This shapeliness has earned it the nickname 'The
Matterhorn of Wales', although, to be fair, it looks nothing like the Matterhorn. Even so, it is a
devilishly attractive and inviting mountain despite not linking comfortably with any other summits,
except perhaps Moelwyn Mawr. Yet as a mountain in its own right it offers a splendid yomp blessed
with excellent views that embrace the whole of the National Park.*

The Route

Leave the car park, turning right along the lane
through Croesor, and climb out of the village, continuing to the end of the lane where a ladder-stile-
gate gives onto a stony track climbing into broadleaved woodland.

The village of **Croesor** is small, sitting at the end of
a glaciated valley accessed by a narrow lane that
runs past the stylish structures of Plas Brondanw,
the old family home of Clough Williams-Ellis, the
man behind the lavish creation of Portmeirion.
Apart from a few farms, all is quiet in the valley
now, but it once resounded to the mayhem of

↑ *The final slopes up to Cnicht summit*

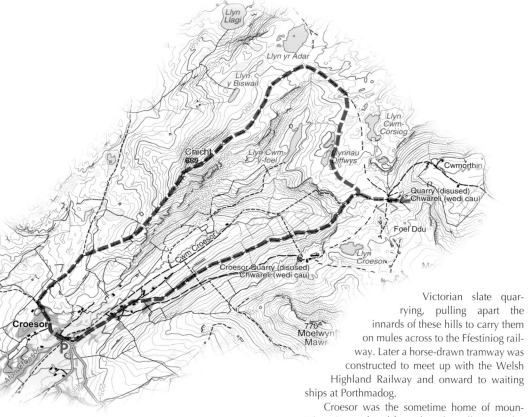

ROUTE INFORMATION

Distance	11km/7 miles
Height gain	620m (2035ft)
Time	4 hours
Grade	moderate
Start point	SH632447

Getting there
National Park (Pay and Display) car park at Croesor, reached by a narrow lane running north-east from Garreg on the A4085.

Maps
(Harvey Superwalker) Snowdon and the Moelwynion; (Ordnance Survey) OL17 Snowdon/Yr Wyddfa, and OL18 Harlech, Porthmadog and Bala

After-walk refreshment
Café at the entrance to Cwm Croesor, directly accessible from the car park

Victorian slate quarrying, pulling apart the innards of these hills to carry them on mules across to the Ffestiniog railway. Later a horse-drawn tramway was constructed to meet up with the Welsh Highland Railway and onward to waiting ships at Porthmadog.

Croesor was the sometime home of mountain writer and prolific author Showell 'Pip' Styles (1908–2005), one of the last links with the great descriptive writers who frequented the hills during the inter-war years. In Croesor, Styles kept the village post office until it closed in the 1960s.

At a high point in the path the track divides. Bear right through a gate and now follow a fine, stony track that steers you towards that splendid profile of Cnicht. The ascent is by way of an interesting rocky ridge, steep in places but only moderately narrow, with the summit beckoning you on like an impatient child the whole time. The track climbs steadily, and eventually comes to a ladder-stile in a wall, with a view northwards across a gap to the Snowdon Horseshoe. From the stile, the path crosses a short stretch of rock downfall before gaining the final pull to the summit of **Cnicht**.

The name '**Cnicht**' – 'Cynicht' on early maps and guidebooks – is said to have derived from the Anglo-Saxon for a knight, supposedly given by sailors in the estuary from its fanciful resemblance to a helmet from those distant times.

141

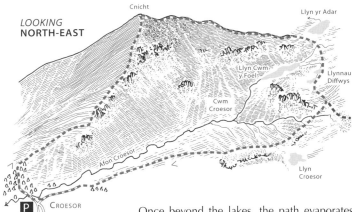

LOOKING **NORTH-EAST**

The summit is a neat, rocky point from which the ridge runs onward in a north-easterly direction, with a number of grassy paths splaying out to give you a choice of route to a cairn at a dip at SH657478, just above **Llyn yr Adar**.

At the cairn you start heading in a south-easterly direction, following a clear path that runs across a hummocky landscape eventually to descend towards the complex plateau that holds the quarry site of Rhosydd. In a few places the path is vague, but a useful target, once you have crossed the head of the Afon Cwm y Foel are the twin lakes of **Llynnau Diffwys**, although initially only one, containing a small island, is visible. There is another path branching more directly towards Rhosydd, but that passing the lakes offers the prospect of a few moments dallying on the lake shores, or even on its little island if you can get there dry-shod.

Once beyond the lakes, the path evaporates altogether, but with the Rhosydd quarry buildings soon coming into sight below and to the south-east, you can descend trackless ground to join the broad and prominent bed of a tramway that served the quarry.

A short **extension** to visit the quarry remains would not be out of order, and Walk 25 contains information about Rhosydd. It is a simple enough stroll to the east, crossing a ladder-stile by an isolated store, possibly a powder storehouse, to reach the ruins, and then return.

Leaving the summit of Cnicht

Llynnau Diffwys and Cnicht

Having reached the old tramway, head west (right) for a short distance, keeping an eye open for a small cairn just at the side of the track on the left. This marks the start of a path descending initially through a few rocky outcrops, but then turning into a most splendid, steadily descending traverse of the north slopes of Moelwyn Mawr, high above **Cwm Croesor** with Cnicht rising magisterially on the other side of the valley. Gradually walled fields appear as you descend into the tamed lower part of the valley, and the cultivated enclosures yield a most intense greenness and vibrancy.

The path eventually comes down to a gate and stile at SH643452. Here, cross the stile and descend a sloping pasture, roughly parallel with a collapsed and turfed wall. This feeds into a farm track that leads down to another stile/gate just above the first of the farm buildings (Moelwyn Banc). Cross the stile and walk on a few strides to join a more substantial access track that now leads out of the valley, concluding at a convenient café serving light refreshments, after which bear right to return to the car park.

143

Moelwyn Mawr and Moelwyn Bach

*G*azing down on so much industrial dereliction, the Moelwyns, on the face of it, are far from appealing. But there is much of interest here, not least those industrial remnants, which will fascinate anyone with an interest in Victorian endeavour. But the wider landscape also yields some of the finest walking in Snowdonia, a place for which the word tortuous seems to have been coined. Fine hilltops offer splendid walks across a countryside of heathery hummocks and hollows, many filled with lakes, that enable you to walk for hours without the slightest hint of quarrying and mining. The two Moelwyns do not have this luxury, but they are excellent viewpoints, arguably the best in Snowdonia, their conquest other than by the simple grassy ridges that descend to the west is anything but straightforward, testing the route-finding mettle of the best. The complexities of the terrain, and the surfeit or shafts, holes, adits and assorted ironmongery make this a hazardous place in poor visibility: save it for a good day.

↑ *Moelwyn Mawr and Moelwyn Bach*

ROUTE INFORMATION

Distance	11km/7 miles
Height gain	810m/2660ft
Time	4–5 hours
Grade	energetic
Start point	SH632447

Getting there
National Park (Pay and Display) car park at Croesor, reached by a narrow lane running north-east from Garreg on the A4085

Maps
(Harvey Superwalker) Snowdon and the Moelwynion; (Ordnance Survey) OL17 Snowdon/Yr Wyddfa, and OL18 Harlech, Porthmadog and Bala

After-walk refreshment
Café at the entrance to Cwm Croesor, directly accessible from the car park

The Route
The difficulties of this route, such as they are, lie between the ruins of the Rhosydd quarry and Moelwyn Bach. First it will be industrial remnants that queer the pitch, then the craggy nature of the two hills themselves, which call for careful route-finding; no amount of route description is going to be helpful here. But outwith this hiatus all is sweetness and light, a fine, steady rise above **Cwm Croesor** followed by a long grassy descent of Moelwyn Bach's west ridge.

Go through the car park at Croesor, taking the path to the café, and there turn left along a surfaced lane. Maintain the same direction when passing farms until you reach Moelwyn Banc, the last of a line of farmsteads. Just as you reach the farm, bear right to a ladder-stile and follow a track and collapsed wall up the field to another stile, where you join a splendid path that slants across the northern slopes of Moelwyn Mawr. This is the path used in descent in Walk 24.

The path rises in easy stages, until finally it climbs through the headwall of the valley and intercepts an old tramway that served the Rhosydd quarry. Turn right along this and walk to the **quarry ruins**.

Ruins, Rhosydd quarry

Water-filled tunnel, Rhosydd

Rhosydd Quarry, which ceased working in the 1920s, affects everyone. As Jim Perrin puts it in *Visions of Snowdonia*: 'The dereliction, the strange displacement of former industry to a remote and mountainous setting seizes on the imagination'. Long before Perrin wrote his book, I visited this locality, and was moved to poetry.

> 'High
> among encircling hills
> whose hearts you tore for gain
> Remnants
> gaunt and grey still stand
> their walls hard
> against the changing hand of
> Time
> slowly taking back, concealing
> what you stole, or left behind
> to scar this once proud land.'

Clearly I am unlikely ever to be a candidate for Poet Laureate, but this singular offering reflects the atmosphere felt on that first visit more than twenty years ago. It was every bit as potent when visited recently; it is the paradox, the over-burdening sense of the end of a crucial period in man's industrial history contrasted with the implicit ravage and exploitation.

Behind the main quarry buildings is a large and wet tunnel into the hillside, and beside it a slaty ramp by which you gain higher ground (resist the temptation to enter the tunnel). The ascent passes tiny **Llyn Croesor**, which looks forlorn among so much darkness – but with the sun in its heaven, Llyn Croesor sparkles with the best of them.

Once above the ramp, you eventually arrive at a large reedy area framed by spoil that has been shaped into a trackbed. Off to the left, **Moel yr Hydd** looks inviting, but the easiest way to it means trekking far off-route beyond the quarry site to a low col to the south-west of the summit and walking easily up from there. The direct ascent of Moelwyn Mawr bears

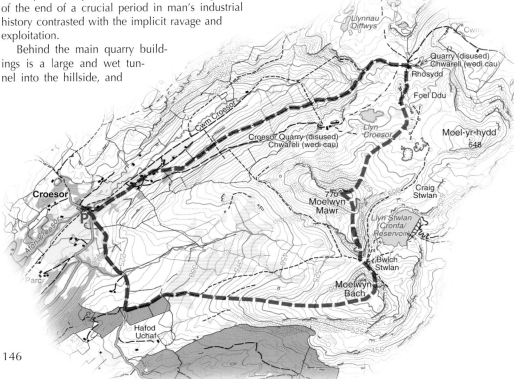

Moelwyn Mawr
Moelwyn Bach
Bwlch Stwlan
Llyn Croesor
Rhosydd
Afon Maesgwm
Cwm Croesor
Afon Croesor
CROESOR
P
LOOKING **SOUTH-WEST**

right from the reedy area, following a clear if damp path towards a ladder-stile, which is not needed, as the path passes to its left, and follows a clear route onto the shallow north ridge of **Moelwyn Mawr** and then steeply up to the squat and tidy trig pillar on the summit, trending right near the top. It is possible to count 15 or more lakes from the top of Moelwyn Mawr, and the view, notwithstanding the dereliction, is one of the finest in Wales for extent, beauty and diversity.

The continuation to Moelwyn Bach will call for some thought. Begin by going east from the trig, but only for about 100m, and then turn right and descend the south ridge in a series of rock steps, crossing the subsidiary summit of Craig Ysgafn, to the pronounced pass of **Bwlch Stwlan**, marked by a large cairn. Above, **Moelwyn Bach**'s crags look impenetrable and shaky, not so much a scramble as a crumble. You can avoid them by ascending a clear path diagonally left that will take you to the grassy eastern spur of the mountain, from where the summit is readily attained.

Finishing the walk simply involves descending the long grassy western ridge of Moelwyn Bach, romping downwards to a small plantation through which you finally gain a narrow lane. Turn right, descend to cross the **Afon Maesgwm** and then climb easily on the other side, following it for about 1.5km (1 mile) back to Croesor.

Mynydd Moel from the slopes of Cnicht

Moel Meirch
and Ysgafell Wen

*T*he area around Moel Meirch on the southern side of Nantgwynant is one of endearing
ruggedness, a place of wild and extravagant beauty that is rarely visited. The ground dips and
twists endlessly, knuckles of rock bare their bones everywhere, the ground is often wet underfoot,
yet it remains a region of great appeal, and without doubt a place to practise the skills of navigation.
The convoluted nature of the terrain means that the walk seems much longer than it is, while the
preponderance of lakes might well earn this hinterland the sobriquet 'The Welsh Lake District'. There
is certainly no shortage of water.

The Route

A fair bit of road walking starts and finishes this walk,
but with what Moel Meirch and Ysgafell Wen have
in store, it will be appreciated, and much easier on
the feet. So, leave the car park at Pont Bethania, turn
left along the road towards Beddgelert and take the
first lane on the left, a narrow road that immediately
crosses the **Afon Glaslyn**. Follow the lane for just
under 2km (1¼ miles), and then, at a right bend, you

can leave the lane down a gravel track at a footpath
sign for 'Edno'. After about 150m, turn left towards
Hafodydd Brithion as the track divides, bearing left
around a small spruce plantation, and then beyond a
ladder-stile-gate, following a broad track around the
edge of rough pasture.

Just as you approach the farm, leave the track by
bearing right through a gate (waymark), onto a path
through the edge of light, broadleaved woodland and

↑ *Moel Meirch*

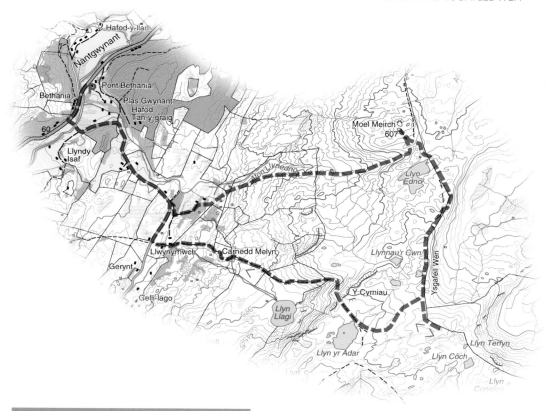

ROUTE INFORMATION

Distance	14.5km/9 miles
Height gain	845m/2770ft
Time	5 hours
Grade	energetic
Start point	National Park car park, Pont Bethania, Nantgwynant (SH628507)

Getting there
Nantgwynant; there is a small car park (Pay and Display) and adjacent toilets next to Pont Bethania

Maps
(Harvey Superwalker) Snowdon and the Moelwynion; (Ordnance Survey) OL17 Snowdon/Yr Wyddfa

After-walk refreshment
Gwynedd Café near the start, along the road towards Beddgelert; pubs in Beddgelert, at Pen y Gwryd, and Pen y Pass

alongside a lush, moss-covered wall. Wander along the path a little further where, at a gate, it gives into another even rougher pasture, fed and crossed by streams. Cross the streams, bearing left to another gate and on to a rising path until just after passing through a wall gap and, beside a large sycamore below a ruined building, you can branch left towards an obvious ravine, and passing two young rowan trees beside a narrow stream (waymark), beyond which a stile crosses a wall.

Over the wall turn left and enjoy a hugely delightful ramble through the gorge, down which flows the Afon Llynedno. The gorge is flanked by numerous rock outcrops among which *rhododendron ponticum* flourishes in abundance. This ravine now steers you along the next stage in the walk. For the most part there is a continuous path, but it is often wet and occasionally unclear. Your objective is simply to head up the ravine and enjoy the experience. Towards the top, you cross the infant **Afon Llynedno**, and press on still higher until, almost at the high point of the ravine, you can bear left and climb onto the pointy top of **Moel Meirch**.

LOOKING
SOUTH-EAST

Moel Meirch is a fabulous viewpoint, and if having a height of 607m gives the mountain more distinction than it would if the height was expressed in feet (1991ft), then metrication was well justified on that count alone. To the north-east Moel Siabod squats on the skyline, while the Glyders, further west, obscure most of the Carneddau. But it is to Snowdon that the eye will be drawn, an unmistakable summit, but seen here from a rather unusual angle.

Moel Meirch, final slopes →

Llyn LLagi

Due south from Moel Meirch lies **Llyn Edno**, a simply perfect spot to linger. The ground at its eastern end is often water-logged, but as you leave Moel Meirch you will see a fenceline running along the line of a parish boundary, and this guides you to a ladder-stile by the lake, by means of which you can cross to drier ground, returning to the fenceline as soon as conditions underfoot improve. In fact, the fence now guides you all the way to the next summit, Ysgafell Wen. Having crossed the fence, however, you are now on the wrong side of it if you want to visit the northern summit of Ysgafell Wen marked by a large cairn, although the fence can be crossed easily, without damage, in many places. But the true summit of **Ysgafell Wen** lies further south along the fenceline, and beyond a gate and cross-path, at a height of 672m.

Having bagged Ysgafell Wen, backtrack to the gate and path and turn towards **Llyn yr Adar**. The going is less clear now, although there is a path to begin with, heading in a south-westerly direction. Your objective is the eastern shoreline of the lake, and in the absence of any discernible path you can simply head down across moderately rough ground towards the lake. Keep to the right of the lake, and beyond its in-flowing streams swing to the right a little to cross a shoulder and continue with an improving path around the head of a steep-sided ravine through which a stream flows down to Llyn Llagi. There is a measure of uncomfortable going for a while, but at a small cairn (SH655486) the path turns to the west, heading down the ravine but at some height above the stream.

Once past **Llyn Llagi**, which has a setting not unlike lakes in the Rhinogs, the path is a variable commodity, but the route remains fairly obvious, and you finally descend to leave Access Land at a ladder-stile and gate (SH637490). From this go forward to a wall and powerline pole, just beyond which you arrive at a cottage, **Llwynyrhwch**. Turn left in front of the cottage and cross a nearby ladder-stile and the ensuing reedy pasture to a wooden gate giving onto a path rising beside another cottage. There turn left to follow its access out to a lane, although the right of way actually runs more directly to the road somewhat less clearly than the access track. Turn right along the lane, and soon rejoin your outward route, retracing your steps to Pont Bethania.

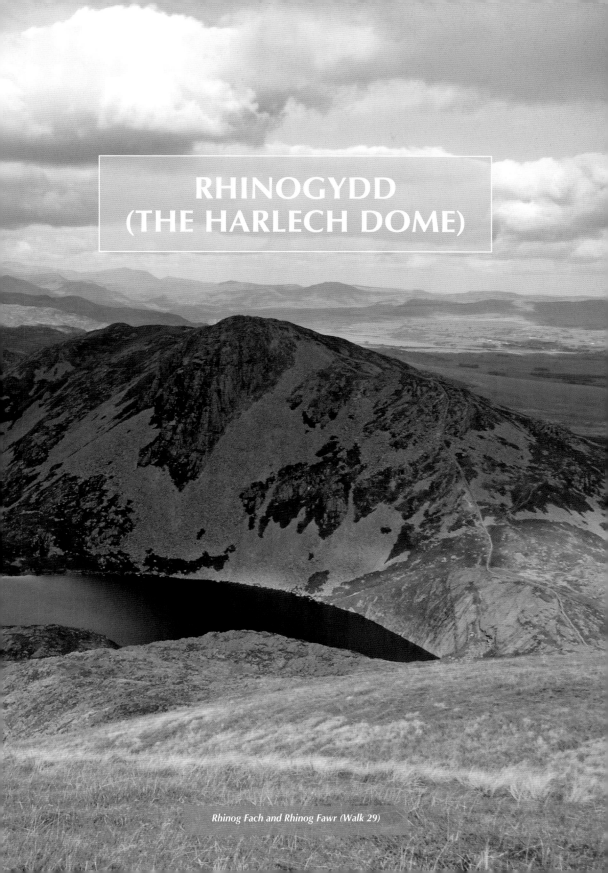

RHINOGYDD
(THE HARLECH DOME)

Rhinog Fach and Rhinog Fawr (Walk 29)

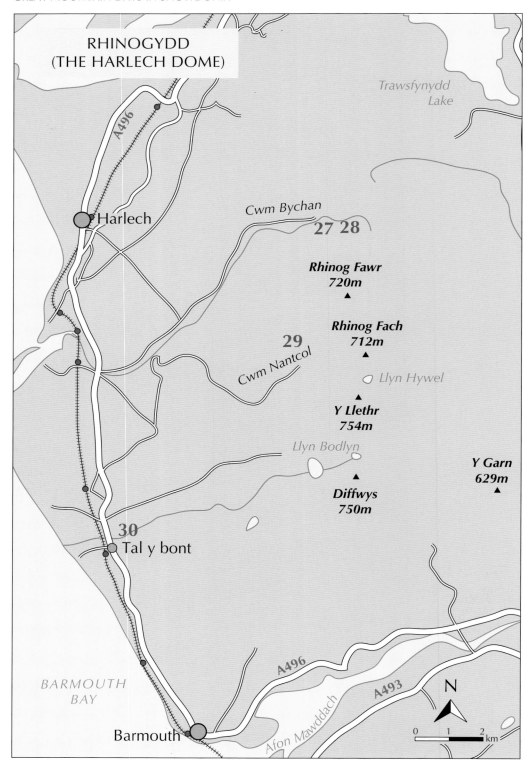

RHINOGYDD
(THE HARLECH DOME)

Trawsfynydd Lake

A496

Harlech

Cwm Bychan

27 28

Rhinog Fawr
720m
▲

Rhinog Fach
712m
▲

29

Cwm Nantcol

Llyn Hywel

▲
Y Llethr
754m

Llyn Bodlyn

Y Garn
629m
▲

▲
Diffwys
750m

30
Tal y bont

BARMOUTH
BAY

A496

A493

N

Afon Mawddach

Barmouth

0   1   2 km

RHINOGYDD (THE HARLECH DOME)

From the Mawddach Estuary in the south, the Rhinogydd push their way northwards to the Vale of Ffestiniog through 24km (15 miles) of the most uncompromising, and roughest, country in the whole of Wales. The hard Cambrian sandstones and gritstones from which they are formed, brought to the surface by an upfold of the rock strata known as the Harlech Dome, favour the growth of heather above all else, and, with the profusion of huge boulders partly buried in peat, give the entire area an appealing, rugged splendour. The coarse, hard Cambrian sandstone resists weathering, so it stands in bold erosional relief as the Rhinogydd. This is a region that geologists rave about, the most complete representation of the Cambrian system in Wales (Cambrian: 490–540 million years ago).

The name 'Rhinog' probably means 'threshold', which is appropriate for a ridge that separates the inland plateaus of central Wales from the lush coastal fringes of Dyffryn Ardudwy. This is an amazing landscape every walker should get to know, a place of boggy hollows, bare rock precipices and knobbly ridge crests, all liberally dappled with lonely sky-mirror lakes. But it is not for the faint-hearted and

places unheard-of demands on navigational skills and endurance the moment you digress from what few pathways exist. Even along the trodden routes, the going is never less than demanding; the sense of place is preternatural, but never unfriendly. It is just that the Rhinogydd do not yield their treasures quite as readily as other groups of mountains. And they are all the better for that.

The northern end of the range rises to a flattish ridge where the bare rock, cracked and broken like the mud of a dried lake, thrusts through the heather. And everywhere the light catches the eye of numerous small, clear lakes. Further south, on either side of Rhinog Fawr, are the only two ways across the range, the notorious Bwlch Drws Ardudwy and, to the north, Bwlch Tyddiad, renowned for its 'Roman' steps, although there is little evidence to show that the Romans were ever interested in the coastal lands of Dyffryn Ardudwy. South again, beyond Rhinog Fach, lies Llyn Hywel, claimed by the peregrinating cleric Gerald of Wales to contain monocular fish, and into which plunge steep, bare rocky slabs planed so smooth they might have seen the passage of glaciers only a century ago rather than a hundred.

ANCIENT HIGHWAY

Thomas Pennant, writing in his *Tour in Wales,* said of **Bwlch Drws Ardudwy**, one of only two practical crossings of the range: 'I was tempted to visit this noted pass, and found the horror of it far exceeding the most gloomy idea that could be conceived of it. The sides seemed to have been rent by some mighty convulsion into a thousand precipices.' The Reverend Bingley, a man perfectly willing to go in search of plants on the fiercesome cliffs of Clogwyn du'r Arduu near Snowdon, nevertheless found the pass 'a place well calculated to inspire a timid mind with terror'. Black's *Picturesque Guide to North Wales* claims that 'Nothing can exceed the dreariness and desolation of this ravine, overshadowed by the rugged, frowning cliffs of *Rhinog-fawr* and *Rhinog-fach.*'

Not exactly what you would call an encouraging picture. Patrick Monkhouse, sometime Deputy Editor of the *Manchester Guardian*, claimed that Rhinog Fawr 'exacted more perspiration to the yard than any other...in Wales, with the possible exception of the other side of the same mountain.' Yet these negative comments are only one side of the picture: the Rhinogydd are fascinating and rewarding, wild Wales at its most wildly splendid.

Y Llethr, the highest of the Rhinogydd, and Diffwys display contrasting sides. On the west, smooth grassland rolls down to the sea, while on the east they revert to type as you struggle through ankle-twisting, heather-covered rocks.

Perhaps, then, there is something to the portrayal of the area as one of ruggedness and bleakness, but there are ways through, and excellent mountain tops, where the walker will be rewarded far more for effort than anywhere else in Wales.

Ancient walls beside the Roman steps in Cwm Bychan (Walk 28)

Bwlch Tyddiad
and Bwlch Drws Ardudwy

*A*s a way of getting to know the lovable old rugosities of the Rhinogydd without taking on more
than you can chew, this walk, which circles Rhinog Fawr like a predator, is as good as you can
get. Only two weaknesses penetrate the high Rhinogs, Bwlch Tyddiad and Bwlch Drws Ardudwy,
both packhorse and droving routes of considerable antiquity, and this walk makes use of them both.
For the most part the route is without undue difficulty, but in such rugged country, where the rocky
skeleton of the land is barely millimetres below your feet, it should be taken as read that the going is
inevitably rough at times, especially in the last third of the route as you work your way back from Cwm
Nantcol to Cwm Bychan. The secret of success among the Rhinogydd is patience and the ability to
navigate and trek across pathless terrain. This walk should not be attempted in poor visibility.

The location of **Llyn Cwm Bychan** is quite
exceptional, and it's highly popular spot for
campers and day visitors during the summer
months. To the south of the lake the slopes of

Carreg y Saeth rise in ragged heather terraces;
glaciation is evident everywhere with unyield-
ing bedrock underfoot and striated boulders
scattered haphazardly.

↑ *The Rhinogydd from Rhobell Fawr* 157

Llyn Cwm Bychan

Distance	14km/8¾ miles
Height gain	745m/2445ft
Time	5 hours
Grade	energetic
Start point	SH645314

Getting there
At the end of the narrow road leading past Llyn Cwm Bychan there is parking in a field at the start of the path leading to the Roman steps (charge for parking)

Maps
(Harvey Superwalker) Rhinogs; (Ordnance Survey) OL18 Harlech, Porthmadog and Bala

After-walk refreshment
There are numerous pubs, cafés, restaurants and hotels in Harlech, and among the coastal resorts of Ardudwy

The lake itself is lovely, silent and brooding, beneath the cliffs of Carreg y Saeth, the 'Stone of the Arrow'. A little further east stands a farm once occupied by Ieuan Llwyd, who claimed lineal descent from Welsh lords living in this region as far back as 1100. Cwm Bychan feels like a world apart – the silence is profound – and indeed it did have visitors from other worlds back in 1983, when episodes from the television drama *Doctor Who* were filmed here. Across the rippling hill slopes you may catch sight of the feral goats, mostly black and white, that have long been established in the area. They are sturdy, independent beasts, a nuisance to farmers but born survivors.

The Route
Leave the parking area through a gate (waymark), and turn right along a path for the so-called **Roman Steps** (see Walk 28), a gently ascending path. Stay by a wall and then a fence to enter ancient oak woodland at a ladder-stile, heading steadily uphill and leaving the woodland at another stile. Once clear

of the woods, the path, which forms into steps at the steeper sections, runs clearly up a narrowing defile to the huge cairn that marks the top of the pass.

At the pass, before reaching the cairn, bear left and then press on along a clear path heading downhill with wide views ahead of mountain and moorland, as you head for an isolated section of the plantations of **Coed y Brenin Forest**. Keep on

The 'Roman' Steps, Cwm Bychan

through grass and heather to the edge of the planta-tion and then follow a path through the conifers.

Coed y Brenin translates as the 'Forest of Kings' and was renamed from the original 'Vaughan Forest' to celebrate the Silver Jubilee of King George V in 1935. It lies at the heart of the Welsh gold prospecting area and is the oldest and most extensive forest in Wales.

Turn right to cross a footbridge over a stream and fol-low waymarks to another foot-bridge. Keep on until you reach a broad forest trail (SH669299), turn right for 800m and then, when the trail divides, take the left branch to reach a T-junction (SH675288). Turn right here, but when the track bends acutely to the left, leave it and maintain the original direction along a grassy path that climbs easily to leave the forest at a gate. Through the gate

Cairn at the summit of Bwlch Tyddiad

you re-enter the Rhinog National Nature Reserve with the two Rhinog summits ahead. Press on across moorland, the path climbing gently to the head of the pass, **Bwlch Drws Ardudwy**.

Pass through a wall gap and then descend gently into the inspiring scenery ahead. Lower down, the path broadens into the gentler spread of **Cwm Nantcol**, and you move on to reach the farm at **Maes y Garnedd** (see Walk 29). At Maes y Garnedd, turn right along a track up to a gate and onward for Nantcol, following the track ahead as it winds gently uphill.

The next section is much more complex in terms of navigation and route-finding than what has gone before. In the early stages of the ascent you are never far from a wall, climbing behind Nantcol and then bearing left, steeply uphill, following occasional marker posts and aiming for a wall junction at SH640280, by now having left the right of way you were following. Go through a wall gap at the junction and forward with the wall on your left, heading gently uphill. From the next wall junction, you need to work out your own route, and that will depend on conditions underfoot, which can be problematic after prolonged rain. Begin by continuing to climb, but have no faith that you will find the path shown on maps. Instead, take a bearing on **Gloyw Llyn**, the Bright Lake, roughly north, and head that way across difficult terrain. Paths appear, but you need to be constantly alert to the possibility of following them blindly in the wrong direction. Eventually you gain a ridge (SH646289) above the lake, where a spectacular view awaits as reward for the effort.

More effort is needed in getting down to the lake, although if you can locate a sheepfold (SH645290) there is a discernible path leading down to it from there. From the sheepfold, keep more to the left of the shallow valley ahead and you come to a ladder-stile, from which the descent steepens as you make

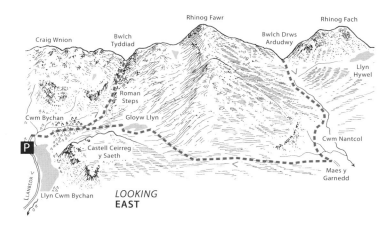

your way down to the lake, just before which the ground becomes rather marshy. Circle to the left of the lake along an improving path to its far end, and then start back on the other side to reach a shallow ravine. Turn left here to locate a path that descends through rocks and heather, crossing a stream and descending to a wall. Beyond the wall, continue descending, crossing and re-crossing an accompanying stream, and before long you rejoin your outward route just below the Roman Steps.

Cwm Nantcol and Drws Ardudwy

Rhinog Fawr

*T*he difficult nature of the terrain makes circular walks in the Rhinogydd beyond all but the most experienced and hardened walkers. But going round in circles isn't always what it's cracked up to be, as this linear conquest of Rhinog Fawr proves. You might reasonably expect that Rhinog Fawr is the highest of the range, but that distinction is reserved for Y Llethr, although if you look at the mountains from the east, you can see why Rhinog Fawr seems a cut above the rest.

The Route

A signposted track heads roughly southwards, climbing first through **Cwm Bychan**, and then entering a narrow gorge leading to the top of Bwlch Tyddiad.

> **Cwm Bychan** is one of two narrow river valleys that penetrate the western flanks of the upland massif of Ardudwy (Cwm Nantcol to the south being the other). Both rivers feed into the Artro, which passes through Llanbedr and out into the sea near Llandanwg. The principal defining characteristic of the valley is the woodland that extends along both flanks for almost its entire length. Coed Dol-wreddiog, Coed Gerddi bluog, Coed Crafnant and Coed Dolbebin are broadleaved woodlands (comprising mainly sessile oak) and represent an important resource. There is little of archaeological interest in the valley, but it is generally thought that the area would have been exploited by man since prehistoric times. The names of the woods (associated with the names of farms) suggest that they originated in the early post-medieval period, although it is conceivable that they had earlier origins.

　　　↑ *The summit of Rhinog Fawr*

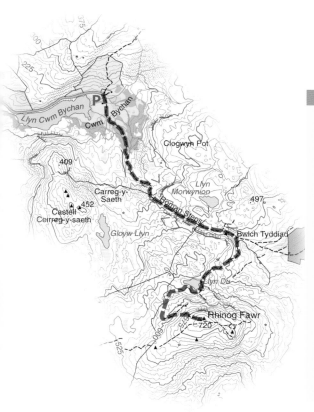

ROUTE INFORMATION

Distance	7km/4½ miles
Height gain	595m/1950ft
Time	4 hours
Grade	energetic
Start point	SH645314

Getting there

At the end of the narrow road leading past
Llyn Cwm Bychan there is parking in a field
at the start of the path leading to the Roman
steps (charge for parking)

Maps

(Harvey Superwalker) Rhinogs; (Ordnance
Survey) OL18 Harlech, Porthmadog and Bala

After-walk refreshment

There are numerous pubs, cafés, restaurants
and hotels in Harlech, and along the coastal
settlements

Rhinog Fawr with the Snowdon massif in the background

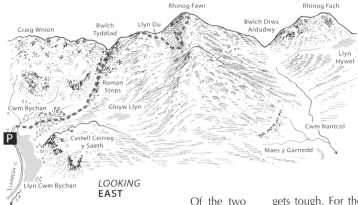

Rhinog Fawr

Rhinog Fach

Bwlch Drws Ardudwy

Llyn Du

Bwlch Tyddiad

Craig Wnion

Llyn Hywel

Roman Steps

Cwm Nantcol

Cwm Bychan

Gloyw Llyn

P

Castell Ceirreg y Saeth

Maes y Garnedd

LLANBEDR

Llyn Cwm Bychan

LOOKING EAST

Of the two breaks in the Rhinog range, **Bwlch Tyddiad** is rather better known.

From Cwm Bychan to the pass, hundreds of large slabs of gritstone have been laid to make a well-defined track, known as the **Roman Steps**. This route across the mountains may well pre-date the Romans, but the paved section is more likely to be early medieval, possibly constructed when Edward I rebuilt Harlech Castle. As an inland route, traversing beyond the open moorland of the Rhinogydd, this crossing would have been important not only politically – Pennant comments on the dependency of Bala on the castle at Harlech – but also as a trade route for wool and other merchandise between Bala and the coastland.

The ascent by the Roman Steps to Bwlch Tyddiad (described in Walk 27) is as enjoyable a route as any in the heather and rock maze of the Rhinogydd, but, from the top of the pass, the going gets tough. For the simplest line, walk beyond the top of the pass and head downhill for about 100m (but not so far as a sign), to locate a narrow path branching on the right, and working around a rocky knoll to climb easily up to **Llyn Du**.

Go left, and cross the outflow of Llyn Du to find the continuing path, which now passes to the west of the lake where a wall delineates the next part of the route climbing to a point almost due west of the summit. From here make directly for Rhinog Fawr, and ascend a short scree slope (which can be avoided). Once above the scree, follow a clear path to the trig point and cairns on the summit.

The safest and surest return to the start is back the way you came.

Rhinog Fach
and Rhinog Fawr

B wlch Drws Ardudwy, between the northerly Rhinog Fawr and the slightly lower Rhinog Fach
to the south, will come to be a fulcrum of indecision on this walk, which seeks, somewhat
artificially and some would say needlessly, to link the two Rhinogs in one walk. The problem is the
sheer awkwardness of the terrain and the effort it calls for, to such an extent that when you reach
Bwlch Drws Ardudwy, you may well set off for one of the summits fully with the intention of coming
back to this high pass and then heading for the other summit. But then indecision sets in: have you
had enough? – do you really want more of the same leg-numbing terrain? – have you got what it
takes to cajole weary limbs on further when the car and comfort is waiting just a short way down
into Cwm Nantcol?

So the bwlch also lets you split the walk into two outings, returning another day for what you
left untouched. And for many that would be a more preferable solution, not because you were not
'up to it', but because this is such stunning scenery, such pure, untameable mountain ruggedness,
that you just can't get enough of it.

↑ *Rhinog Fach and Llyn Hywel*

ROUTE INFORMATION

Distance	11km/6¾ miles
Height gain	910m/2985ft
Time	5 hours
Grade	strenuous
Start point	Maes y Garnedd (SH641270)

Getting there

Leave the A496 at Llanbedr or Dyffryn Ardudwy, and follow lanes inland to Cwm Nantcol. Continue up the lane to Maes y Garnedd, an isolated farm at the roadhead, where parking is available for a small fee

Maps

(Harvey Superwalker) Rhinogs; (Ordnance Survey) OL18 Harlech, Porthmadog and Bala

After-walk refreshment

Numerous cafés and pubs all along the coastal settlements between Barmouth and Harlech

The Route

This walk is an out-and-back excursion, with the stretch from Maes y Garnedd to Bwlch Drws Ardudwy, the wild col between Rhinog Fawr and Rhinog Fach, also common to both summits. The scenery is awesome, a mixture of rock, half-concealed boulders and heather and with incomparable views throughout.

An ordinary looking farmhouse, **Maes y Garnedd** does not betray its bloody past, for this was the home of Colonel John Jones, born nearby in Llanbedr, a member of Cromwell's army, who married Cromwell's sister and was one of the signatories of Charles I's death warrant. He was an avid Republican at a time when Wales was largely Royalist, a quality that made him 'the most hated man in Wales'. In his role as Parliamentary Commissioner for Ireland, he was a ruthless persecutor of the Irish, Catholic and Protestant, native and settlers alike. As one of the 59 signatories to the king's death warrant, however, his action brought him his comeuppance on 17 October 1660, when he too had an appointment with executioner, and was hanged, drawn and quartered.

Go through the gate on the east side of the track and take the clear path that heads north-east into **Cwm Nantcol**.

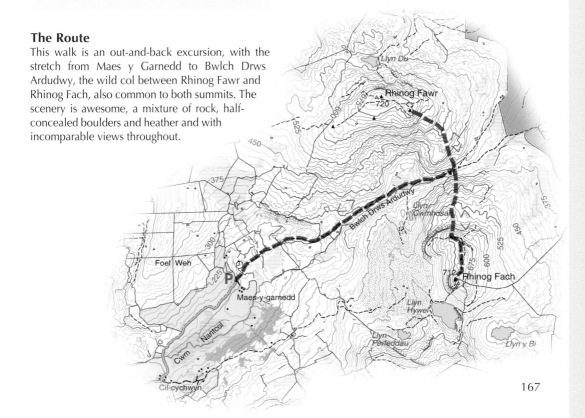

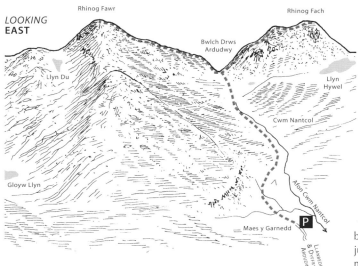

LOOKING EAST

Rhinog Fawr

Rhinog Fach

Bwlch Drws Ardudwy

Llyn Du

Llyn Hywel

Cwm Nantcol

Gloyw Llyn

Afon Cwm Nantcol

P

Maes y Garnedd

LLANBEDR & DYFFRYN ARDUDWY

or jug used for pouring water) in the shape of a stag, to bronze skillets and a small water jug – but also their date. Most metalwork hoards found in Wales tend to be prehistoric, but this one was late medieval.

In 1918, a remarkable **hoard of treasure** was discovered by a man mining for manganese in Cwm Nantcol. The hoard had been concealed in a cavity beneath a large stone on rough ground on the south side of the valley. What makes the hoard especially attention-grabbing is not only the wide range of objects – from a fine aquamanile (a ewer

As you progress up the valley, all you need to do is follow the path until you reach the col, **Bwlch Drws Ardudwy**, which is marked by a large cairn. At times the way is a little marshy, but generally offers no particular difficulties, and after a brief widening the valley narrows again towards

Heading into the Rhinogs from Cwm Nantcol

Rhinog Fach and Llyn Hywel

the conclusion. On reaching the bwlch there is an excellent view across to Lake Trawsfynydd and the Arenigs.

This is also the time to mull over whether the Rhinogydd reflect your idea of quality walking; looking south from the bwlch you can see the steepness of the path heading to the summit of Rhinog Fach. The Rhinogydd do offer great routes, exceptional scenery and constantly changing panoramas. Don't let the roughness of the landscape put you off. But equally, don't stray from such paths as exist – only grief lies that way.

From the top of the pass turn southwards for **Rhinog Fach**, climbing steeply at an angle that eases only as the northern end of the summit ridge is reached. From here the safest option is to retrace your steps to Bwlch Drws Ardudwy, but first make time to take in the marvellous view southwards to Y Llethr, and west to the coastal sand dunes and the sea.

On arriving back at the saddle, if you decide to tackle **Rhinog Fawr**, take to a narrow path from the

cairn on the pass that rises a tad east of north to intersect a wall that crosses the top of the pass a little higher up the slope. At the base of this wall there is a large hole through which most walkers should be able to shimmy, if not altogether elegantly.

Beyond the wall climb through a convoluted landscape of rocks to a slightly more level stretch, keeping an eye open for a prominent cairn on the skyline. Climb up to this via a stone shoot to arrive on the summit plateau of rock slabs and heather. Now simply retrace your steps and reprise your wall-crossing technique to Bwlch Drws Ardudwy, and back down to Maes y Garnedd.

What this excursion into the heart of the Rhinogydd achieves is a respect for the difficult nature of the terrain. There are other paths, and variations of routes, including routes coming in from the east. But all the going is difficult and you need the sort of experience this walk imbues before venturing more widely. Difficult it is, but hugely enjoyable and it more than amply repays the effort and care.

Y Llethr and Diffwys

T his long circuit of the southern summits of the Rhinogydd could not be more different from routes to the north. Here, smooth profiles and grassy slopes replace the deep heather and boulders of the north. If height supremacy is a reason for climbing mountains, then the ascent to Y Llethr, the highest of the Rhinogydd, is justified. But even without such a hallmark, this round is outstanding. It's demanding, too, but never desperately so, and a fine summer's day will have you strolling across the summits without a care in the world.

The Route

From the car park, take a path to the Ysgethin Inn. Go behind this to locate a narrow path leading into the pleasant woodland of Coed Cors y Gedol, a Site of Special Scientific Interest. The time spent in the woodland is a delight with the noisy **Afon Ysgethin** a constant companion, but finally you emerge at a cottage, **Lletty-lloegr**. Go immediately left for a few strides to a signed path through bracken, and then pass to the rear of the cottage. At the next sign, behind the cottage, turn left, this time through bracken and

↑ *Crib y Rhiw, leading to Diffwys*

ROUTE INFORMATION

Distance	22km/13¾ miles
Height gain	975m/3200ft
Time	6–7 hours
Grade	strenuous
Start point	Car park at SH590218

Getting there
Although it is possible to begin the walk
from the end of a minor road near Dyffryn
Ardudwy, a start at Tal y Bont, beside the Afon
Ysgethin, is preferred

Maps
(Harvey Superwalker) Rhinogs; (Ordnance
Survey) OL18 Harlech, Porthmadog and Bala

After-walk refreshment
Numerous cafés and pubs all along the coastal
settlements between Barmouth and Harlech

gorse, roughly following a wall upwards. Once
above the gorse, everything is more evident, and you
can follow a clear path to a through-stile in a wall
bounding a wide track.

Cors y Gedol hall lies off to the left, one of the
many places where Charles I stayed while fleeing
the Roundheads during the Civil War in the 1640s.
It is said that there is a tunnel linking the hall with
a farmhouse on Shell Island, and that the tunnel
may have been used as a smuggling route.

171

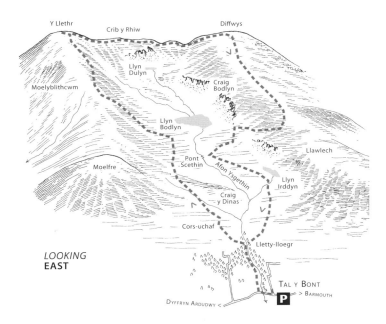

LOOKING **EAST**

Turn eastwards (right) along the track which, after a couple of dog-legs, reaches open country below the rounded mound of Moelfre on your left. Stay with the ongoing track, ignoring the branch that leads down to Pont Scethin from a waymark pole. Along the way you pass below a small, remnant woodland, not far from which a scatter of ruins is all that remains of a coaching inn that served the London–Harlech stage-coach route. As you draw level with the low point linking Moelfre with Y Llethr, an indistinct path forks left (from about SH640242) and heads up to the col on the eastern side of **Moelfre**. The point of

Moelfre from the slopes of Moelyblithcwm

Afternoon light on Crib y Rhiw, with Diffwys in the background

departure is not clear, but what is in view are quad bike tracks higher up the grassy slope. Once you feel able to, simply cross the lower grassy section to gain the track.

> Strong walkers will have no difficulty including **Moelfre** in the round, and it adds an interesting start to the day, being topped by an ancient cairn built by the mysterious people who inhabited the Vale of Ardudwy at its feet. Legend also relates that from Moelfre, the ubiquitous King Arthur cast a large quoit into the valley, which must have been something of a regal pastime given the preponderance of 'Arthur's Quoits' dotted about the landscape of Wales.

The path improves with height and swings to the right, up to a wall that puts you on the **Moelyblithcwm** ridge. Follow this wall, at varying distances from it, as it climbs steadily towards the rounded summit of Y Llethr to the south of which it intercepts the ridge wall. From here, over a ladder-stile in a corner, it is but a short haul to the top of **Y Llethr**, marked by a squat cairn on a flat, grassy summit plateau, which may come as something of a minor disappointment

– that this, the highest of the Rhinogydd, doesn't have an impressive cairn and rugged summit; but it hasn't, alas. For the best views, you will need to walk north-east along the summit to get a stunning view of Llyn Hywel and Rhinog Fach.

> Llyn Hywel is renowned as the haunt of **monocular fish**, but since they seldom swim near the surface of the impressive lake with its tilted slabs, the truth of the assertion is difficult to confirm. Gerald of Wales (Giraldus Cambrensis), that roving cleric who travelled around Wales in 1188, observed of the lake: 'It abounds in three different kinds of fish, eels, trout and perch, and all of them have only one eye, the right one being there but not the left.' Gerald, alas, left no explanation of this phenomenon, nor is there any evidence that he went to the lake to see for himself.

Retrace your steps across the top of Y Llethr, and drop down to the wall junction to the south. With the wall on your left a sure and certain guide, head roughly south and climb easily to cross the top of **Crib y Rhiw**, effectively the headwall of the splendid Ysgethin valley. From Crib y Rhiw's summit-linking heights, steep

Diffwys and Llyn Bodlyn

crags plummet to the spacious Eden valley below, while onward the ongoing path meanders in undulating fashion through scattered rock outcrops before climbing more seriously to the summit of **Diffwys**. A path shortcuts the final section, but it is more entertaining to stay along the crest as much as possible

From Diffwys top, marked by a robust, squat trig pillar, there is a superb view across the Mawddach estuary to the Cadair Idris range. Stay with the wall as you head initially south from the trig pillar, before turning west and following the wall over smooth upland to the 642m **spot height** at SH648229. Remain on the ridge path, later crossing a wall to intercept a path on the **Llawlech** ridge that heads north and down towards Pont Scethin. At the point where the path descending from Diffwys meets the Llawlech ridge path, there is a gate and a stile in the wall, and a cairn marking the descent a little to the right of the path.

The path you intercept is the old Dolgellau to Harlech road, once plied by stagecoaches on the journey north from London, although it is difficult to image that today. The descent to **Pont Scethin** is straightforward, and crosses the extravagantly wild moorland that frames Llyn Bodlyn. From the bridge, and without crossing it, strike off to the south along a path that improves as you go to reach a broad track passing to the north of **Llyn Irddyn**. Continue along this, and it will guide you to Pont Fadog, spanning the Afon Ysgethin, just beyond which you climb to join the outward route at Lletty-lloegr. Now simply branch left and retrace your way through the woodland, back to Tal y Bont.

MIGNEINT
AND THE ARANS

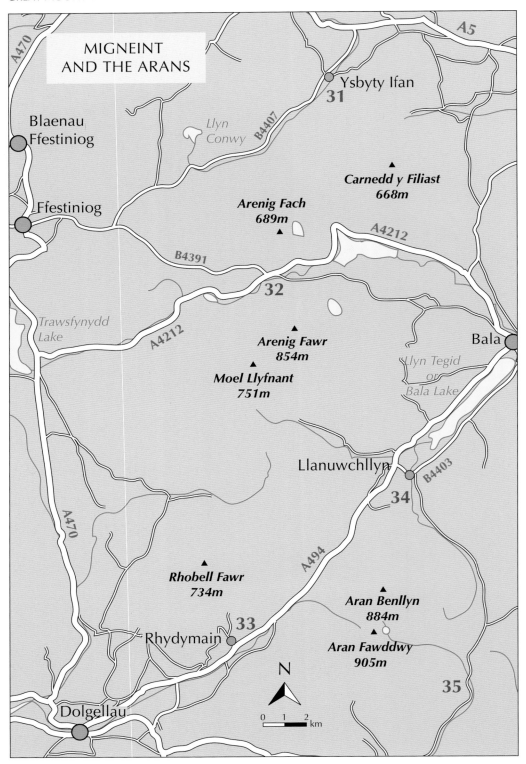

MIGNEINT
AND THE ARANS

A470

A5

Blaenau
Ffestiniog

Llyn
Conwy

B4407

Ysbyty Ifan

31

Carnedd y Filiast
668m

Ffestiniog

Arenig Fach
689m

A4212

B4391

32

Trawsfynydd
Lake

A4212

Arenig Fawr
854m

Bala

Llyn Tegid
or
Bala Lake

Moel Llyfnant
751m

Llanuwchllyn

B4403

34

A470

A494

Rhobell Fawr
734m

Aran Benllyn
884m

Rhydymain

33

Aran Fawddwy
905m

Dolgellau

N

35

0   1   2
km

MIGNEINT AND THE ARANS

Those whose perspective of Snowdonia is one of range upon range of craggy summits tapering into the distance will have that view skewed dramatically by the Migneint. For here, while there are indeed mountains worthy of attention, the abiding impression is of endless moorland, possibly the largest cotton-grass moor in Wales. Nothing could be further from the commonplace view of Snowdonia; yet this is a region, nearly 200km², that holds much for the intrepid walker whose mentality isn't crag-bound, whose perception embraces the whole gamut of walking terrain and not just a few pods of mainstream cragginess.

For those with the willingness to embrace the wide bounds of Migneint, the discovery will be one of a fascinating area, a true moor in the restricted ecological sense, largely devoid of human habitation, of a rough, bare land of old quarries, abandoned farmsteads, reservoirs, broken hill slopes, deep valleys and rocky hills with sharply defined crags.

Few books have much to say about the Migneint, but walkers with a liking for the Pennine moorlands of England will feel very much at home here, a place of acid moorland and dappling cloud shadows rolling across the grassland. As a rough guide, the Migneint is bounded in the west by the A470 and the Coed y Brenin Forest, in the south by the A494 linking Dolgellau and Bala and in the north by the A5, and even that is a guess for the map makers also have some uncertainty about this amorphous land.

During the preparation of this book I met the farmer from Blaen-y-Cwm, north of Carnedd y Filiast. He was so surprised to see someone that he drove over in his tractor, stopped the engine, opened the windows and passed the time of day. Had I been on the mountain? Yes. Had I seen anyone? No. I asked whether I should expect to see anyone. He said, no, it was unusual, although some 4x4 roadsters had ripped up the byway we were on a week or so ago to prove that their monster machines could climb hills and make a lot of noise.

↑ *The summit of Rhobell Fawr (Walk 33)*

Most of the time, of course, it is not like that. What you get here is peace, nature in the raw, huge skies, wide, grassy, peaty voids that have won every contest in the human occupation stakes hands-down, and a sense of being so far away from civilisation that at times it might be unsettling.

Principal among the mountains here is Arenig Fawr, one of only nine summits of note in such a vast area of austere beauty, and oddly comforting in its dominance of the scenery. It is an uncomplicated landscape, hiding nothing but its exquisite lakes, not least that below Arenig Fawr, and another east of its sibling, Arenig Fach to the north.

Southernmost of this peaty desert is Rhobell Fawr, a strong, rugged, inviting shape set in a wild landscape. Across the valley of the Afon Wnion, south of Llyn Tegid, a long ridge rises steadily southwards across the Arans, Benllyn and Fawddwy, vanguard of a hotch-potch of rounded hills that extend to the Dyfi valley and Dinas Mawddwy before slipping across the boundary of the National Park. There is peaty bogginess here, too. But on the Arans nothing awaits but sheer delight, a fine romp from north or south, onto lofty heights where crag and turf interplay, and steep sides slip effortlessly down to the Dyfi the Twrch.

Aran Fawddwy from the slopes of Erw y Ddafad Ddu (Walk 35)

Carnedd y Filiast

*T*his lonely mountain, 'Cairn of the Greyhound', lies at the eastern end of the Migneint-Arenig-Dduallt Special Area of Conservation, an area characterised by bogs, marshes and water-fringed vegetation. Carnedd y Filiast squats to the north of the man-made Llyn Celyn, gazing westwards to Arenig Fach and the Rhinogs, and north to the whole panoply of northern Snowdonia mountains from Tal y Fan above Conwy to the Moelwynion. The view alone is reason enough to make this jaunt, but while the largely featureless landscape of blanket bog may seem unappealing, it will prove to be a gem, especially by this circuitous approach from the delightful village of Ysbyty Ifan. If you want company on the hills, then on this walk you will have to take it with you. Oddly, perhaps, amid so much emptiness, this walk proves to be safer than most in poor visibility – not that you would choose such a day – as there are either good tracks or fencelines to guide you.

↑ *Migneint moors: Arenig Fach and Arenig Fawr*

ROUTE INFORMATION

Distance	16km/10 miles
Height gain	650m/2130ft
Time	5 hours
Grade	energetic
Start point	SH843488

Getting there

Small parking area south of the bridge in Ysbyty Ifan (there are toilets 50m from the parking area in the direction of the walk)

Maps

(Ordnance Survey) OL18 Harlech, Porthmadog and Bala

After-walk refreshment

Pub and café at Pentre Foelas; full range of services at Betws y Coed

The Route

From the bridge walk towards the telephone box and then take the first lane on the right (a turning just before this leads to the toilets).

Ysbyty Ifan, until 1189, was known as Dôl Gynwal. Then, as the name 'ysbyty', meaning 'hospital' or 'hospice', implies, it came to the attention of the **Knights of St John**, who set up a hospice. Very much at the centre of North Wales, Ysbyty Ifan was at an important cross-roads linking Anglesey, Bardsey Island, London and Chester, and as gouged and grooved rocks along the mountain tracks testify great use was made of this region by drovers, pilgrims and merchants. The church marks the spot where the old hospice stood, and it contains many remnants that tell of the area's rich history. Before 1974 the village was divided between counties by the infant Afon Conwy, part in Caernarvonshire and part in Denbighshire.

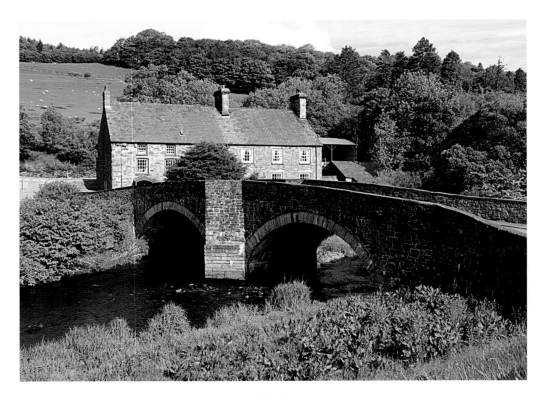

Ysbyty Ifan and the infant Afon Conwy

When you reach the church, bear left, still walking up a narrow lane and climbing gently. Stay on the ascending lane when you reach a junction at the access to Ty Nant farm.

At **Ty'n-y-ffridd**, the road surfacing ends but the route continues as a rough vehicle track, and just as you pass the farm you get a view northwards that takes in Moel Siabod, Tryfan and the

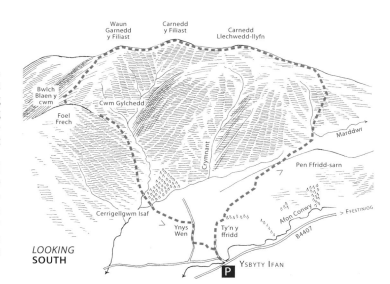

LOOKING **SOUTH**

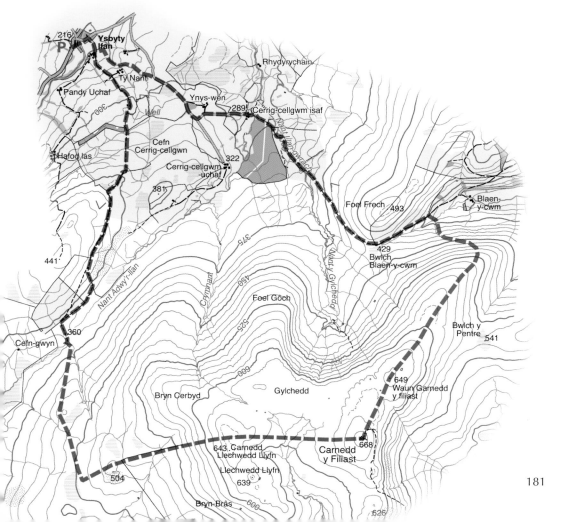

181

Carneddau. Higher up at a gate and ladder-stile you enter Access Land, not that you would want to wander freely here. In good conditions, with a warm sun on your face, it all looks sweetly benign, but in its darker moods this huge area of sticky peatiness can be an evil place.

The ongoing track is clear throughout and straightforward; in places you can see where ancient iron-rimmed cart wheels have gouged a groove in the underlying rocks. As you walk along so the bulk of Carnedd y Filiast defines the boundary to the south-east, while to the south-west your attention is caught by the fine outline of Arenig Fach.

In due course the track descends to run along a broad moorland valley, that of the **Nant Adwr'y-llan**, which drains north-eastwards to the Conwy. At SH840458, the track changes direction and goes down to cross the valley. At the low point you step over a small stream, the **Marddwr**, a feeder of the Afon Gelyn, which flows west and south, indicating that you have just crossed a minor watershed. Once across you then do the best you can with the gate beyond, before continuing with the rising vehicle track.

The track briefly runs beside a fence but soon bears away onto a hill slope and very soon disappears altogether. The actual course of the ongoing route is not discernible underfoot, and you can spend much unprofitable time going off in search of it. In places a very narrow path does materialise, but the surest and safest course is to follow the fence on your left, beside the Nant y Fuddai. This guides you up to intercept a fence running east-west, which is easy enough to cross without risk of either damage or personal injury. Close by there is an old boundary stone with barely legible writing: RP 1866, possibly.

Carnedd y Filiast now lies about 2.5km (1½ miles) east along the fenceline across a long stretch of bilberry, heather, bog cotton, tussock grass and reeds. On the way you cross intermediate fences besides which, lying in the heather, ladder-stiles await assembly, and may well be in place by the time this book is published. But the fences are not difficult to cross, and, at the time of writing, the ladder-stiles-in-waiting are known to have been waiting for at least two years. (If they ever are erected, please let us know!).

What makes this vast region so fascinating is the vegetation, among which the white bobs of bog cotton grass tell a tale. But, while the continuing walk is no Sunday stroll in the park, neither is it especially arduous, and soon you pass over a minor top – **Carnedd Llechwedd-llyfn** – marked by a smart cairn of boulders, although the highest ground lies about 200m to the south.

An easier pull now leads up to the trig, cairns and shelter of **Carnedd y Filiast**. A slate slab in a cairn bears the initial 'TI'. It marks an amazing place with a view of just about every mountain embraced within this book, that clearly points up the contrast between the clustered mountains of northern Snowdonia and those, more widespread, to the south.

From the top of Carnedd y Filiast, set off in an east-north-easterly direction alongside the continuing fence. A broad track, one that has risen from the south, instantly appears, but is of little use. Leave it when it bears right, and return to parallel the fence. You soon pass across a minor bump, **Waun Garnedd y Filiast**, with nominal re-ascent, and which sometimes has a shallow lake and sometimes doesn't.

The next 2km (1¼ miles) provide the most difficult going, devoid of any distinguishing features save for the guiding fenceline and the occasional self-seeded spruce. At an intermediate fence, at SH878457, cross to the northern side of the ongoing fence, which is in rather better condition than all those around it, having been repaired in 2007.

Gradually, the ground starts to fall away more steeply. Stay with the fence until you intercept another at SH883466, and now turn left, in a north-westerly direction alongside the fence, descending across the fall of slope that is **Bwlch y Pentre**, and heading for a clear track on the far side of the valley that has now appeared. Underfoot, for most of the way, lies an earth-covered collapsed wall, an ancient boundary, and a narrow path runs along the top of this, guiding you ever downwards.

By following the old wall downwards, a little awkwardly in its lower reaches, you come to the inevitable stream crossing and boggy patch, followed by a brief pull up to a gate giving on to a clear and part-surfaced track that leads south-west to **Bwlch Blaen-y-cwm**, a gentle ascent now being needed.

↑ *The ancient track across the moors; Arenig Fach in the background*   183

On the summit of Carnedd y Filiast

At this pass, you gain a fabulous view of the great bowl below Carnedd y Filiast, drained by the **Nant y Gylchedd**. It is feasible to descend through this bowl directly from Carnedd y Filiast to the bwlch, but this is very difficult going, and unless you keep to the west of the fenceline running along the National Park boundary you will not find any convenient crossing points lower down. This is a very demanding descent, and probably best shunned.

Beyond the gate at the bwlch, a descending track cuts across the flank of **Foel Frech**. At a gate you quit Access Land, and continue to walk alongside the **Nant Llan-gwrach**, crossing a couple of shallow fords before reaching the farmyard at **Cerrigellgwm Isaf**.

The surfaced road-head lies just beyond, and you should follow the road past **Ynys Wen** farm and then in the direction of Ysbyty Ifan.

Continue to follow the lane until, just as it bends right (north) at SH850484, you can leave it, on the left, to walk to the first of a number of black, metal kissing-gates. Through the gate, go forward along the top edge of pasture, walking above the wooded ravine, and repeating this as you descend more pastures to a footbridge and another gate. Keep forward with a wall on your left, to locate yet more gates that finally take you out to rejoin the outward route near the church. Now simply retrace your steps to the village bridge.

Arenig Fawr
and Moel Llyfnant

U nlike mountain groups further north, the summits to the north and south of Bala are spread out, and provide excellent scope for extended days. Arenig Fawr and Moel Llyfnant prove the point; this is splendid walking country, largely uninhabited, wild, untamed and with a great sense of remoteness. Good-ish paths tend to cover most of this walk, although there is a little free range bog-bashing in the middle, but that should deter no one. Choose a fine day and your reward will be one of the great unsung rounds of Snowdonia, with almost every Snowdonian mountain in view at some stage. All very exceptional, and satisfying.

The Route

After parking, amble along the lane in an easterly direction for a further 1.5km (1 mile), passing a number of houses on the way. Just after **Pant-yr-Hedydd**, leave the road (SH846395) for a rising grassy track on the right that initially heads south-west, but turns to head south-east and levels off as the waters of Llyn Arenig Fawr come into view.

Press on along the track, passing to the east of **Llyn Arenig Fawr**, with the cliffs of the mountain rising abruptly on your right in a truly wild setting, until you come to a small building near the dam outflow. (The lake's primary purpose is to supply water to the nearby town of Bala and the numerous small villages in the surrounding area.)

Turn right down a path and through a gate at the rear of the building. Cross the outflow and move ahead, following a path that rises along the ridge above the southern shore of the reservoir. The climb is steady and the path easy to follow. When you

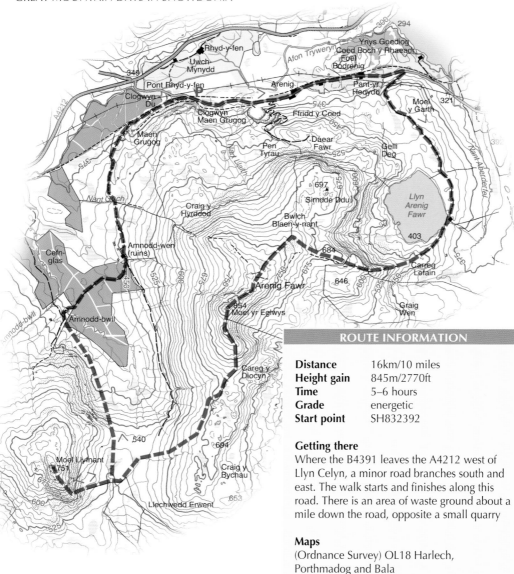

ROUTE INFORMATION

Distance   16km/10 miles
Height gain   845m/2770ft
Time   5–6 hours
Grade   energetic
Start point   SH832392

Getting there
Where the B4391 leaves the A4212 west of Llyn Celyn, a minor road branches south and east. The walk starts and finishes along this road. There is an area of waste ground about a mile down the road, opposite a small quarry

Maps
(Ordnance Survey) OL18 Harlech, Porthmadog and Bala

After-walk refreshment
Bala offers a wide range of pubs, hotels, restaurants and cafés

reach a fence above **Y Castell**, cross it and maintain the same approximate direction until another fence is approached, this time at an acute angle. Cross this fence, too, and then continue the climb, taking the easiest line westwards until you intercept a fenceline that runs along the summit ridge. From

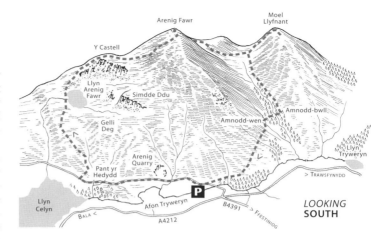

the fence there is a narrow path trending to the left, but this does not climb directly onto the ridge ahead, instead contouring across the south-eastern flank of **Arenig Fawr**, gradually climbing. This can be used, but it is easier simply to maintain the original direction and climb up to the ridge fence. There turn left and follow the fence to the top of the mountain, which is marked by a crumbling trig pillar, a stone shelter and a memorial to an American Flying Fortress that crashed here in 1943 with the loss of all six crewmen. The very top of the mountain is also known as **Moel yr Eglwys**, the hill of the church.

However long it took you to reach the summit, it is likely to have been somewhat longer than the fell runners who tackle the **Arenig Fawr race** each October, with some runners completing the race in a little over 53 minutes. From the top the view is superb especially to the north, embracing all the high mountains of Snowdonia including Snowdon, the Glyders and the Carneddau, and commanding a panoramic view across the expanse of mountain, lake and moorland that is the Migneint.

George Borrow, writing in *Wild Wales*, said 'Arenig is certainly barren enough, for there is neither tree nor shrub on it, but there is something majestic in its huge bulk. Of all the hills I saw in Wales none made a greater impression upon me.'

Continue to follow the fenceline south from the top of Arenig Fawr to descend across minor tops, largely on grass and following a fence for some of the way. From Craig y Bychan, you need to descend to the wide, marshy col below Moel Llyfnant. You can decide whether to include Moel Llyfnant, of course, but it does make an interesting addition to the day, even though its status as a Marilyn gives it an attraction not everyone might feel.

Arenig Fawr (right) and Moel Llyfnant

The pull onto **Moel Llyfnant** is best achieved by sticking fairly close to the line of a collapsed wall. As you near the ridge, aim left to the summit. The highest point is on the far side of the fence, a rocky knoll crowned by a cairn. After a rather tedious ascent, the short turf of the summit with its rocky outcrops comes as a pleasant surprise. A stroll south to a little promontory gives an aerial view of the Afon Lliw valley, a route used by the Romans during their invasion of this area.

Go back down by the same route to the col, and there turn northwards, picking up a path that leads to **Amnodd-bwll**. Here, take the track heading north-east through woodland to **Amnodd-wen**, and from there follow a path heading northwards towards the course of a dismantled railway. Just before reaching this, turn north-east along a track that eventually leads out to the minor road, a short distance from the parking area near the quarry at the start.

Rhobell Fawr

*R*hobell Fawr sits in rather splendid isolation north of the Bala fault, poking its head above a ring of farmland and forest plantation. The approach is along minor lanes and forest trails, twisting and turning, and seeming never to be going in the right direction. But then, as the mature rash of plantation is left behind, the mountain appears, girt by crags that never quite throw down a challenge rock climbers would take up, but which present the walker with a modest amount of artful dodging. With nothing to get in the way, Rhobell Fawr commands excellent views, and that alone is justification for making the ascent. There are two ways to finish the walk: the shorter is the more demanding and involves a certain amount of thrashing around in a lovely but boggy setting, while the longer keeps it simple.

The Route

The first stage of the walk involves finding a way through farmland. From the parking area a lane leads into the village of **Rhydymain**, a lovely little backwater. You soon cross the **Afon Eiddon**, and immediately turn right towards the chapel. There, go left onto a steeply rising track above the chapel graveyard to a gate. Beyond the gate, branch right onto a rising stony track that turns out to be a fine old walled lane of some antiquity. As you walk on, Rhobell Fawr, and its neighbour, Dduallt, ease into view above sheep pastures, a quite lovely image.

Eventually, the lane emerges onto a narrow surfaced back road. Turn right, but soon leave the road

↑ Rhobell Fawr peers above sheep pastures, Rhydymain

ROUTE INFORMATION

Distance	12km/7½ miles
Height gain	650m/2132ft
Time	4–5 hours
Grade	energetic
Start point	SH805221

Getting there
The walk begins in the village of Rhydymain, just off the Bala to Dolgellau road. There is a parking area on the left, just as you turn off the A-road

Maps
(Ordnance Survey) OL 23 Cadair Idris and Llyn Tegid

After-walk refreshment
There are numerous pubs, cafés, restaurants and hotels in Bala, and Dolgellau

(at SH797222), by stepping up to a gate on the right. Cross the lower end of a pasture to a step-stile below a mature sycamore tree. Cross the stile, and go left towards a gate; through the gate, turn right to follow a fenceline to Braich-y-fedw farm. (At the time of writing, the farmer is putting in fencing to enclose the right of way; when completed this will slightly modify the route description, but not the route.)

At the farm, emerge onto another lane. Turn right, and follow this lane through a number of twists and turns: the hedgerows here, in season, provide quite a feast, being made up of hazel (for nuts), blackthorn (for sloes) and wild raspberries. Holly appears too, and the impression is of a very ancient hedgerow bounding an equally ancient highway.

Continue to a gate, and sheepfold and barn, at SH796232, and, beyond the gate, take the surfaced lane that rises gently, following this as it later swings round to reach the edge of a mature plantation at

Walled lane, and the Arans

Rhobell Fawr

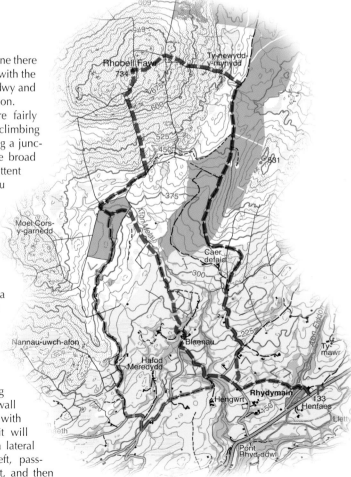

SH795237. As you walk this splendid lane there is time to take in the view to the south, with the mountains of Aran Benllyn, Aran Fawddwy and the Cadair Idris range forming the horizon.

The confines of the plantation are fairly short-lived, and you soon break free, climbing along the edge of the forest and passing a junction at SH797249. Keep following the broad forest trail, with Rhobell Fawr's intermittent crags temptingly rising on the left. You are heading towards a lonely habitation – **Ty Newydd y Mynydd** – now demolished; it has been many years since this was the 'new' house in the mountains. Before reaching the site of the house, you reach a gate on the left, at SH798255.

Go through the gate and follow a fence, wall and narrow path to a stream crossing, which you may have to leap. Beyond, the fence and wall find an easy way through crags above, and are a sure guide in poor visibility. Higher up the slope, beyond a couple of minor scrambly bits where crag and wall come close together, the wall and fence go their separate ways. Stay with the fence, without crossing it, and it will guide you to a ladder-stile spanning a lateral wall (SH790258). Over this, bear left, passing across a wall at a collapsed point, and then walking easily, obliquely across easy, gently rising

ground towards the robust trig pillar now in view on the summit of **Rhobell Fawr**. You cross another ladder-stile just below the summit, before the final few strides up to the top.

> The **view** is stunning. To the north-east you can pick out Moel Llyfnant and Arenig Fawr; north lie the great mountains of northern Snowdonia; south lie the Arans and Cadair Idris, but it is the shapely silhouette of the Rhinogydd that really catches the eye. All splendid stuff.

Leave the summit heading south to a ladder-stile across a wall. Cross this and turn right beside the wall until it reaches a junction in a dip. Now keep left, following the descending wall and using an accompanying path at varying distances from the wall, and not always plainly evident. But the direction is simple: down, parallel with the wall, to intercept a broad track close by a gate.

Turn right through the gate, now on level ground for the first time on the walk. A broad trail leads across rough sheep pasture, and finally curves left to re-enter plantation. After only about 100m, when you reach a footpath sign on the left (SH784241), you have a choice of routes to finish the walk. The following description covers the more difficult of the options, one that involves some hard going across trackless terrain. The alternative finish, described below, gives the easier, but longer, route back to Rhydymain.

The signposted path sends you into dense plantation, but this brief skirmish with gloom is short-lived, and you emerge to a lovely view across the gathering grounds of the **Afon Melau**. From the moment you leave the plantation until you reach the isolated homes at Blaenau there is no footpath worthy of the name, and a lot of rough going over a distance of 1.5km (1 mile). But the scenery is splendid, and if you can take your mind off the effort, it can be readily appreciated.

The river, to your left, is your guide, but easier going is found by staying well away from it, albeit parallel with its course. Fight your way valiantly onwards and down to eventually find a gate above the riverbank, and then keep on in the same direction, a little more easily. You soon reach another gate, beyond which an optimistic cart track appears.

The track has moments of doubt, but then regains confidence and continues clearly across rough pasture, guiding you round to a cluster of gates near a ruined barn.

Pass through the gates (going left), and then bear right across the corner of another rough pasture to a gate in a fence. Beyond the gate, once more without a path, keep on in the same direction over a slight rise, before descending to two gates (one wooden, one metal) at a wall corner (SH791230). Through the wooden gate you enter an enclosed pasture, marginally improved, where the going is a little easier, but still uncertain. Although a green path will be found to descend through bracken and isolated blackthorn and ash, it requires good navigation, or good luck, to reach a gate in a moss-covered wall at SH791228.

Through the gate, bear right below the wall, and then left, heading briefly downhill through bracken to another gate giving onto a surfaced lane. Turn left and follow the descending lane to **Blaenau**. Just after a gate you reach a road junction. Here, turn left and follow the lane finally to cross the Afon Melau, beyond which the lane climbs gently. At a broad road junction, keep right and then walk downhill to meet the old walled lane used in the early part of the walk. Turn into this and follow it back to Rhydymain.

Alternative finish: This alternative conclusion to the walk takes the overall distance up to 13.2km (8¼) miles, with no significant additional height gain.

From the forest signpost, simply stay on the broad trail, following this in a southerly direction until you intercept a lane at SH786218. Now turn left. The actual route you take back to the start is a matter of choice. There are narrow lanes, old walled tracks, field paths, any of which will help you construct a route back to the bridge over the Afon Melau at SH795223.

↑ *The summit of Rhobell Fawr*

Aran Benllyn

*O*f the two vast hills of Aran, the lower, Aran Benllyn, is arguably better known than its neighbour Aran Fawddwy, since it is the dominating feature of the skyline rising enticingly beyond the end of Llyn Tegid (Bala Lake). Making circular walks that aren't painfully long is difficult, but that is of little consequence because the simple process of walking up Aran Benllyn and back down again is so hugely rewarding, and markedly different in descent, especially as the sun moves around and distant mountains take on changing forms and shapes. For a longer day, you can simply tack on Aran Fawddwy.

The Route

From the car park, head towards the bridge and cross the road to a ladder-stile beside a gate (do not cross the bridge).

Llanuwchllyn was the birthplace of Owen Morgan Edwards, Welsh language author and educationalist. Just north of the main road, Caer-gai is a Roman fort later associated with Arthurian legend as the home of Cei, King Arthur's foster brother and one of the first Knights of the Round Table.

Follow a narrow, surfaced lane beyond as far as a bridleway signpost and ladder-stile beside a gate at SH878292. Ascend diagonally up-field following a shallow, grooved track to another stile, beyond which the continuing bridleway lopes around the northern end of Garth Fach. Already there a fine views northwards, notably at this stage of Arenig Fawr and Moel Llyfnant.

At the next gate and stile you enter Access Land, still following the sunken bridleway, until it divides at a low waymark at SH875288. Here bear left,

↑ *Aran Benllyn from Erw y Ddafad Ddu*

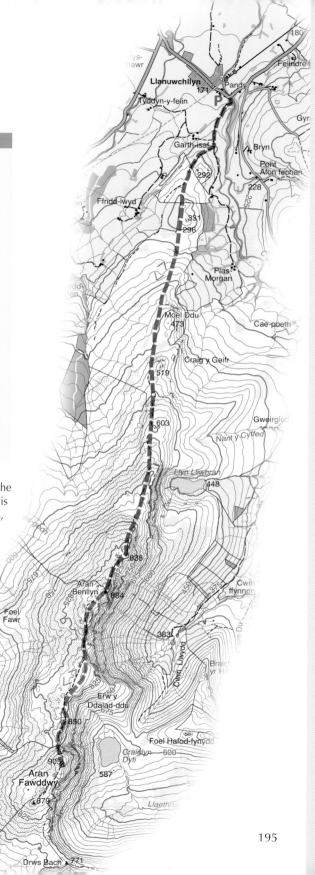

ROUTE INFORMATION

Distance	13km/8 miles: including Aran Fawddwy 17.8km/11 miles
Height gain	740m/2425ft: including Aran Fawddwy 995m/3265ft
Time	4–5 hours, 6–7 hours including Aran Fawddwy
Grade	moderate
Start point	Pont y Pandy SH879298

Getting there

There is a small National Park (free) car park at Pont y Pandy in Llanuwchllyn

Maps

(Ordnance Survey) OL 23 Cadair Idris and Llyn Tegid

After-walk refreshment

There is a pub in Llanuwchllyn, and all the refreshments you could want both in Bala and Dolgellau

climbing steadily to cross a wall, after which the path is accompanied by a fence. Aran Benllyn is renowned for a whole repertoire of false summits, so, tempting as it might be to suppose that you can see the summit ahead, any such thoughts should be quelled for quite some time. In many ways, not least the constantly changing views and skyline, this characteristic makes the ascent more pleasurable as you tackle Moel Ddu, Craig y Geifr and Moel Ffenigl to come. The fenceline, too, is a friend to be trusted, as it will lead you to the very summit of the mountain, and beyond. It does not quite touch upon the highest point of Benllyn, but it is a near thing.

The first stages of the ascent are easy enough, dropping quite early on through a dip to a stile at the end of a wall, after which the path now starts to climb more energetically. To the east, by way of diversion, the rolling, lush, patterned

The final approach to Aran Benllyn; Aran Fawddwy is just visible in the background

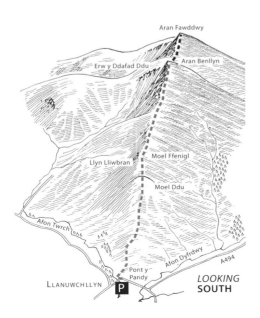

pastures of Cwm Cynllwyd and its hill farms are an especial delight.

The path is rarely in doubt, and always keeps the fenceline in sight, climbing to a stile at SH872262 on the edge of **Moel Ffenigl**. A short way further on, you cross to the opposite side of the fence as you start the final pull up on to Aran Benllyn, and cross it back again a little later. None of this fence-hopping is really necessary, but it ensures that you follow the predominant path. A small lake, **Llyn Pen Aran**, at SH869247 comes as a pleasant surprise, and from it you make the final pull across to the summit, crown by a neat cairn of mainly quartz rocks.

Aran Benllyn is technically a subsidiary summit of the higher Aran Fawddwy which rises temptingly to the south, but it commands presence itself and feels every bit an independent mountain. The top of the mountain has a spread of rocky outcrops, and the makings of a wall, although the function of a wall hereabouts is unclear. The view, as might be

The summit trig on Aran Fawddwy →

The summit of Aran Benllyn

supposed, is quite splendid and embraces virtually all of the northern Snowdonian mountains.

The simple act of retracing your steps to Pont y Pandy will conclude a marvellous day, high among the mountains.

Alternative route: The continuation to Aran Fawddwy is not at all difficult in either direction, and again you could follow the fence, which continues to be a reliable guide. But there is an interesting diversion across a minor top, **Erw y Ddafad Ddu**, the Acre of the Black Sheep,

to a lovely cairn overlooking the eastern face of Aran Fawddwy and Craiglyn Dyfi, the source of the River Dyfi (Dovey).

After a final dip, crossed by a wall and fence, with two ladder-stiles, a brief rocky pull leads up to the trig set on a pile of stones that marks the summit. It is a fine, exhilarating moment, with Cadair Idris looming to the south-west like some great ship about to set sail. To the north-west lie the Rhinogs, and closer still, the isolated summits of Rhobell Fawr and Dduallt.

Aran Fawddwy

*A*ran Fawddwy is the highest summit along the range of mountains from the border with England to the sea, a frontier that formed the southern boundary of ancient Gwynedd, the strongest of the old Welsh states. With the River Dfyi (Dovey), which rises directly below Fawddwy's summit in Craiglyn Dyfi, forming a natural barrier, this line is traditionally the division between North and South Wales. Aran Fawddwy is rather less accessible than its northerly neighbour, ascents to its summit beginning in enclosed Cwm Cywarch, which lacks the openness of Benllyn. Even so, the valley can soon be escaped and what then follows is a fine walk up the mountain.

The Route

From the lane through Cwm Cywarch, a way-marked route crosses a bridge (SH853187) and then ascends, traversing across the north-facing slopes of **Pen yr Allt Uchaf**, above the deep trough of **Hengwm**, to a quartz cairn on the low col between **Waun Goch** and Drysgol. From here a path crosses boggy ground and leads to the top of **Drysgol** and on, following a fenceline to **Drws Bach**.

You may puzzle at the sight of a moss-covered **cairn/monument** on this insignificant top, placed in memory of a member of the RAF St Athan Mountain Rescue Team, who was killed by lightning near this spot in 1960.

From Drws Bach a gentle stroll, still following a fenceline, takes you to the base of the final pull up to **Aran Fawddwy**. Now the going changes abruptly

↑ *Aran Fawddwy*

ROUTE INFORMATION

Distance	12.5km/8 miles: including Aran Benllyn 17km/10½ miles
Height gain	900m/2955ft: including Aran Benllyn 1130m/3710ft
Time	4–5 hours: including Aran Benllyn 6–7 hours
Grade	energetic
Start point	SH853184

Getting there
Turn off the A470 Mallwyd to Dolgellau road at Dinas Mawddwy. Turn left at Abercywarch, off an unclassified road signed Llanymawddwy, Bala and Llyn Llanwddyn. Follow the narrow lane up Cwm Cywarch to an open area of grass where parking is available

Maps
(Ordnance Survey) OL 23 Cadair Idris and Llyn Tegid

After-walk refreshment
Pubs in Dinas Mawddwy and at Cross Foxes; cafés, restaurants, pubs and hotels in Dolgellau

from grass to rock, and the route is marked by a line of cairns. As you approach the south top, so the fence you have been following joins with another for the final assault on the summit, although it does not actually pass directly over the summit, being about 100m to the west of it.

Aran Fawddwy is named, like Aran Benllyn, from ancient territorial divisions, known as cantrefs, which once belonged to the Middle Kingdom of Powys. Aran Benllyn rises to the north, beyond a minor top Erw y Ddafad Ddu. To the west, the mountains offer only soft slopes running down to the Afon Wnion, but to the east the cliffs are dramatic, steep, craggy and laden with bilberries and heather.

You can return to Cwm Cywarch by the simple expedient of retracing your steps. But if you want a slightly longer completion, return just as far as the point where the fencelines met. Here cross a ladder-stile on the right, and then follow the ongoing fenceline,

Aran Fawddwy and Craiglyn Dyfi from Erw y Ddafad Ddu

Aran Benllyn

valley. The path soon passes a small lake, and leads you into a narrow and steep-sided cwm. Cross a stream and follow it downhill, passing below overhanging crags.

The rocky path is consistently steep and awkward in a few places, heading initially in a south-westerly direction across featureless moorland. Keep the fence on your left throughout what is quite a long descent, crossing more fences on the way down to a boggy col north-east of **Glasgwm**, across which an ancient right of way runs. The fence does not continue all the way to the col, so when it changes direction, just keep on until you intercept the right of way. Here you change direction, now heading south-east, encountering and crossing a fence as you descend steeply below **Creigiau Camddwr** and **Craig Cywarch** to return to the

201

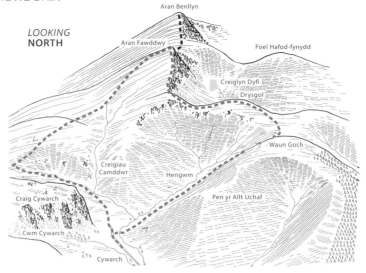

LOOKING **NORTH**

with the rocks proving slippery when wet. Keep going down to a footbridge and turn right over it, and then left still beside the stream, now following an easier path down to a ladder-stile. Cross the stile and go ahead a short distance to meet a track, and turn right along this, crossing mores stiles and eventually running out, past a farm to join a lane that takes you back to the start.

Continuation to Aran Benllyn: Many walkers reaching Aran Fawddwy opt to continue along this outstanding ridge to Aran Benllyn, and there is no difficulty in doing so. Just north of Aran Fawddwy's summit, a rocky descent leads to a narrow and unsuspected col crossed by a wall, a fence, and two ladder-stiles. Beyond these, it is an easy and gentle pull up beside the fenceline to Aran Benllyn, crossing and re-crossing the fence a few times at ladder-stiles. It is worth diverting, going or coming back, to **Erw y Ddafad Ddu**, a minor top, but one with a splendid cairn perched high above **Creiglyn Dyfi**, the source of the River Dyfi (Dovey), and a stunning profile of the east-facing cliffs of Aran Fawddwy. The summit of Aran Benllyn is marked by a large cairn.

On the summit of Aran Fawddwy looking back to Aran Benllyn and Bala lake

CADAIR IDRIS
AND THE TARRENS

Pen y Gadair and Llyn Cau (Walk 38)

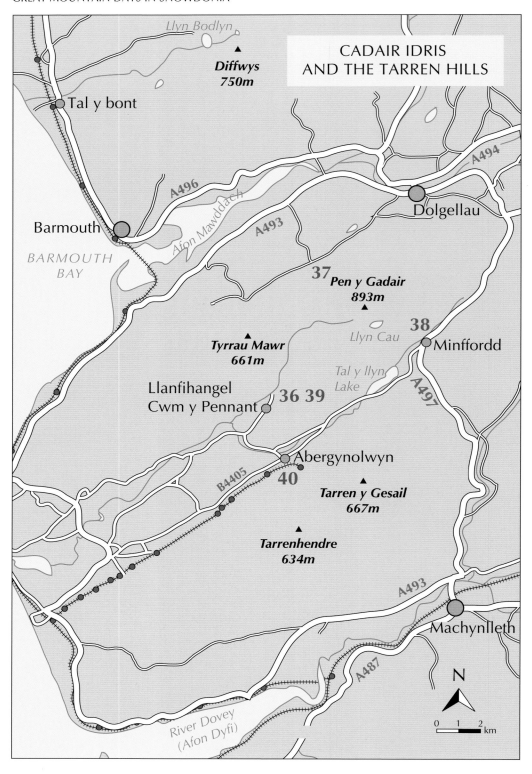

CADAIR IDRIS
AND THE TARREN HILLS

Llyn Bodlyn

▲ Diffwys
750m

Tal y bont

A494

A496

Dolgellau

Afon Mawddach

A493

Barmouth

BARMOUTH
BAY

37 Pen y Gadair
893m
▲

38

▲ Tyrrau Mawr
661m

Llyn Cau

Minffordd

Tal y llyn
Lake

A497

Llanfihangel
Cwm y Pennant

36 39

Abergynolwyn

B4405

40

▲ Tarren y Gesail
667m

▲
Tarrenhendre
634m

A493

Machynlleth

A487

N

River Dovey
(Afon Dyfi)

0   1   2
km

CADAIR IDRIS AND THE TARREN HILLS

The distinctive character of the Cadair Idris range derives from the way ice has gouged great corrie basins from the volcanic rocks, with impressive results. One such corrie, in which reposes Llyn y Gadair, is the legendary Chair of Idris, from which the range takes its name, the highest point of which is Pen y Gadair, although it is more commonly referred to as Cadair Idris, or the anglicised Cader Idris.

The whole area around Cadair Idris has long been popular with tourists. For over fifty years in the 18th century, Robin Edwards of Dolgellau guided clients across the mountains, while the arrival of the Cambrian Railway at Barmouth in the 19th century opened up the countryside to a new wave of enlightenment-seeking Victorian excursionists. Such was the force of Victorian enterprise that a refreshment

THE REALM OF IDRIS

Idris, in some accounts, is a mythical giant; in others he is a local worthy given to much contemplation among the mountains in true bardic fashion. Yet other tales portray him as a giant warrior poet killed in battle against the Saxons in 630. The reality is more likely to be that Idris is a name invented to adorn mythology and folklore. Belief in the existence of elves or fairies in the caves of Cadair Idris has long been held. But they are good spirits, in spite of the often malevolent and grim aspect of the

mountain, and, according to one account in Welsh mythology, Cadair Idris is also said to be one of the hunting grounds of Gwyn ap Nudd (King of the Tylwyth Teg, the Fairy Folk), and his Cwn Annwn. The howling of these huge spectral hounds foretold death to anyone who heard them, the pack sweeping up that person's soul and shepherding it into the underworld. Part of an explanation, then, of why it is said that anyone who sleeps on the mountain will wake up either a madman or a poet.

hut was built hut on the top of Pen y Gadair, the scant remains of which (now containing a personalised memorial plaque) cluster below the summit, and might easily be passed without notice.

To the north, Dolgellau is an ancient market town set in a wide and fertile valley through which flows the river Wnion. Roman roads meet here – the Romans conquered the tribal lands of the Ordovices in 77–8. After the Romans left, the area came under the control of Welsh chieftains, although Dolgellau was probably not inhabited until the late 11th or 12th century, when it was established as a serf village (or maerdref), which it remained until the reign of Henry VII (1485–1509), the first Tudor monarch. In 1404, Owain ap Gruffudd Fychan, better known as the charismatic Owain Glyndwr, a descendant through his mother of the last native Prince of Wales, Llywelyn the Great, assembled the last Welsh Parliament here, from which Glyndwr issued letters patent in sovereign style appointing ambassadors to go to France to a sign a treaty of alliance with Charles IV against the English.

To the south nothing but delight awaits. Here, the Dysynni valley is picture postcard perfect, and focuses on the small village of Abergynolwyn. This is part of the old county of Merionnydd, a component of Gwynedd, the strongest of the Welsh kingdoms, and one that often imposed unity on the war-faring princelings of medieval Wales. The nearby Castell y Bere, close by the confluence between the Afon Dysynni and the Afon Cadair, was the last castle to fall to Edward I, in 1283, defended to the last by the enigmatic Dafydd, brother to Llywelyn ap Gruffudd, the Prince of Gwynedd.

Further south, forming the most southerly rampart of this book, lie the Tarren Hills, although that name is a tautology – 'Tarren' means 'hill'. But the phrase has stuck and made a convenient label for quite a few hills. These wood-cloaked summits, of which only two exceed 600m in height, are a delight to explore, possessing an esoteric, almost fragile, quality that places the walker at one with nature. Start your exploration of Snowdonia here, and it may be a long time before you go anywhere else.

Foel y Geifr, the grassy ridge linking the two Tarrens (Walk 40)

Cyfrwy, Pen y Gadair and Mynydd Pencoed

*T*his is the gentlest of the ways onto the Cadair Idris range, but it is the longest. The so-called Pony Track runs from the hamlet of Llanfihangel y Pennant, over the eastern shoulder of Tyrrau Mawr and down the other side to Ty Nant. This was the most direct way for parishioners to get to Dolgellau, their nearest market town and seat of Quarter Sessions. Today, the track serves recreational walkers, and leads easily through a peaceful pastoral setting that is a delight to explore, lush and green, its hedgerows bright in springtime with red campion and honeysuckle, and the air filled with the sound of larks, curlew and young lambs.*

The Route

Follow the narrow lane up the valley, passing Ty'n y Fach farm. A short way further on, cross the bridge over the **Afon Cadair** and turn right.

A ruined cottage – **Ty'n y Ddôl** – by the river contains a commemorative stone. This was the home of Mary Jones, who in 1800 walked barefoot, 25 miles over the mountains to Bala to buy a Welsh Bible from the Reverend Thomas Charles. It is said that her devotion inspired him to found the British and Foreign Bible Society.

Keeping Mary Jones' cottage to your right, continue along the metalled road, parallel with the river. You press on up the lane, enjoying the surroundings,

↑ *Cyfrwy and Llyn y Gadair*

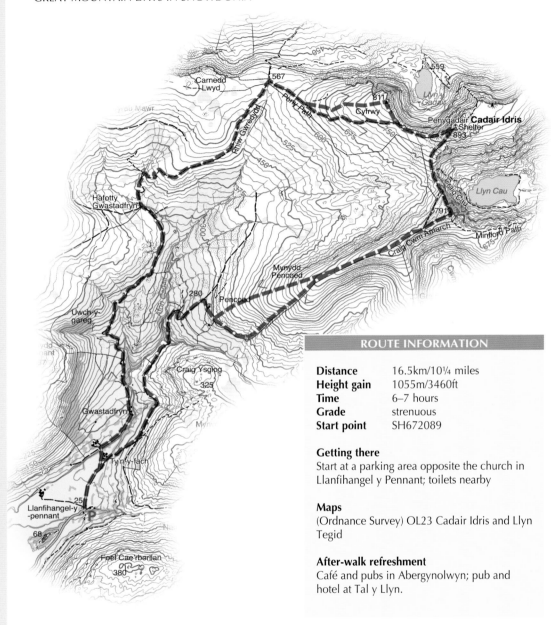

ROUTE INFORMATION

Distance   16.5km/10¼ miles
Height gain   1055m/3460ft
Time   6–7 hours
Grade   strenuous
Start point   SH672089

Getting there
Start at a parking area opposite the church in Llanfihangel y Pennant; toilets nearby

Maps
(Ordnance Survey) OL23 Cadair Idris and Llyn Tegid

After-walk refreshment
Café and pubs in Abergynolwyn; pub and hotel at Tal y Llyn.

and soon reach the old farmhouse of Gwastadfryn, where the road surfacing ends. From here on the track is rougher, and climbs to a gate. The shapely profile of **Craig Ysgiog** is on your right set against the smoother and more distant shape of Mynydd Pencoed, and shortly you pass a larch plantation on the steep slope beneath the track.

The fields you are walking through are part of **Ty'n y Fach** farm. Typically, a mountain farm is divided into three parts: the lowest consists of the intensively managed land around the house, where grazing and crops of hay or silage are focused. Higher up is the 'ffridd', below the mountain wall, an enclosed area of rougher land under a degree of management. Above the mountain wall is a large area of open mountain grazing.

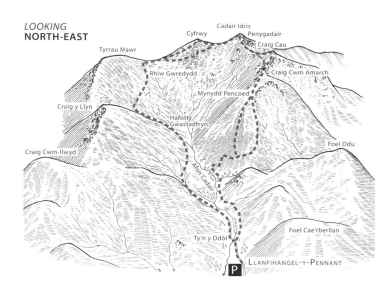

As you pass through another gate above the larch plantation you will see the rounded hump of Mynydd Pencoed on your right. A little further on you reach another gate close by a stone barn on your left.

The track you are walking eases steadily up the valley, with lovely retrospective views. Down in the valley, beyond your starting point there is an excellent view of Castell y Bere, and ahead to Pen y Gadair, the summit of Cadair Idris.

Castell y Bere was built by Llewellyn the Great around 1221 to protect the mountain trade routes, but following the invasion of Wales by Edward I in 1277 the castle was besieged, in 1283, by English forces. Its key position meant that, after its capture, Edward I ordered it to be refortified and garrisoned, and a small settlement was then encouraged to develop around its base.

Eventually, you reach the site of the old farm of **Hafotty Gwastadfryn**.

In the 18th and 19th centuries, mountain farmers used to follow a practice called **transhumance**, much as they did across Europe, notably in the Alps and the Pyrenees. The entire family would move to a mountain home, or 'hafod', in the

Cyfrwy and Pen y Gadair from Rhiw Gwredydd

On the summit of Pen y Gadair

summer, taking their stock to graze on the rich mountain grasses, so letting the lowland fields grow a crop of hay. In autumn, they all returned to the winter house ('hendre').

Continue along the track, bearing right over ladder-stiles just before you reach the sheep pens in the old farmyard, still in use today. Soon after crossing a stream, the track begins to climb steeply. When the track divides you take the right-hand branch; the left one goes only a little further, to a small quarry. Continue to follow the track, now grassy and becoming progressively narrower, until it meets the crest of the ridge, at **Rhiw Gwredydd**, and turns right to an intersection of fences with a gate and a stile. The path on the other side of the fence to your left is the **Pony Path** going down to Ty Nant, but you must follow it right. The track is perfectly clear, broad and well-trodden, climbing steadily and without undue difficulty through a bleak but fascinating terrain of frost-shattered rock.

The track reaches a level section high above Llyn y Gadair, and it is from here that you briefly turn northwards to walk up to the rocky summit of Cyfrwy. There is a more direct route to the top of Cyfrwy from just above Rhiw Gwredydd; this is cairned and rocky for most of the way.

Although the summit of **Cyfrwy** is undistinguished, it provides arguably the finest view there is of the cliffs of Pen y Gadair, perched as it is at the top of steep crags with blue **Llyn y Gadair** way below. One section of the northern arm of this outlying top has shattered in such a way as to create, below half height, a pedestal of rock known as Idris' Table.

Return to the main path and follow it around the edge of the cliff, taking great care, especially in snow and icy conditions. Do not go too close to the edge, as cornices – overhanging masses of snow – regularly form here. Soon you come to a cluster of peculiarly shaped rocks with the path winding between them. It is now only a few minutes' enjoyable, easy scrambling to the summit of **Pen Y Gadair**, marked by a trig pillar perched high on a pile of rocks and accessed by a short flight of steps. Close by is a squat, stone-built shelter maintained by the Snowdonia National Park Warden Service, a dry, safe haven in poor weather.

The route now continues southwards, but not directly. Your objective is the dip above **Craig Cau**. Take care as you leave Pen y Gadair to ensure that you have the correct line, as, from the summit, it is not instantly obvious. But if you do miss it, it is not difficult to swing left and cross to join the correct path. The view down into Cwm Cau and of the crags above the lake is quite eye-catching.

From the dip, a short climb leads to a rocky top crossed by a fence and ladder-stile. This small summit, with its stupendous plunge to the lake below, has a minor identity crisis, as it goes by various names, most of them linked to crags below the summit. Pen Craig Cau or Pen Cwm Amarch are arguably the only plausible names, but it is not so named. Instead, as the summit comes at the eastern end of a long and lovely ridge bearing the name of **Mynydd Pencoed**, this is the name used here.

Once at the summit, you need to follow the fenceline that runs roughly in a south-westerly direction, following a clear, narrow path around a few rocks, and on through short turf and bilberries. When the path veers away above **Cwm Amarch**, remain beside the fence until you reach a junction and ladder-stile. Here, cross to the north side of the fence. Now maintain the original direction, with the fence on your left, a delightful and easy prospect with fine views across to the summits of Tyrrau Mawr, Craig y Llyn and the Rhinogydd north of the Mawddach Estuary.

When the fence makes a slight change of the direction, the descent increases significantly. You have a choice: (a) continue to follow the fence, ever more steeply, and eventually losing the path amid a great spread of bilberries, but continuing downwards to meet a right of way at SH689108, beside a wall. Now follow the wall, keeping it to your left until at a ladder-stile you can cross the wall and head for another stile close by the farm building at Pencoed; (b) from the bend in the fenceline take a bearing on Pencoed, and make directly for it. The going underfoot is mainly grass, bilberry and heather, becoming steeper the closer you get to Pencoed. There are a few low outcrops of rocks, easily avoided; with care over the placement of feet you can target the ladder-stile in the wall, and from there walk to Pencoed.

At Pencoed, you find a broad access track, and this provides a lovely walk down into the valley, briefly crossing a neck of Access Land, and then continuing in delightful fashion to Ty'n y Fach farm. Just above the farm, as the track swings right to go down to the farmyard, leave it on the apex of the bend and pass through the right-hand one of two gates, to follow a broad grassy track out to meet the valley road. Now simply turn left and walk the short distance back to the start.

Pen y Gadair from Mynydd Pencoed

Pen y Gadair
from Ty Nant

*T*he Pony Track from Ty Nant, an ancient thoroughfare between adjacent valleys, today forms
the main path up Cadair Idris from the north. It is a reasonably safe and straightforward route,
*which also provides the most rewarding views. From the north you are faced with the impressive
escarpment of the range, which looks impenetrable, and for the most part is. But the mountain has
long been popular, and for over fifty years in the 18th century, Robin Edwards of Dolgellau guided
clients across the Cadair Idris range. The walk is a simple up-and-down ascent of the mountain; Walk
38 offers a circular route over the mountain from the south, while Walk 39 can easily be extended
to visit Pen y Gadair.*

The Route

As you leave the car park, Ty Nant farmhouse lies
to your left, and towering above it the bastions of
Cadair Idris ridge – Mynydd Moel, Pen y Gadair and
Cyfrwy, with the conspicuous notch that is the so-
called Idris' Table.

Follow the track up to **Ty Nant**, and go through
a kissing-gate. Soon you cross a concrete bridge
over a stream and pass through mixed, broadleaved
woodland of ash, birch, hawthorn, hazel and sycamore. Woodland is vital to mountain farms like Ty
Nant, providing much-needed shelter for stock in

ROUTE INFORMATION

Distance	9km/5½ miles
Height gain	735m/2410ft
Time	4 hours
Grade	energetic
Start point	Entrance to Ty Nant farm on the 'Cader' road about 5km (3 miles) out of Dolgellau (SH697153)

Getting there
National Park car park and toilet block at Pont Dyffrydan almost opposite the start point

Maps Ordnance
Survey OL23 Cadair Idris and Llyn Tegid

After-walk refreshment
Dolgellau is always worth a visit and has numerous cafés and pubs

Ascending the Pony Track from Ty Nant

bad weather. But constant grazing by sheep prevents young trees from growing, and this has resulted in a serious decline in Snowdonia's native woodlands.

The path is rocky but climbs gently. Many sections have suffered from erosion and slates have been sunk across the path to prevent hill-slip and to drain off surface water. Shortly you come to three large chestnut trees, where you turn right. Pass through another kissing-gate and cross a stream by a stone bridge. Presently the path starts to climb more steeply as it ascends the grassy hillside. Again, slates have been placed across the path, and further up, where the gradient is even steeper, steps have been built to prevent erosion.

On passing through a gap in a wall by a stream, you may notice that **the terrain** has become more open. Gone are the fine broadleaves and ancient chestnuts: now the only trees around are dwarfed and gnarled old hawthorns, like wizened hags bent on trouble. This is largely because the climate is more harsh the higher up the mountain you go, a change that few species are able to withstand.

Keep to the steps and eventually you pass through a gate and over a small bridge. To your left are the dark cliffs of

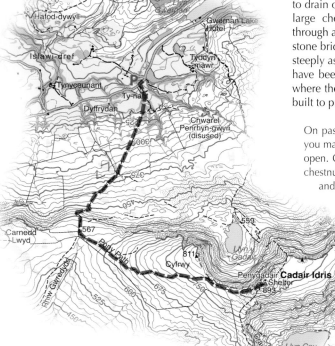

213

The summit: Pen y Gadair

Cyfrwy. Soon you will come to another gate in the wall with a stream nearby.

The path climbs very steeply by some stone sheep pens on your right. On this steep section erosion has been a serious problem in the past. At the top of the stone steps a barrier fence stops you going straight ahead. Turn left here and zigzag up the steep slope to the pass known as **Rhiw Gwredydd**. There is much anti-erosion work in evidence here: stone steps have been laid and gabions placed in gullies to prevent landslip damaging the path. After a steep climb the path levels out until it reaches an intersection of fences with a gate and stile.

Turn left and continue for a while along a level path. In some places there has been considerable erosion and

there are several areas where the peat has been deeply exposed. The path soon starts to climb again, and cairns mark the route, as the path follows a series of lazy zigzags until you top the rise and are rewarded by a view of Pen y Gadair. To the left is the **Cyfrwy** ridge and behind you the Pony Path down into the Pennant valley.

Passing through a landscape of frost-shattered rock, you are on top of the cliffs overlooking **Llyn y Gadair**. Follow the path to the right around the edge of the cliff, taking great care in the vicinity of the north-facing gullies, particularly in winter conditions. It is now only a few minutes rocky rambling to the summit, which is marked by a trig pillar set on a little plinth and ascended by a flight of steps, setting it apart from the rash of boulders, a cairn and shelter.

The summit of Cadair Idris, properly **Pen y Gadair**, is quite a tumbled affair among which are the remnants of the Victorian commercial initiative that built a stone refreshment hut here, where, according to one contemporary writer, visitors could partake of refreshments 'while waiting the dispersion of the misty clouds in order to enjoy the exquisite prospect'. The clouds are often still there, but the refreshments are not.

Pen y Gadair is the highest summit of the range, one stretching from Craig y Llyn in the west to Gau Craig in the east. It is a highly individual mountain, in spite of many similarities with Snowdon, and named after a someone who was killed in battle against the Saxons around the year 630. At one time it was considered to be the highest mountain in Britain, and although its true stature is somewhat less, its attraction to walkers, ancient and modern, has lessened not one jot.

As you retrace your steps, make sure you keep to the right hand path from the summit. The left hand path will take you down towards Bwlch Cau and the south side of the mountain.

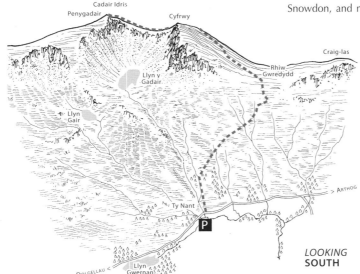

LOOKING **SOUTH**

214

Retrospective to Tyrrau Mawr from the Pony Path up to Pen y Gadair →

Mynydd Pencoed,
Pen y Gadair and Mynydd Moel

*T*he ascent of Cadair Idris from Minffordd is the shortest route, but one that involves the greatest amount of height gain. Moreover, it begins with a brutal flight of steps up through ancient woodland that seems to be saying 'If you can't do the steps; you can't do the hill', and so it seems. Set against that, this is a fine mountaineering route, possessing all the attributes of ruggedness, beauty and geologically fascinating scenery. Cwm Cau is a magical place worthy of a journey in itself, cradled by high mountain slopes and with a calm that is persuasive.

The Route

Go to the far end of the car park, through a gate and follow a broad track to Ystradllyn. Turn left in front of this sometime visitor centre until you cross Nant Cadair and can turn right through a gate into a fine example of a 'relic' (8000 years old) oak wood, now a National Nature Reserve.

Follow a stepped footpath steeply up through the woods, crossing a small stream along the way, until at a drystone wall and gate marking the end of the wood you enter Access Land. Mercifully, the gradient now eases as the path winds up to Cwm Cau passing a couple of ruined buildings on the left, and with the river and slopes of Mynydd Moel to the right. Just above the woodland boundary, you see that the river is crossed by a slate footpath; this is the way down from Mynydd Moel, the path to which can be seen rising across the lower slopes.

↑ *Mynydd Pencoed and Llyn Cau*

Distance	9.25km/6 miles
Height gain	945m/3100ft
Time	5–6 hours
Grade	energetic
Start point	SH732115

Getting there
National Park (Pay and Display) car park at
Dôl Idris, Minffordd, just after the junction of
the A487 and the B4405 Dolgellau to Tywyn
road (toilets)

Maps
(Ordnance Survey) OL23 Cadair Idris and Llyn
Tegid

After-walk refreshment
There is a pub and hotel at Tal y Llyn;
otherwise Abergynolwyn or Dolgellau

As the cliffs of Craig Cau come into view the
path becomes less distinct, but the scenery no
less impressive. Bear left around the marshy hollow immediately in front of you, in which you may
notice the landscape dotted with large 'erratic' boulders, deposited by the last Ice Age.

When you reach a large cairn the path divides.
Here, you can go forward, passing the long, smooth
profile of a *roche moutonnée*, and continue past it to
the shores of **Llyn Cau**.

A *roche moutonnée* is an elongated mound of
bedrock worn smooth and rounded by glacial
abrasion. It has a gently sloping, striated side
facing the direction from which the glacier origi-
nated, and a steeper side facing the direction of
glacial movement.

The crater-like depression containing **Llyn Cau**
has given rise to speculation that it is part of an
extinct volcano. But this is not so, and the theory
was discounted as early as 1872, when Charles
Kingsley commented in his book *Town Geology*:
'I have been told, for instance, that that wonderful

Roche moutonnée, Cwm Cau

Pen y Gadair from the ridge above Cwm Cau

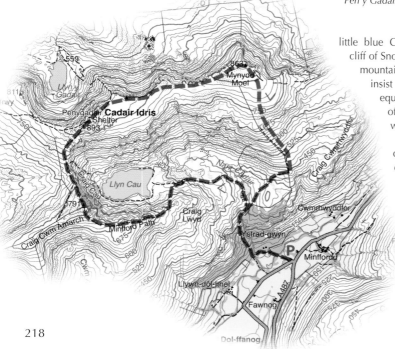

little blue Glas Llyn, under the highest cliff of Snowdon, is the old crater of the mountain; and I have heard people insist that a similar lake, of almost equal grandeur, in the south side of Cader Idris, is a crater likewise. But the fact is not so.'

In fact, Cwm Cau is a classic example of a 'corrie' or 'cirque', the result of both volcanic and later glacier activities, producing superb scenery and an ideal habitat for alpine plants.

The diversion to Llyn Cau is splendid, not least because from it you can see the path that takes you out of the cwm

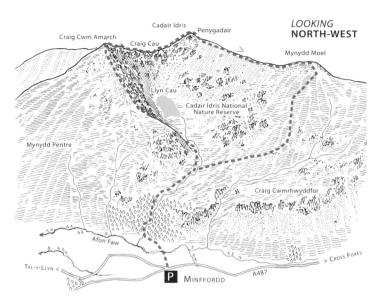

and onto the long, undulating ridge leading up to Mynydd Pencoed. The short climb, on slate steps, leads to fine views of the Tarren Hills to the south. Well-marked by cairns, a broad path winds steeply upwards, passing a band of white quartz in the rocks to your right.

A short detour to the left provides stunning views of Tal y Llyn Pass and the lake, part of the 30-mile long Bala fault, created 400 million years ago when the south side of the pass moved 3km (2 miles) in a north-easterly direction.

As you plod up the ridge, it levels out as Cwm Amarch comes into view on your left. The long rounded ridge ahead is **Mynydd Pencoed**.

There is some confusion over naming here. **Mynydd Pencoed** is probably better known as *Craig Cau*, the top of that impressive wall of rock rising vertically from Llyn Cau. Local knowledge and established opinion among mountaineers assert that Craig Cau is the abrupt terminus of the long ridge rising from Nant Pencoed and Cwm Pennant, which is named both *Mynydd Pencoed* and *Daear Fawr*. Craig Cau means the 'enclosed crag', which clearly it is, but a crag as such is not a summit. *Daear Fawr*, the 'large ground', may refer to the side of the ridge, but *Mynydd* clearly means 'mountain'. So, Mynydd Pencoed, which derives

from a small farmstead in Cwm Pennant, would seem to be the name not only of the tumbled mass of rocks and grass that form the summit but also of the whole grassy ridge extending south-west-wards. And while on the topic, Cadair Idris is the name of the whole range of mountains, the highest point of which is Pen y Gadair.

The path up to Mynydd Pencoed is well trodden and steep, and from it there are two routes down to Bwlch Cau before the final pull to Pen y Gadair. One follows the edge of the cliff and the other bears to the left.

The final section of the path up to Pen y Gadair is steep, slippery and suffering badly from erosion. Please keep to the footpath to prevent the erosion from spreading. A short zigzag finally brings you to the summit cairn and shelter.

No one is certain where the name **Cadair Idris** (Idris' chair) originates. Some maintain that Idris was a national hero, killed in battle against the Saxons round about the year 630. Some insist that he was a giant (Idris Gawr) said to be skilled in poetry, astronomy and philosophy, and yet others link Idris with the legend of Arthur.

It is also attested that anyone who sleeps on its slopes will supposedly awaken either a madman or a poet. This tradition (of sleeping on the summit of a mountain) stems from bardic traditions, when bards would sleep on mountain tops in hope of inspiration.

Mynydd Moel is linked to Pen y Gadair by a broad and grassy ridge with steep drops on both sides, but there is a good path between the summits. In fine weather you might consider taking to a narrow path along the very edge of the north-facing escarpment; this is much more exciting and gives excellent views over Dolgellau to the Mawddach Estuary in the west and the Arans in the east.

From the top of Mynydd Moel, set off initially in a south-easterly direction (but don't go too far that way, or you'll end up heading in the wrong direction), soon turning southwards to connect with a path that steers you down to the path you will have noticed as you climbed up into Cwm Cau. This eventually leads down to a ladder-stile, beyond which the path slips easily downwards to the slate bridge spanning the **Nant Cadair**, and a return through the oak woodlands of Dôl Idris.

The continuation to Mynydd Moel from Pen y Gadair

Tyrrau Mawr and Craig y Llyn

*N*ormally the remote hamlet of Llanfihangel y Pennant is used to effect a long but relatively easy ascent to Pen y Gadair. But to the south-west of the high summit a couple of grassy hills with fine, north-facing cliffs makes an excellent and easy variation on a theme, taking you into a region that is delightful at all times of year, and especially attractive during the summer months when most folk are heading for the heights. The early stages of the walk are replicated on the return leg, but the valley of the Afon Cadair is such an agreeable place of pastoral loveliness that to retrace your steps is no real hardship.

The Route

This walk shares the long but easy ascent to Rhiw Gwredydd with Walk 36, setting off up the lane to Ty'n y Fach farm, passing Mary Jones' cottage, Ty'n y Ddôl, and continuing all the way to the summer shieling of **Hafotty Gwastadfryn**.

The **memorial** at Ty'n y Ddôl, which commemorates the long walk 16-year-old Mary Jones (1784–1864) took to Bala in 1800 to procure a Welsh Bible, was erected in 1921 by the Sunday Schools of Merioneth.

↑ *Tyrrau Mawr from Carnedd y Lwyd*

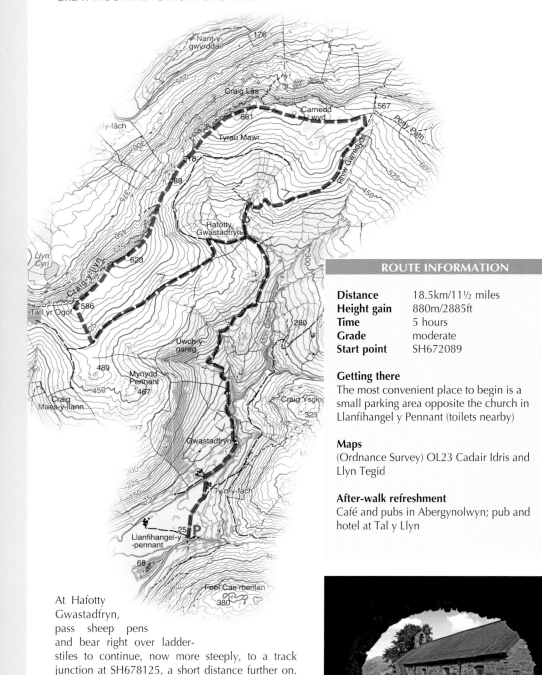

ROUTE INFORMATION

Distance	18.5km/11½ miles
Height gain	880m/2885ft
Time	5 hours
Grade	moderate
Start point	SH672089

Getting there
The most convenient place to begin is a
small parking area opposite the church in
Llanfihangel y Pennant (toilets nearby)

Maps
(Ordnance Survey) OL23 Cadair Idris and
Llyn Tegid

After-walk refreshment
Café and pubs in Abergynolwyn; pub and
hotel at Tal y Llyn

At Hafotty
Gwastadfryn,
pass sheep pens
and bear right over ladder-
stiles to continue, now more steeply, to a track
junction at SH678125, a short distance further on.
Bear right at the junction, continuing now along a
broad grassy track which, as height and distance are
gained, becomes narrower. It leads to the obvious
cross-path at **Rhiw Gwredydd**, where the Pony Path
arrives from Ty Nant to the north, and a broad track
strikes eastwards for Pen y Gadair. Thomas Pennant

Llanfihangel y Pennant church

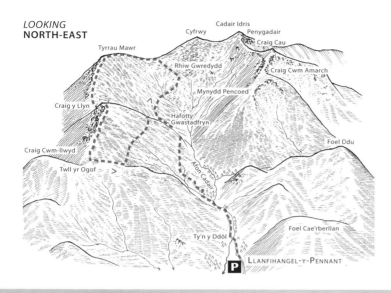

LOOKING **NORTH-EAST**

describes the cross-mountain route as 'a narrow steep horse-way, perhaps the highest road in Britain, being a common passage even for laden horses, into Llanfihangel-y-Pennant, a vale on the other side.'

Here, turn left alongside a fence, taking a narrow path through rough grassy terrain, and targeting a couple of conspicuous mounds of stones to the west. This is **Carnedd Lwyd**, and a clear indication of prehistoric occupation both of the hills and the valleys below. Here, too,

Craig y Llyn

you find a small stone shelter, built into the mound of stones. To the north, an impressive rack of cliffs, **Craig Las**, peers down on the Mawddach Estuary, and the best impression of these is gained by trotting up to the top of Tyrrau Mawr. Pennant considered that these cliffs were '... the highest rock [he] ever rode under'.

The highest point of **Tyrrau Mawr**, easily reached by staying beside the ongoing fenceline, is marked by a cairn of slaty stones on the very edge of the precipice, a location that requires sure footing, or, better, an approach to the rim that is not too close.

Once across Tyrrau Mawr, a steady descent leads onward, the fence being crossed by ladder-stiles in a few places before a surprisingly stiff little pull up to **Craig y Llyn**, the top of which is marked by a small stone cairn. Cradled in a wild hollow below, the jewelled eye of Llyn Cyri lies somewhat forlorn beneath **Twll yr Ogof**, a minor top which would be insignificant were it not for a curious circular mound of stones on its top.

Beyond, as Richard Fenton describes in *Tours in Wales*, the ridge peters out and 'the Mountains change into fine Downy Hills, though of great height; extensive sheep walks... for some miles not a habitation, unless here and there, in some sheltered situation, an Havodty.'

Tyrrau Mawr and Craig y Llyn are almost identical summits with imposing steepness to the north contrasting markedly with the smooth flanks by which route you have ascended from the south. And it is into the embrace of those smooth slopes that the route now returns.

Due south from Twll yr Ogof, down steep grassy slopes you intercept a broad track, an extension of tracks used earlier in the walk. Having reached the track, turn left (north-east) along it and it will take you down to a track junction (SH674121), a short distance to the west of Hafotty Gwastadfryn, where you join the outward route. All that remains is to turn right, heading south, and enjoy the walk down this delectable valley.

The valley of the Afon Cadair

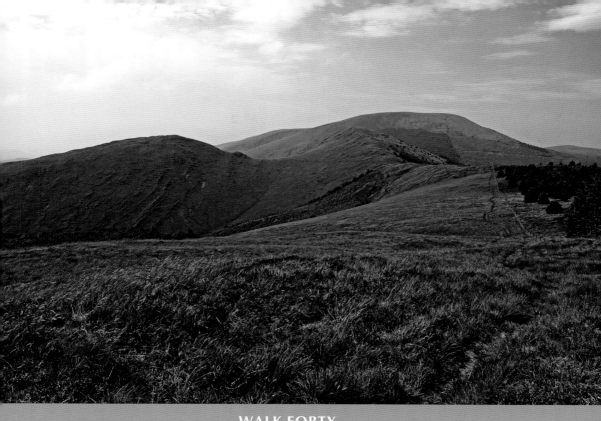

The Tarrens

*E*ncircling the Bryn Eglwys quarry, the Tarrens form a great headwall to this side valley; they are little visited by walkers, often deserted and somewhere you can enjoy invigorating, leg-swinging freedom as you gallop along forest trails or the superb grassy ridge linking the two main summits. On a warm day with a gentle breeze this is a place of great delight high above Machynlleth to the south and the delectable Dysynni valley to the north.

The walk falls into three distinct sections, the first and last making use of wide trails that serve the forests hereabouts, although there has been a great deal of clear felling and replanting in recent years which means that virtually throughout the walk the views are high, wide and handsome, rarely inducing the claustrophobia associated with mature plantations. Between the two you romp along grassy summits and linking ridges in a manner nothing short of soul-refreshing. There are few places in Snowdonia where you can so readily enjoy the harmonious sounds of silence; the Tarrens lay a fair claim to being the best.

↑ *The Foel y Geifr ridge; heading for Tarrenhendre*

View from the slopes of Tarrenhendre, looking over Mynydd Rhyd-galed to Tarren y Gesail

ROUTE INFORMATION

Distance	18.5km/11½ miles
Height gain	1060m/3480ft
Time	6–7 hours
Grade	energetic
Start point	SH678069

Getting there
There is a small car park near the post office in Abergynolwyn (toilets nearby)

Maps
(Ordnance Survey) OL23 Cadair Idris and Llyn Tegid

After-walk refreshment
Café behind the post office, and pub across the road, in Abergynolwyn

The Route
Set off by walking up the lane running south-east from the post office, climbing steeply for some time.

Abergynolwyn was formerly a major centre of the slate industry, founded in the 1860s to house workers at the Bryn Eglwys quarry; today it is hill farming, forestry and tourism on which the village's economy is founded. Before this development, what is now Abergynolwyn was just two tiny hamlets, Pandy and Cwrt, at opposing ends of the present village.

As you climb the lane, you come to the entrance on the right, at a gate, to Coed Cadw (SH681068), a new woodland through which a path runs parallel with but lower down the hill slope from the lane. You can go this way if you want to shun the hard surfacing of the road; at a number of points, paths lead up to stiles giving back onto the lane.

Otherwise, continue up the lane, which at a gate enters a brief wooded section, on leaving which the gradient now eases as the smooth profile of Tarrenhendre comes into view on the right. You finally leave the lane at SH691058, by doubling back on a broad trail, ascending steadily. Had you used the alternative path, you would find that in due course it curved back up to the road, not far from this key turning point.

In the valley below you can see the spoil from the **Bryn Eglwys slate quarry**, first worked on a small scale in the 1840s. In 1864 William McConnel, an industrialist and mill owner from Lancashire, leased the quarry, forming the Aberdovey Slate Company Limited, planning to increase production. The limiting factor was the need to transport finished slates to the wharves

at Aberdovey by packhorse. To overcome this, McConnel built the Talyllyn Railway, a narrow-gauge line running from the quarry to Tywyn, whence slate could be transhipped to the newly built Aberystwyth and Welsh Coast Railway. In the event, neither the quarry nor the railway were great commercial successes, and by 1879 the company had run out of money.

Follow the broad trail upwards at an easy gradient until you finally enter the forest, Coed Tyglas, at a gate and stile (SH698065). The forest is mature, although the trees are well set back from the track. There is one main trail through the forest, with a couple of diverging trails that are less pronounced. Stay on the main trail throughout, and this will bring you out of the forest and onto the western slopes of **Tarren y Gesail** at a stile (SH704055). Climb steeply left, along the forest boundary for a short distance further until you can bear off along a grassy path that will take you to the crumbling trig pillar next to a low stone shelter near the top of the mountain.

Press on along the top of the hill, following the fenceline and adjacent path in an easterly direction, and later stay beside the fence when it changes direction and descends steeply to an obvious pass (bwlch) below.

Tarren y Gesail

From the pass (SH717054), cross a stile and keep on in the same direction to follow a fire break through young spruce. This finally emerges on the end of a fine grassy ridge, **Foel y Geifr**, which leads on to a gate at SH703046, through which a speedy descent may be made, if needed, to the Bryn Eglwys quarry site.

Otherwise, press on and climb over a grassy lump that marks the highest point of **Mynydd Rhyd-galed**. Finally, you engage the pull up onto **Tarrenhendre**, with an intermediate stile looking from below like it might be the top of the ascent; alas, it isn't, and more uphill work awaits before the fence guides you to a junction with a large cairn off to the left pretending to be the summit of the mountain. Cross the fence at this point and walk on a little further to another fence junction. Here you need to cross the fence on the right, preferably without damage to the fence or injury to yourself. Nearby, a low cairn on the edge of a peat hag marks the undistinguished summit of the mountain.

From the summit, a line of poles sets off in a north-easterly direction, accompanied by a narrow grassy path. This is the surest way off the mountain, unless you choose to backtrack to the gate at SH703046. The descending path is continuous throughout; the waymark poles rather less so, although they do appear whenever you feel in need of reassurance. Lower down the path is becoming encroached upon by a random spread of what looks like self-seeded spruce, but eventually it guides you down to intercept a broad forest trail, largely at this point devoid of forest (SH688047).

Turn left along the trail to begin a long, open and serpentine return to Abergynolwyn, with virtually no scope for effecting shortcuts. The trail winds round below Tarren-fach, on the steep slopes of which the debris of clearance effectively prevents a descent north from Tarrenhendre, had you thought of going that way. The trail passes to the south of **Foel Fawr**, passing two trails on the left, and then one merging from the right. Shortly after this third junction you leave the woodland behind and soon arrive at a blue waymark belonging to one of the walking trails from Abergynolwyn.

If you need a shorter return, then at this blue waymark double back onto a narrow path, descending into a wooded ravine, and later changing direction to run as a clear path to Nant Gwernol Station, the Talyllyn Railway terminus.

Otherwise, stay on the higher, broader forest trail until (at SH678065) you reach a third blue waymark at which you leave the forest trail by diving down to the right into woodland, following a path that emerges from the trees at another broad trail. Now turn right and follow this trail to its end at a turning circle from which a path leads on (red and blue waymarks) through bracken, and then as a terraced path across a steep wooded slope high above Nant Gwernol.

Finally, when the path divides, descend steps on the left to Nant Gwernol Station; go right and cross a footbridge, and on the other side continue descending to conclude with a lovely path beside the stream, with numerous small cascades and plunge pools. The path finally pops out on the lane used in the early part of the walk. Turn down this to complete the walk.

The summit of Tarren y Gesail looking to Tarrenhendre

APPENDIX 1
Concise walk reference and personal log

WALK		DISTANCE	HEIGHT GAIN	TIME	GRADE	WALKED
1	Snowdon Horseshoe	11km/6¾ miles	1110m/3640ft	5–6 hours	arduous	
2	The Rhyd Ddu Path and the Snowdon Ranger	14km/8¾ miles	970m/3182ft	5–6 hours	energetic	
3	The Watkin Path and Yr Aran	12.6km/8 miles; including Yr Aran 14.5km/9 miles	1070m/3510ft; including Yr Aran 1320m/4330ft	5–6 hours; with Yr Aran 6–7 hours	arduous/ strenuous	
4	The Pyg Track and the Miners' Track	11.5km/7 miles	840m/2755ft	4–5 hours	strenuous	
5	Moel Eilio Horseshoe	13.8km/8½ miles	990m/3250ft	4–5 hours	energetic	
6	The Glyders by the Bristly Ridge	8.5km/5¼ miles	845m/2772ft	4–5 hours	arduous	
7	Y Garn to Elidir Fawr and Carnedd y Filiast	14km/8¾ miles	1150m/3770ft	6+ hours	strenuous	
8	Tryfan	3.75km/2½ miles	585m/1920ft	3–3½ hours	arduous	
9	Bwlch Tryfan, Y Foel Goch, Gallt yr Ogof and Cefn y Capel	16.5km/10¼ miles	840m/2755ft	6+ hours	moderate	
10	Conwy Mountain	9.5km/6 miles	370m/1215ft	3 hours	moderate	
11	Tal y Fan	15.5km/9¾ miles	640m/2100ft	5 hours	moderate	
12	Drum, Foel Fras, Carnedd Uchaf, Drosgl and Aber Falls	18km/11¼ miles	1035m/3395ft	6+ hours	energetic	
13	Llyn Anafon and the eastern Carneddau	10km/6¼ miles	690m/2265ft	3–4 hours	moderate	
14	Pen yr Ole Wen, Carnedd Dafydd, Carnedd Llywelyn and Pen yr Helgi Du	16km/10 miles	1170m/3840ft	6+ hours	arduous	
15	Cwm Eigiau Horseshoe	16.5km/10¼ miles	1075m/3525ft	6–7 hours	arduous	
16	Creigiau Gleision and Llyn Cowlyd	15.4km/9½ miles	760m/2495ft	5 hours	energetic	
17	Llyn Geirionydd and Llyn Crafnant	13.7km/8½ miles	570m/1879ft	5 hours	moderate	
18	The Carneddau: end-to-end	29km/18 miles	1555m/5100ft	9–10 hours	strenuous	
19	Mynydd Mawr	10km/6½ miles	550m/1805ft	3–4 hours	moderate	
20	The Nantlle Ridge	13km/8 miles	1025m/3360ft	5–6 hours	energetic	
21	Moel Hebog, Moel yr Ogof and Moel Lefn	12.5km/8 miles	945m/3100ft	4–5 hours	energetic	
22	Aberglaslyn, Llyn Dinas and Cwm Bychan	8.5km/5¼ miles	540m/1770ft	3 hours	moderate	

WALK		DISTANCE	HEIGHT GAIN	TIME	GRADE	WALKED
23	Moel Siabod	9km/5½ miles	760m/2495ft	4–5 hours	energetic	
24	Cnicht and Cwm Croesor	11km/7 miles	620m/2035ft	4 hours	moderate	
25	Moelwyn Mawr and Moelwyn Bach	11km/7 miles	810m/2660ft	4–5 hours	energetic	
26	Moel Meirch and Ysgafell Wen	14.5km/9 miles	845m/2770ft	5 hours	energetic	
27	Bwlch Tyddiad and Bwlch Drws Ardudwy	14km/8¾ miles	745m/2445ft	5 hours	energetic	
28	Rhinog Fawr	7km/4½ miles	595m/1950ft	4 hours	energetic	
29	Rhinog Fach and Rhinog Fawr	11km/6¾ miles	910m/2985ft	5 hours	strenuous	
30	Y Llethr and Diffwys	22km/13¾ miles	975m/3200ft	6–7 hours	strenuous	
31	Carnedd y Filiast	16km/10 miles	650m/2130ft	5 hours	energetic	
32	Arenig Fawr and Moel Llyfnant	16km/10 miles	845m/2770ft	5–6 hours	energetic	
33	Rhobell Fawr	12km/7½ miles	650m/2132ft	4–5 hours	energetic	
34	Aran Benllyn	13km/8 miles: including Aran Fawddwy 17.8km/11 miles	740m/2425ft: including Aran Fawddwy 995m/3265ft	4–5 hours: 6–7 hours including Aran Fawddwy	moderate	
35	Aran Fawddwy	12.5km/8 miles: including Aran Benllyn 17km/10½ miles	900m/2955ft: including Aran Benllyn 1130m/3710ft	4–5 hours: including Aran Benllyn 6–7 hours	energetic	
36	Cyfrwy, Pen y Gadair and Mynydd Pencoed	16.5km/10¼ miles	1055m/3460ft	6–7 hours	strenuous	
37	Pen y Gadair from Ty Nant	9km/5½ miles	735m/2410ft	4 hours	energetic	
38	Mynydd Pencoed, Pen y Gadair and Mynydd Moel	9.25km/6 miles	945m/3100ft	5–6 hours	energetic	
39	Tyrrau Mawr and Craig y Llyn	18.5km/11½ miles	880m/2885ft	5 hours	moderate	
40	The Tarrens	18.5km/11½ miles	1060m/3480ft	6–7 hours	energetic	

231

APPENDIX 2
Bibliography

Bingley, W
North Wales (London: Longman and Rees, 1804)

Black's Picturesque Guide to North Wales
(Edinburgh: Adam and Charles Black, 1857,
and subsequent editions)

Borrow, George
Wild Wales (London: John Murray, ed, 1901)

Camden, William
Britannia (London: John Stockdale, 1806)

Carr, Glyn *Death on Milestone Buttress*
(London: Geoffrey Bles, 1951)

Carr, Herbert RC, and Lister, George A
The Mountains of Snowdonia
(London: Crosby Lockwood & Son Ltd, 1948)

Condry, William.
– *Snowdonia*
(Newton Abbot: David and Charles, 1987)
– *The Snowdonia National Park*
(London: Collins, 1966)

Firbank, Thomas
I Bought a Mountain (London: Harrap, 1940)

Godwin, Fay, and Toulson, Shirley.
The Drovers' Roads of Wales
(London: Whittet Books Ltd, 1987)

Hilling, John B. *Snowdonia and Northern Wales*
(London: BT Batsford Ltd, 1980)

Hughes, Cledwyn
Portrait of Snowdonia (London: Robert Hale, 1967)

Hughes, Harold, and North, Herbert L
The Old Cottages of Snowdonia
(Capel Curig: Snowdonia National Park Society,
1979)

Jenkinson, Henry Irwin
Jenkinson's Smaller Practical Guide to North Wales
(Bibliolife, 2008)

Jones, Jonah
The Lakes of North Wales
(London: Whittet Books Ltd, 1987)

Lovins, Amory
Eryri, the Mountains of Longing
(New York: Friends of the Earth)

Marsh, Terry
– *The Summits of Snowdonia*
(London: Robert Hale, 1984)
– *The Mountains of Wales*
(London: Hodder and Stoughton, 1985)

Millward, Roy and Robinson, Adrian
Landscapes of North Wales
(Newton Abbot: David and Charles, 1978)

North, FJ *et al*
Snowdonia: The National Park of North Wales
(London: Collins, 1949)

Pennant, Thomas
A Tour in Wales (Henry Hughes, 1783)

Perrin, Jim
Visions of Snowdonia: Landscape and Legend
(London: BBC Books, 1997)

Senior, Michael
Portrait of North Wales (London: Robert Hale, 1973)

Styles, Showell
The Mountains of North Wales
(London: Gollancz, 1973)

Williams, Mervyn
Snowdonia: The Official National Park Guide
(Newton Abbot: Pevensey Guides, 2000)

APPENDIX 3
Glossary of Welsh Words

Welsh is an ancient, complex, rich and bardic language, spoken as a community language by almost 750,000 people. You are unlikely to encounter anyone who has no English whatsoever, but knowing the meaning of just a few words, especially as they apply to the mountain landscape, will give you the component parts of many place names, and, through this, an insight into the terrain being covered. It won't make you fluent in Welsh, but it will at least enable you to identify the places you want to visit.

One tricky little feature of the Welsh language is mutation, an aspect common to all Celtic languages, and one likely to make it difficult to find words in dictionaries. Understanding when, where and how to use mutations is a linguistic issue, but in the list below words in brackets are the mutated form of the original, and mean the same thing.

Here are some of the most commonplace words for hillwalkers.

WELSH	ENGLISH
aber	river mouth, estuary
allt	wooded hillside, cliff
afon	river
bach (fach)	small
bwlch	pass, col
caer	fort
carnedd (garnedd)	cairn
castell	castle
coed	wood
craig (graig)	crag
crib	narrow ridge, crest
cwm	valley, corrie
drws	gap, pass
dyffryn	valley
eglwys	church
ffridd	mountain pasture
ffynnon	spring
hen	old
isaf	lowest
llan	church, parish

WELSH	ENGLISH
llwybr	path
llyn	lake
maen	stone
mawr (fawr)	big
melin (felin)	mill
moel (foel)	(rounded) hill
mynydd	mountain
nant	stream
pen	top, head
pont (bont)	bridge
pwll	pool
rhaeadr	waterfall
rhiw	hill, slope
rhyd	ford
sarn	causeway
traeth	beach
ty	house
uchaf	highest
ynys	island

INDEX

MORE TO EXPLORE
RELATED CICERONE GUIDEBOOKS

Wales and Snowdonia

Backpacker's Britain: Wales
Graham Uney

Hillwalking in Snowdonia:
Glyders, Carneddau and Outlying Areas
Steve Ashton

Hillwalking in Wales – Vol 1: Arans to Dovey Hills
Peter Hermon

Hillwalking in Wales – Vol 2: Ffestiniog to Tarrens
Peter Hermon

Ridges of Snowdonia:
The Best Ridge Walking in Snowdonia
Steve Ashton

Scrambles in Snowdonia: A Scrambling Guide
Steve Ashton

The Mountains of England and Wales:
Vol 1 – Wales
John and Anne Nuttall

The Ridges of England, Wales and Ireland:
Scrambles, Rock Climbs and Winter Routes
Dan Bailey

Walking on the Brecon Beacons
Andrew Davies and David Whittaker

Welsh Winter Climbs
Malcolm Campbell

Walking in the South Wales Valleys
Mike Dunn

Walking in the Forest of Dean
Mike Dunn

Walking on Gower
Andrew Davies

The Wye Valley Walk
The Wye Valley Walk Partnership

General mountaineering guides

The Hillwalker's Manual:
A Definitive Source of Reference
Bill Birkett

The Hillwalker's Guide to Mountaineering:
Essential Skills for Britain's Classic Routes
Terry Adby and Stuart Johnston

Map and Compass:
A Comprehensive Guide to Navigation
Pete Hawkins

Navigation: Using your Map and Compass
Pete Hawkins

Mountain Weather:
Understanding Britain's Mountain Weather
David Pedgley

Pocket First Aid and Wilderness Medicine
Jim Duff and Peter Gormly

Outdoor Photography
Chiz Dakin and Jon Sparks

Geocaching in the UK
Terry Marsh

Other large format guides

Great Mountain Days in the Lake District
Mark Richards

Great Mountain Days in the Pennines
Terry Marsh

Great Mountain Days in Scotland
Dan Bailey

Scotland's Mountain Ridges
Dan Bailey

The National Trails
Paddy Dillon

← *On the ascent of Moel Cynghorion (Walk 5)*

LISTING OF CICERONE GUIDES

BRITISH ISLES CHALLENGES,
COLLECTIONS AND ACTIVITIES
The End to End Trail
The Mountains of England and Wales
  1 Wales & 2 England
The National Trails
The Relative Hills of Britain
The Ridges of England, Wales and Ireland
The UK Trailwalker's Handbook
The UK's County Tops
Three Peaks, Ten Tors

MOUNTAIN LITERATURE
Unjustifiable Risk?

UK CYCLING
Border Country Cycle Routes
Cycling in the Hebrides
Cycling in the Peak District
Cycling the Pennine Bridleway
Mountain Biking in the Lake District
Mountain Biking in the Yorkshire Dales
Mountain Biking on the South Downs
The C2C Cycle Route
The End to End Cycle Route
The Lancashire Cycleway

SCOTLAND
Backpacker's Britain
  Central and Southern Scottish Highlands
  Northern Scotland
Ben Nevis and Glen Coe
Great Mountain Days in Scotland
Not the West Highland Way
Scotland's Best Small Mountains
Scotland's Far West
Scotland's Mountain Ridges
Scrambles in Lochaber
The Ayrshire and Arran Coastal Paths
The Border Country
The Cape Wrath Trail
The Great Glen Way
The Isle of Mull
The Isle of Skye
The Pentland Hills
The Scottish Glens 2 – The Atholl Glens
The Southern Upland Way
The Speyside Way
The West Highland Way
Walking Highland Perthshire
Walking in Scotland's Far North
Walking in the Angus Glens
Walking in the Cairngorms
Walking in the Ochils, Campsie Fells
  and Lomond Hills
Walking in Torridon
Walking Loch Lomond and the Trossachs
Walking on Harris and Lewis
Walking on Jura, Islay and Colonsay
Walking on Rum and the Small Isles
Walking on the Isle of Arran
Walking on the Orkney and Shetland Isles
Walking on Uist and Barra
Walking the Corbetts
  1 South of the Great Glen
  2 North of the Great Glen
Walking the Galloway Hills
Walking the Lowther Hills
Walking the Munros
  1 Southern, Central and Western Highlands
  2 Northern Highlands and the Cairngorms

Winter Climbs Ben Nevis and Glen Coe
Winter Climbs in the Cairngorms
World Mountain Ranges: Scotland

NORTHERN ENGLAND TRAILS
A Northern Coast to Coast Walk
Backpacker's Britain – Northern England
Hadrian's Wall Path
The Dales Way
The Pennine Way
The Spirit of Hadrian's Wall

NORTH EAST ENGLAND,
YORKSHIRE DALES AND PENNINES
Great Mountain Days in the Pennines
Historic Walks in North Yorkshire
South Pennine Walks
St Oswald's Way and St Cuthbert's Way
The Cleveland Way and the
  Yorkshire Wolds Way
The North York Moors
The Reivers Way
The Teesdale Way
The Yorkshire Dales
  North and East
  South and West
Walking in County Durham
Walking in Northumberland
Walking in the North Pennines
Walks in Dales Country
Walks in the Yorkshire Dales
Walks on the North York Moors
  Books 1 & 2

NORTH WEST ENGLAND
AND THE ISLE OF MAN
Historic Walks in Cheshire
Isle of Man Coastal Path
The Isle of Man
The Lune Valley and Howgills
The Ribble Way
Walking in Cumbria's Eden Valley
Walking in Lancashire
Walking in the Forest of Bowland and Pendle
Walking on the West Pennine Moors
Walks in Lancashire Witch Country
Walks in Ribble Country
Walks in Silverdale and Arnside
Walks in the Forest of Bowland

LAKE DISTRICT
Coniston Copper Mines
Great Mountain Days in the Lake District
Lake District Winter Climbs
Lakeland Fellranger
  The Central Fells
  The Far-Eastern Fells
  The Mid-Western Fells
  The Near Eastern Fells
  The Northern Fells
  The North-Western Fells
  The Southern Fells
  The Western Fells
Roads and Tracks of the Lake District
Rocky Rambler's Wild Walks
Scrambles in the Lake District
  North & South
Short Walks in Lakeland
  1 South Lakeland
  2 North Lakeland
  3 West Lakeland

The Cumbria Coastal Way
The Cumbria Way and the Allerdale Ramble
Tour of the Lake District

DERBYSHIRE, PEAK DISTRICT
AND MIDLANDS
High Peak Walks
Scrambles in the Dark Peak
The Star Family Walks
Walking in Derbyshire
White Peak Walks
  The Northern Dales
  The Southern Dales

SOUTHERN ENGLAND
Suffolk Coast & Heaths Walks
The Cotswold Way
The North Downs Way
The Peddars Way and Norfolk Coast Path
The Ridgeway National Trail
The South Downs Way
The South West Coast Path
The Thames Path
Walking in Berkshire
Walking in Essex
Walking in Kent
Walking in Norfolk
Walking in Sussex
Walking in the Isles of Scilly
Walking in the New Forest
Walking in the Thames Valley
Walking on Dartmoor
Walking on Guernsey
Walking on Jersey
Walking on the Isle of Wight
Walks in the South Downs National Park

WALES AND WELSH BORDERS
Backpacker's Britain – Wales
Glyndwr's Way
Great Mountain Days in Snowdonia
Hillwalking in Snowdonia
Hillwalking in Wales
  Vols 1 & 2
Offa's Dyke Path
Ridges of Snowdonia
Scrambles in Snowdonia
The Ascent of Snowdon
Lleyn Peninsula Coastal Path
Pembrokeshire Coastal Path
The Shropshire Hills
The Wye Valley Walk
Walking in Pembrokeshire
Walking in the Forest of Dean
Walking in the South Wales Valleys
Walking on Gower
Walking on the Brecon Beacons
Welsh Winter Climbs

INTERNATIONAL CHALLENGES,
COLLECTIONS AND ACTIVITIES
Canyoning
Europe's High Points
The Via Francigena
  (Canterbury to Rome): Part 1

EUROPEAN CYCLING
Cycle Touring in France
Cycle Touring in Ireland
Cycle Touring in Spain
Cycle Touring in Switzerland
Cycling in the French Alps

For full information on all our guides, and to
order books and eBooks, visit our website:
www.cicerone.co.uk.

Walking – Trekking – Mountaineering – Climbing – Cycling

Over 40 years, Cicerone have built up an outstanding collection of 300 guides, inspiring all sorts of amazing adventures.

Every guide comes from extensive exploration and research by our expert authors, all with a passion for their subjects. They are frequently praised, endorsed and used by clubs, instructors and outdoor organisations.

All our titles can now be bought as **e-books** and many as iPad and Kindle files and we will continue to make all our guides available for these and many other devices.

Our website shows any **new information** we've received since a book was published. Please do let us know if you find anything has changed, so that we can pass on the latest details. On our **website** you'll also find some great ideas and lots of information, including sample chapters, contents lists, reviews, articles and a photo gallery.

It's easy to keep in touch with what's going on at Cicerone, by getting our monthly **free e-newsletter**, which is full of offers, competitions, up-to-date information and topical articles. You can subscribe on our home page and also follow us on **Facebook** and **Twitter**, as well as our **blog**.

Cicerone – the very best guides for exploring the world.

CICERONE

2 Police Square Milnthorpe Cumbria LA7 7PY
Tel: 015395 62069 info@cicerone.co.uk
www.cicerone.co.uk